The Reptiles
of Northern and Central Europe

THE REPTILES OF NORTHERN AND CENTRAL EUROPE

Donald Street

B. T. Batsford Ltd   London

First published 1979
© Donald Street
ISBN 0 7134 1374 3

Filmset by Elliott Bros. & Yeoman Ltd., Speke, Liverpool L24 9JL
Printed and bound in Great Britain by
Redwood Burn Limited, Trowbridge & Esher
for the publisher B. T. Batsford Ltd.
4 Fitzhardinge Street, London W1H 0AH

Contents

List of Illustrations

vii

Preface

This book deals in detail with all the species of reptiles living in northern and central Europe. It is intended mainly for field workers with a specialized interest in reptiles, and for naturalists with more general interests who may like to expand their knowledge of some of the species which they have encountered in the field. The area reviewed includes the British Isles, Scandinavia, and the northern and central parts of the European mainland, extending from the Atlantic, through the Alps and Pannonian plain (north of the River Sava), up to and including the Carpathian region. The remaining species of reptiles living in southern France (south of 45° N.), Italy, the Iberian and Balkan peninsulas, as well as Europe east of the Carpathians are not dealt with except briefly in an appendix.

Every species is dealt with systematically, each account consisting of a description of its physical appearance, its habitat, behaviour, and an up-to-date report on its distribution. The sections concerning distribution cover the entire range of the species concerned, not merely with northern and central Europe. Finally, the local European names are listed (mainly in the language of the country in which the particular species occurs).

For over twenty years I have studied reptiles, having made many visits to both western and eastern Europe. In this way I have become familiar with all the species described in the text. This present work is based partly upon my own observations, as well as the available literature. The classification used is based on that of Mertens and Wermuth (1960) in their checklist of European amphibians and reptiles, though minor amendments have been incorporated, to allow for a few new discoveries and changes of status. The main part of the book is preceded by a brief account of these reptiles as a class.

Although this book deals with the species of northern and central Europe, many of them also occur in southern Europe. For example, of the 25 species described, 17 occur in Spain, 20 in Italy and 21 in Yugoslavia. In fact much of my research was done in these countries, where some of these species are more abundant and widely distributed.

Although our knowledge of reptiles has increased considerably within the present century, a great deal has still to be learnt, and even our basic information concerning certain species is still very sketchy. In order to gain a full understanding of any species, it is necessary to have comprehensive details of its ecological background, and it is only quite recently that such studies have been made.

The intention of this book is to bring together for the first time a substantial

amount of information now known about European reptiles. It has of course
not been possible for me to verify personally all the statements made in this
book, and during the course of time certain details may have to be rejected, or
at least modified. For the present however I hope that this work will help to fill
the gap that exists.

Acknowledgements

I am greatly indebted to Mr. Hugh Sainsbury, Miss Anne Bracht, Mr. W. L. Chick, Mr. Sdeuard Bisserôt, and especially Mr. Eric Hosking for supplying the photographs; to Mrs. Gabriella Dombay, Mr. Sándor Kenéz, Dr. F. Calin, Mrs. T. Skaller, Mrs. Ursula Fahr and Mr. G. Dedopulos for their kind assistance in translating texts from various foreign languages; to Dr. Robert Stebbings for his helpful comments and criticism on reading the manuscript; and to the ever-helpful library staff of the British Museum of Natural History. To Miss Anne Bracht I am particularly grateful for typing the manuscript, and for the constant help and advice that she gave while the book was in progress.

All the reptiles shown in the illustrations were specially captured by myself for study purposes. The majority of them were subsequently released in the wild.

Of the black and white plates, nos. 1, 2, 3, 4, 5, 6, 7, 8, 9, 12, 13, 14, 15, 16, 18, 19, 21, 23, 24, 25, 26, 28, 30, 31, 35a–d, 36, 39, 40, 41, 42, 43 and 44 were taken by Eric Hosking; nos. 17, 20, 29 and 34 by Sdeuard C. Bisserôt; no. 10 by W. L. Chick, no. 22 by Anne Bracht and no. 33 by Hugh Sainsbury. Nos. 11, 27, 32, 37 and 38 were taken by the author.

Of the colour plates those illustrating the sand lizards, eyed lizard, viperine snake, and the aspic viper with its young, as well as the southern smooth snake displayed on the dust jacket, were taken by Eric Hosking. Those of the blue-spotted slow worm, the juvenile and adult dark green whip snakes, and the adders were taken by the author.

Introduction

Reptiles are predominantly cold-blooded or *ectothermic* vertebrates, their body temperature fluctuating like that of the amphibians and fishes, in accordance with the surrounding temperature. In the evolutionary chain, they form a link between the amphibians and the warm-blooded birds and mammals. They were in fact the first vertebrates to adapt themselves to a completely terrestrial way of life. The name *reptile* is derived from the Latin word *reptilis*, meaning a creeper. The Greek word for creeper is ἑρπετὸυ (= herpeton) from which is derived the word *herpetology*, meaning the study of both reptiles and amphibians.

Reptiles, when adult, possess an almost fully ossified skeleton, though parts of the skull in particular are cartilaginous. Compared with the amphibians, particularly frogs, they have considerable freedom of head movement. The skin, unlike that of the amphibians, is not wet and slimy, but quite dry, and is covered with plates or scales. Fertilization is always internal, there being no external larval stage or metamorphosis, and the embryos develop in foetal membranes. From the moment of birth they breathe through lungs.

Today the Class *REPTILIA* comprises some 6000 surviving species, these often being divided into six groups or *orders*. The first three groups, SAURIA (the lizards), AMPHISBAENIA (small worm-like, burrowing reptiles, until recently classified among the lizards), and SERPENTES (the snakes), are considered by some authorities as being sub-orders of the order SQUAMATA, because their bodies are covered with scales. The lizards and snakes are particularly rich in numbers of species, some 3000 of the former and 2700 of the latter being recognised at present. The order TESTUDINES, with 212 species, comprises the tortoises, terrapins and turtles, while the order CROCODYLIA consists of the crocodiles and their allies. The final order, RHYNCHOCEPHALIA is represented today by a solitary lizard-like species known as the tuatera, which is endemic to a few islands off the New Zealand coast.

Most reptiles live in the Tropics. Further north and south the number of species, and abundance of individuals often decline. In Europe reptile life is conspicuously more abundant in the Mediterranean regions. As a whole however, Europe is not very rich in reptilian fauna, there being just over a hundred species, made up of some 63 species of lizards, 35 species of snakes, and 11 species of tortoises, including turtles. Less than a quarter of these occur in northern and central Europe: twenty-five species of reptiles are described in this book.

13

Nomenclature and Classification

A species may be defined as a population of interbreeding organisms. However, during the course of thousands of years, the representatives of a species living in some isolated area may develop certain distinctive features regarding their structure, appearance and perhaps behaviour, which distinguish them from other populations of the same species. Such variations are known as *races*, sometimes termed *sub-species*. These terms refer both to the 'parent' and the 'offspring' populations. A race is often a step towards the evolution of a new species. 'Speciation' is attained when such organisms are no longer able to breed freely with allied forms, without resultant infertility.

In 1739 the Swedish botanist Karl von Linné, better known as Linnaeus, published the first version of his *Systema Naturae*. In this work he attempted to catalogue and classify all living organisms. Both Latin and Greek-derived words were used in his nomenclature. Species closely resembling one another were grouped together to form a *genus*, and to each species he gave a fixed *generic* and *specific* name.

However many inaccuracies have been discovered in Linnaeus's catalogue and many amendments and countless additions have subsequently been made and continue to be made. None the less the system begun by Linnaeus is universally accepted. Often the name of the describer of a new species is added after the scientific names, e.g.: *Lacerta agilis* **Linnaeus.** If the classification is subsequently found to be inaccurate a new name is given, but the name of the original describer is still retained but placed in parenthesis, e.g.: *Lacerta viridis* (**Laurenti**). A third name is frequently present, and this denotes the racial identity. In such cases the describer indicated is the one who described the particular race in question, e.g.: *Natrix natrix helvetica* (**Lacépède**).

For every species I have given the year when it was first described, as well as the locality where the original specimen was described, that is, the *Terra typica*.

Lizards

Of all the various groups of reptiles, it is the lizards which exhibit the greatest diversity in form. Typical lizards are readily distinguished from snakes in possessing limbs, a short body, a relatively long tail, movable eyelids, an external ear opening, a short, notched (as opposed to deeply-forked) tongue, and a lower jaw, whose two halves are firmly fused. Furthermore, lizards lack the broad ventral plates characteristic of most snakes. However many species of lizards, to a greater or lesser degree, show a tendency towards a snake-like appearance, and identification has to be made on the basis of a combination of several of the above features. There are also less easily ascertainable differences regarding the formation of the skull. The skeleton of lizards is rather mammal-like, and there are in addition tiny rib-like projections on the upper part of the tail. While at rest or in movement, the belly remains on the ground. Lizards are partly aided in their movements by their long tail.

Lacertids   Members of the family *LACERTIDAE* are typical lizards having a comparatively short body, a distinct head, and a very long tail. Male lacertids often grow larger than the females and can be distinguished from the female by a swelling at the base of the tail. The limbs are well developed, and project more or less sideways from the body, as far as the elbows and knees. Five digits with claws occur on each limb. In such lizards the tympanic membrane (ear drum) is clearly visible. All three of the eyelids are movable and are closed during sleep. The third eyelid is periodically used to moisten and cleanse the cornea. In reptiles it is the lower eyelid, when present, which is larger and more flexible.

The members of the family *LACERTIDAE* are found in Europe, Asia, and in Africa, north of the Equator. The genera *Lacerta* **Linnaeus** and *Podarcis* **Wagler** belong to this family, and all species possess a distinctive scaly collar. The species which form the genus *Podarcis* were formerly also placed within the genus *Lacerta*, though sometimes classified in the subgenus *Podarcis*. Arnold (1973) has presented them as new genus on the basis of certain skeletal and hemipenial characteristics.

Skinks   The skinks (family *SCINCIDAE*), which have a fairly cosmopolitan range, have a tendency towards a rounded, somewhat cylindrical body, which in some species is rather extended and snake-like. Many species, for example the three toed skink, show a reduction in the size of limbs and in the number of digits. Sometimes the fore and hind limbs can be widely spaced. Some skinks are even devoid of legs. There is frequently no distinct neck, and thus the head, like the tail, is often not clearly set off from the rest of the body.

Members of the genus *Ablepharus*, **Lichtenstein**, as the name indicates, have no eyelids, the eye being covered with a transparent skin similar to that of snakes. Four species are currently recognised, occurring in Europe and south-west Asia.

The ten species of the genus *Chalcides* **Laurenti** are found in Europe, south-west Asia, and in Africa north of the Sahara. The lower eyelid has a transparent disc, and the ear cavity is more or less distinct.

Slow worm   A parallel evolution towards a snake-like form is seen among some species of the family *ANGUIDAE*, and this is well illustrated in the case of the slow worm. Like other members of its family it has a long body and a fairly long tail. Neither the head nor the tail are distinctly set off from the body in this species, and there are no visible traces of limbs. Its method of locomotion is similar to that most frequently used by snakes. Despite its serpentine appearance, it has a lizard-like skull, and there are vestiges of a pectoral and a pelvic girdle. The eyelids are movable, and the ear cavity is either tiny or invisible. It is the only species of its genus. Other species of this family inhabit Europe, Asia, north Africa, north and south America.

Snakes

Snakes show some degree of variation in form, though all possess an elongate flexible body. Limbs are invariably absent, though a few primitive snakes, such as the boas and pythons, possess vestiges of a pelvic girdle and hind legs. Snakes have no eyelids, nor is there any trace of an outer ear. In aquatic species the nostrils are directed upwards.

Males have hemipenial swellings at the base of the tail. The male's tail is relatively longer than the female's. Females usually grow a little longer than males and some individual female snakes grow much longer. This does not apply in the case of the aspic and horned vipers however, where the males reach the greater length.

The skeleton of more advanced snakes has only a skull, backbone and ribs. A pair of ribs is attached to each of the vertebrae of the body, and as in lizards, rib-like projections occur on the upper part of the tail. The number of vertebrae is approximately the same as the total ventral and paired subcaudal scales.

The absence of legs in snakes and in the slow worm has resulted in highly specialised methods of locomotion. The large number of ribs allows for a great degree of flexibility during movement. In the most frequently used method, snakes progress forward in an undulatory manner, taking advantage of irregularities on the ground or in the vegetation. Leverage is gained from these points of resistance, and the path taken by the fore part of the body is followed fairly closely by the rest of the snake. When placed on a totally smooth surface however, these reptiles move only with difficulty.

Another method sometimes used by snakes in slow movement, especially on flat surfaces, is known as caterpillar movement. In this method the ventral plates are raised one by one by the muscles attached to the ribs, moved forward and lowered, starting from the neck, and working towards the tail. In this way snakes are able to travel forward in a straight line without any side undulations.

Snakes also employ this form of movement while climbing. Short, heavy-bodied snakes, such as the vipers, are relatively slow in their movements. Long, slender snakes, such as the whip snakes, are noted for the rapidity of their movements. Some snakes, particularly arboreal species, have prehensile tails; of the European snakes, the smooth snake's tail is remarkably prehensile.

The elongate form of snakes has inevitably resulted in a corresponding elongation of all the important body organs. Where such organs are paired, the right one is larger than, and extends in front of, the left one. This applies to snake-like lizards also.

Colubrids   Members of the family *COLUBRIDAE* may be regarded as typical snakes, possessing a long body and tail. They have a cosmopolitan range, and comprise some two-thirds of all known species of snakes. Four genera of this family are found in northern and central Europe. Members of the genus *Natrix* **Laurenti** have a head that is fairly distinct from the neck, a more or less elongate body and a moderately long tail. They occur in Europe, Asia, north and north-east Africa, northern and central America as well as northern Australia.

Snakes of the genus *Elaphe* **Fitzinger** possess an elongate head which is fairly distinct from the neck, and a moderately slender and elongate body. They are found in Europe, Asia, north and tropical America. Also noted for their elongate heads are members of the genus *Coluber* **Linnaeus**. Their bodies and tails are also very elongate. They inhabit Europe, Asia, north Africa, north and central America.

The representatives of the genus *Coronella* **Laurenti** have a head that is only slightly distinct from the neck. The body and tail are quite small and moderately elongate. They occur in Europe, Asia and north Africa.

The European representatives of this family are sometimes separated into two sub-families: *COLUBRINAE* and *BOIGINAE*, the latter being distinguished by possessing a pair of grooved back fangs. Only three species are European, and are restricted to southern Europe.

The Vipers   The venomous vipers (family *VIPERIDAE*) have relatively short bodies. Their head is often somewhat triangular in shape, and the short tail stands out clearly. They inhabit Europe, Asia and Africa. The members of the genus *Vipera* **Laurenti** possess a moderately large head which is distinct from the neck, and a shortish body and tail. Their range is similar to that of the family as a whole.

Tortoises
Tortoises are of course distinguished by their shell, into which the head, limbs and tail can be withdrawn completely or at least partially. Tortoises' ribs, such as they are, are immovable and greatly reduced, and, like a large part of the spine and the shoulder girdle, merge into the shell. A pair of sacral ribs is

however free. The pelvis is set on top of the lower part of the shell. Being encased within their shells, tortoises are considerably restricted in their body movements, though the neck is quite mobile. The eyes are protected by eyelids, and the outer ear is clearly visible. European tortoises and terrapins belong to the sub-order CRYPTODIRA. These are distinguished by the way in which the head and neck make an S – shaped curve on being withdrawn into the shell.

Land tortoises   The genus *Testudo* **Linnaeus**, of which the Greek tortoise is a member, belongs to the family *TESTUDINIDAE*. These are typical land tortoises, having a highly domed *carapace* (upper shell). Members of the genus *Testudo* possess a *carapace* which is firmly and broadly connected to the *plastron* (lower shell). The tail is relatively short in both adults and young. The cylindrical limbs are formed as club feet; the digits are stumpy and do not move freely. They are provided with claws. The representatives of this family live in Asia, Africa, Madagascar, north and south America, the Galapagos Islands as well as Europe.

Pond tortoises   The European pond tortoise (family *EMYDIDAE*) is in fact a terrapin. Such species have an elliptical *carapace* which is only moderately domed. The well developed limbs have movable, webbed digits, provided with long claws. The species of this family occur in Europe, Africa, Asia, north and south America. Nowadays only the European pond tortoise is recognized as a member of the genus *Emys* **Duméril.** The carapace and plastron of this species are united by a ligament of cartilage, and the plastron is in two slightly movable parts, being hinged behind the third pair of plates.

Scalation and plates

Reptiles, being the first fully terrestrial vertebrates, developed a tough skin to protect them from exposure to the air and the heat of the sun. The outer skin or *epidermis* is composed of hardened, dead cells which form a transparent cuticle. Underneath there is a tough, elastic *mesodermal* skin, composed of living cells. Here pigment granules are present, giving the reptile its colouration.

The number and positions of the head plates in reptiles are generally consistent in each species, and afford an important and reliable guide to identification. The number of body scales per species are subject to some variation. Individual specimens however occasionally show further aberrations.

Lizards and snakes   The scales of lizards and snakes can be either smooth or rough to the touch. The roughness is due to the presence of a tiny and narrow longitudinal ridge, known as a keel, which runs across each of the scales. Keels, which are usually stronger in male specimens, are again consistently arranged according to the species, though many species of reptiles are devoid of them.

LIZARDS *Lacertids* The dorsal and lateral scales of the lacertids are very numerous and tiny, though they become larger on the sides. Those on top of the back are usually well keeled, while those of the sides are more feebly keeled. The top of the head is covered with hard bony plates known as

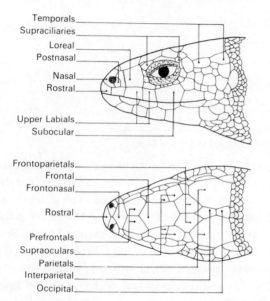

Head plates of a typical lacertid (common lizard).
Profile (upper) and top of head.

osteoderms. A transverse row of scales, forming a collar, is present on the underside of the neck. This collar conceals many very tiny scales underneath. The scales of the belly are smooth, comparatively large and wide. They are arranged in from six to ten longitudinal rows. The number of transverse rows is greater in females than in males. The anal plate is quite large.

Skinks Skinks possess longitudinal rows of smallish, fairly uniform, smooth and polished scales, extending completely around their body. The largest scales occur on top of the head. Osteoderms are present beneath the scales.

Slow worm The slow worm is similarly covered by longitudinal rows of smallish smooth, shiny scales. These are also of fairly uniform size, and as in the skinks the largest plates are those on top of the head. The osteoderms, which are situated beneath all of the scales, are united by tissue, and this allows for a certain degree of flexibility. Those osteoderms beneath the upper surface of the head are united to the bones of the skull.

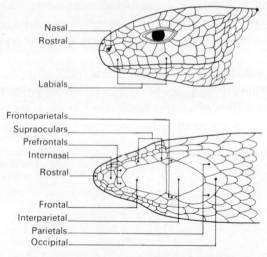

Nasal
Rostral

Labials

Frontoparietals
Supraoculars
Prefrontals
Internasal
Rostral

Frontal
Interparietal
Parietals
Occipital

Head plates of a slow worm (western race).
Profile (upper) and top of head.

SNAKES   The scales of snakes are small and somewhat elliptical, and they overlap one another slightly, like tiles on a roof. Because of the elasticity of the skin, they become separated whenever the skin is stretched. The scales of the back and sides are generally narrowest on top of the back, and largest near the belly. They are arranged diagonally across the back in straight longitudinal rows. There is almost always an odd number of such rows. When counting the number of longitudinal rows of scales extending along the back, it is usual to count in the mid-body region. In most species of snakes the number of rows becomes reduced towards the tail.

The belly has a single longitudinal row of wide plates, which slightly overlap one another. They extend as far as the vent, and are known as *ventral* shields. The *anal* shield is normally divided into two adjacent parts in the colubrids, and is single in the vipers. The underside of the tail, which begins immediately after the anal shield, is covered by plates similar to the ventral shields, but these are arranged in pairs, and are known as *subcaudal* shields. Occasionally freak specimens have been found where the subcaudals are not paired, but are arranged singly like the ventral shields.

The eye is covered by a transparent window knows as the *brille*. This forms part of the skin and is eventually sloughed along with it. Osteoderms are not present in snakes.

Colubrids   Some colubrids, such as the members of such genera as *Coluber* and *Coronella*, have smooth, polished scales. Only members of the genus *Natrix* are well keeled among the European colubrids. There are nine large plates on top of the head and several smaller ones.

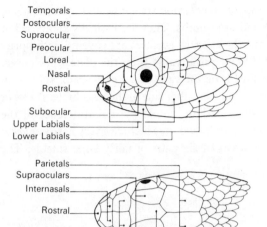

Temporals
Postoculars
Supraocular
Preocular
Loreal
Nasal
Rostral
Subocular
Upper Labials
Lower Labials

Head of a typical colubrid (Dark
green whip snake).
Profile (upper) and top of head.

Parietals
Supraoculars
Internasals
Rostral
Prefrontals
Frontal

Vipers   European vipers have strongly keeled scales, especially on top of the
back. There is a maximum of only five large plates on top of the head, as in the
meadow viper, while in the horned viper there are often only two large plates
(the *supraoculars*). Most of the upper surface of a viper's head is covered by

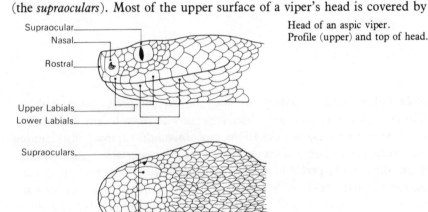

Supraocular
Nasal
Rostral
Upper Labials
Lower Labials

Head of an aspic viper.
Profile (upper) and top of head.

Supraoculars

small, smooth or feebly keeled scales. The plates on the side of the head are
generally smaller and more numerous than those of colubrids.

Apical pits   The *apical* pits, present on both the colubrids and vipers, are
very tiny, shallow impressions, arranged singly or paired, at the rear part of
each scale. They are frequently difficult to see with the naked eye. Their exact
significance is not yet understood, and it is possible that it is of a sensory
nature.

Tortoises In tortoises the *carapace* and *plastron* are connected by cartilage on both sides between the fore- and hind-limbs. They are basically composed of hard, dermal, bony plates, but the external surfaces are covered with horny shields, whose arrangement differs considerably from the plates they cover. Most tortoises have 13 large shields on the carapace: five *vertebral* shields on top of the back and four *costal* shields on either side of the vertebrals. A row of small shields is always present extending around the circumference of the carapace. These are known as *marginals*, and they include a very narrow *nuchal* (neck) shield. The plastron consists of six pairs of fairly large shields. The

Carapace (left) and plastron of a European pond tortoise.

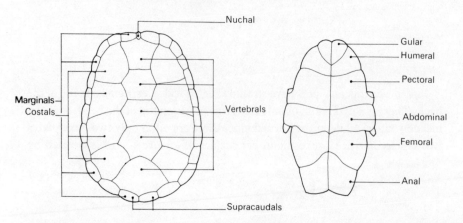

limbs, tail, neck, throat and head are scaly, but certain species, for example the European pond tortoise, have a head covered with smooth skin. Faint ridges are present, extending in rings all the way around the carapace. By counting these ridges a rough idea of the tortoise's age can be ascertained, for each ridge marks the end of a period of growth, which normally ceases every year when the tortoise disappears into hibernation. Such a method of assessing age is not however completely reliable, as prolonged illness may prevent any visible growth. In addition, wear may also partially erode this feature.

Ecdysis

Lizards, snakes and tortoises shed or slough the outer layer of their skin (the *epidermis*) several times a year. This process, known as *ecdysis*, occurs most frequently in summer, the period of maximum food intake. The first sloughing takes place shortly after emergence from hibernation. Whereas in lizards and snakes the epidermis covers the entire surface of the body, in tortoises it covers only the scaly parts, these peeling off in fragments. In lizards the skin also flakes off in fragments, though occasionally there may be one very substantial piece, which can include the entire body, except for parts of the head, limbs and tail.

Lizards SLOW WORM   The slow worm casts its skin rather like a snake. First of all, with the aid of rough vegetation, the old skin is loosened from the head, and then is folded backwards as the slow worm makes its way slowly forward. Normally however, the skin of this species collects to form thick rings as it is folded backwards. Rarely is it shed in once piece. I have seen similar rings formed from the cast skin of the two species of skink.

Snakes   Snakes often shed their skins in one piece, though due to their frailty, these frequently become torn in the process. Specimens in poor health tend to cast their skin in fragments, and tattered pieces may remain attached to the snake after the bulk of the skin has been removed.

Some two or three weeks before shedding, the general colouration of snakes and lizards becomes duller, and the pattern less distinct. In such species where sexual variation in colour is normally well marked, the characteristic differences can become blurred. Melanic snakes, uniformly black both above and below, develop a pale blue belly prior to ecdysis. At this time the brille covering the eye becomes opaque and bluish in colour. About three or four days before sloughing the eye becomes clear again. By now the new epidermis has formed beneath, and a moist secretion helps to loosen the old skin all over the body.

The skin is normally peeled off at the upper and lower lips first of all, and the snake rubs its snout against rough objects in order to do this. Once this has been achieved the skin is usually quite quickly loosened from the entire head, and the snake wedges itself between thick vegetation, pulling itself slowly forward with a regular expansion and contraction of the body, just before the point where the old epidermis is being detached, and turned slowly backwards, inside out. The entire process can be accomplished within five minutes, given ideal facilities. At first the skin is moist due to the secretion already mentioned. As the skin becomes somewhat distended during the sloughing process, the scales no longer overlapping one another, the cast skin is always longer than the snake itself.

Being composed of dead cells, the cast skin does not retain the colouration of the living reptile. Though thin and transparent, the original pattern may be clearly visible as a shadowy brown imprint, which is particularly well marked in the skins of lizards and also of the vipers.

Reptiles which have recently shed their skins have strikingly distinct markings. Young reptiles, whose growth rate is greatest, shed their skins most frequently. Although the amphibia may sometimes devour their cast skins, those of the reptiles are discarded.

Colouration and pattern

The colouration of reptiles is often quite variable among individuals of the same species, even specimens from the same locality showing a considerable degree of variation. The basic pattern however is normally consistent, and all species can usually be readily identified with reference to the markings alone. Sometimes one can find a similarity of pattern among several closely related species.

Cases of albinism and melanism, either partial or total, and other aberrant forms occur occasionally—more frequently in some species than in others—and in such cases identification may have to be made with reference to the general structure and scalation.

Sexual dimorphism in adult reptiles is commonly found in lizards, more rarely in snakes. The males of certain reptiles, such as the sand lizard and adder, are particularly vivid in colour during the mating season, and their brilliant colouration is believed to be of use in displays of rivalry with other males, and not a means of attracting the female.

In some species the markings may fade in elderly adults. Young reptiles often have different colouration and patterns from their parents.

Skin glands

There are few or no skin glands in reptiles, though lacertids do have a number of small indentations on the underside of the thighs, known as femoral pores. They secrete mainly cellular debris, though their exact function is unknown.

Snakes, unlike lizards, possess a pair of sac-like anal glands, which lie at the base of the tail and lead into the vent. Their secretion is produced throughout the year, though most abundantly in spring. There is some evidence that it is used to bring the sexes together during the mating season. Freshly caught grass snakes regularly discharge this secretion.

Senses

Reptiles like other animals are sensitive to pressure, temperature and moisture, possessing nerve endings beneath the outer skin. Rarely having an internal means of controlling their temperature, they are unable to tolerate extreme heat or cold, and the preferred body temperature, which varies from species to species is sustained by constant changes of location.

Sight   This sense is well developed in lizards and tortoises, while in snakes it is rather limited, being effective only at short range, and over greater distances only movements can be detected.

Harmless European colubrids have round pupils. Those of the vipers are noted for their elliptically vertical shape. Pupils of this shape are often associated with nocturnal behaviour, though European vipers are largely diurnal in their habits. In the dark the pupil expands to become round in shape.

A vestigial third eye (the parietal or pineal eye) is present on top of the head of some reptiles. It is particularly prominent in the common lizard and slow worm. Even so, it is small enough to go unnoticed. Recent evidence suggests that it is able to monitor solar radiation, thereby influencing the amount of time spent basking.

Hearing Many lizards, such as the lacertids, have an acute sense of hearing. Basking specimens can be observed to turn their heads towards the direction of any disturbance. Snakes possess neither ear drum, middle ear, nor Eustachian tube, and have been assumed to be unable to hear sounds conducted through the air. The inner ear bones are however present, and connect with the quadrate bone at the back of the jaw. Snakes, though in a sense deaf, are extremely sensitive to ground vibrations, these being transferred via the jaw and skull bones to the inner ear.

More recent investigations however suggest that the inner ear of snakes can also respond electrically to airborne noise, being sensitive to low wave-length sound—from 100 to 500 Hz. (Bellairs and Attridge, 1975). Tortoises are sensitive to relatively low frequencies only.

Smell and the use of tongue Lizards have a good sense of smell. So probably have tortoises. The sense of smell is supplemented in a few lizards, and more especially in snakes, by a highly developed structure known as Jacobson's organ. This is situated in the roof of the mouth, between the nasal cavity and the palate, and is used in combination with the tongue. In snakes the tongue is a long, thin and deeply forked organ. When not in use, as when snakes are lying completely relaxed or feeding, it rests in a sheath situated below the glottis. Otherwise it is constantly flickering in and out of the mouth through the small notch in the upper lip. This flickering becomes more agitated as the snake becomes aware of movement around it. The fork of the tongue contains sensory corpuscles, and picks up scent particles from objects with which it comes into contact, as well as from the air. These are conveyed from the two tips of the tongue to a pair of ducts on the palate, which connects to the Jacobson's organ, where the particles are investigated. It is with the aid of this organ that snakes are able to locate their prey and hibernation dens and in a similar manner, males are able to trace scent particles deposited by the female during the mating season. If a snake is unable to flicker its tongue, it is a sure sign of ill-health. The tongue is not used for licking food.

The slow worm also protrudes the tongue, though much more slowly, and is able to pick up scent particles. The tongue of most lizards is concerned only with touch and taste, though that of the lacertids is also used partially for smelling, and is periodically flicked in and out. All the lizards of northern and central Europe have a short, broad and flat tongue, which is notched, never deeply forked. It does not withdraw into a sheath as does that of snakes. Jacobson's organ is absent from tortoises.

Taste   Many lizards appear to have a good sense of taste, though this sense is not well developed in snakes, which appear to lack taste buds. The sense of taste seems to be better developed in land tortoises than in terrapins.

Intelligence

The reptilian brain is small in proportion to the body and in general reptiles do not display much intelligence, though they are a little more advanced than the amphibia. Most of their actions are instinctive, and their ability to learn and remember is small. Some species can be trained to become quite tame however.

Respiration

In the majority of lizards both lungs are well developed. In the slow worm however the right lung is larger than the left, and extends further forward. The windpipe (*trachea*) divides in two and leads to each lung. Except in primitive snakes, the left lung is merely rudimentary. The well-developed right lung is very elongate. In lizards and snakes the rib muscles draw air into the lungs by expansion and contraction of the body walls. Tortoises have a unique method of breathing, the air being pumped in and out by specially developed muscles, one set of which widens the body cavity, drawing in air, while the other set presses the body organs against the lungs, thus causing the air to be expelled. Compared with mammals and birds, reptiles are able to survive in remarkably airless conditions. The reptilian heart has two auricles, but the ventricle is only partially divided in the lizards, snakes and tortoises.

Reptiles, in contrast to birds and amphibians, lack a well-developed voice-box, and their vocal ability is usually restricted to hissing, although some species are able to squeak or grunt.

Feeding

Most reptiles are principally or exclusively carnivorous although land tortoises are mainly vegetarian. Food is normally recognised by sight, both lizards and snakes as well as terrapins being aroused by the movement of their prey, which is always caught in the jaws.

Individual reptiles sometimes display distinct dietary preferences, which may even include items not normally devoured. It is not unusual for a population of a species in one locality to have a different kind of diet from that of the same species in another area.

All reptiles have salivary glands, whose secretion always keeps the mouth and tongue moist, and lubricates the food, aiding swallowing. The alimentary tract of reptiles consists of a gullet, stomach, small and large intestines, rectum and cloaca. In this respect they are similar to other vertebrates. The gullet and stomach of snakes are very elongate. Digestion is quite a rapid process in reptiles, given sufficiently warm weather. The gastric juices are eventually able to decompose even the hardest of bones, though such items as hairs and feathers are defecated. In many reptiles a reserve supply of food is stored in the tissues known as fat-bodies, and this plays an important rôle in the reproductive cycle.

Lizards Lizards eat every day, sometimes several times. Prey may be devoured at any time during the active hours. In some cases food may be swallowed whole, though it is usually chewed first. The teeth of the members of the families *LACERTIDAE*, *SCINCIDAE* and *ANGUIDAE* are not implanted in sockets but attached to the inner edge of the jaw bone, and are known as *pleurodont*. Members of the genus *Lacerta* frequently have in addition a few teeth on each pterygoid bone. The teeth of the three toed skink are conical in shape. Those of the slow worm are curved slightly backwards. Through constant use the teeth of lizards and snakes become worn or damaged, and are replaced by adjacent reserve teeth. While eating, lizards move both upper and lower jaws, these being hinged in the roof of the skull. After feeding, lacertids can often be seen rubbing the side of their heads against firm objects in order to rid themselves of unwanted particles of food.

Snakes Because snakes eat large prey in proportion to their size, feeding occurs at intervals of several days. A large meal may suffice for a week or more. Little food is taken during the early spring months, snakes then being preoccupied with mating.

The ability of snakes to fast for long periods is well known. Boulenger (1913) refers to an aspic viper which lived, fasting for three years, and a boa (*Boa madagascariensis*) which survived for four years and one month without food.

COLUBRIDS Members of the genus *Natrix*, being partially aquatic, eat mainly fish and amphibia. Unlike poisonous and constricting species, they have little means of subduing warm-blooded prey which may struggle violently. Nestling birds and mammals are occasionally devoured however, as are the adults when found dead.

The fully terrestrial colubrids eat mainly lizards and small mammals, especially rodents. Prey is often held in the coils until the jaws are able to manoeuvre it into a position convenient for swallowing. Most items are swallowed head first, often still alive. Frogs and toads however are usually seized by a hind limb and are then swallowed backwards. Prey is drawn into the mouth by using alternate movements of either side of the jaws.

VIPERS The vipers usually kill their prey, especially warm-blooded prey, by striking it, thereby injecting the lethal venom through a pair of long, highly developed, hollowed (*solenoglyphous*) teeth, usually known as fangs. These occur at the front of the reduced maxillary bone, being the only teeth present on this bone in such species. The fangs in European vipers measure from 3 to 10 millimetres. They each connect via a duct to a modified salivary gland, which is situated in a muscular sheath, below and behind the eye. The fangs are thus not directly in contact with the gland.

Viper venom, a yellow secretion, is a specialised type of saliva, and contains coagulants, *haemorrhagin* and *haemolysin*. It is squeezed by the temporal muscles through the duct into a cavity of the gum at the base of the fangs, and travels through the hollows of the fangs and into the prey. Its function is not only to overpower the latter, but also to assist in its digestion.

The fangs normally lie horizontally, facing the direction of the throat, protected by a layer of skin. When the snake strikes, either at prey or at a potential enemy, the fangs are brought forward into a vertical position. They operate together, rather like a pair of hypodermic needles. The venom outlet is a little higher than the tip of the fang, which tapers very finely, aiding penetration.

The snake strikes with great rapidity, and withdraws instantaneously, having automatically injected the venom into its prey. The fangs are normally restored to the recumbent horizontal position immediately after use. Most animals having been bitten do not stop to put up a fight but scuttle off into the undergrowth. Vipers usually wait for a while until the venom has had time to act, then quite casually, using their tongue and nostrils, they track down their victim, which by then is unable to put up much resistance, and may already be dead. Warm-blooded animals are normally more sensitive to the venom than are cold-blooded prey. The venom will meanwhile have started to break down the tissues, thus aiding digestion.

Periodically, as they become worn or broken, the fangs are shed. There is a small cluster of reserve fangs situated immediately behind the one in use. As soon as this is shed, the succeeding one is ready to function, having almost grown into position before the old one is lost. The replacement fang does not connect to the venom duct until its predecessor becomes detached, this usually having become lodged in its previous meal. The fangs are shed individually, not as a pair.

Many colubrids harmless to man produce a similar venomous secretion in the upper lip glands. This has the effect of stunning prey, thereby aiding the swallowing process.

Both vipers and colubrids have small, pointed and recurved teeth, which face towards the throat. Such teeth are solid and known as *aglyhous*. They are situated on the palatine, pterygoid and dentary bones. The colubrids also possess teeth on the maxillary bone. These increase in size posteriorly (as in *Natrix*, *Coluber* and *Coronella*), or are more or less equal in length (as in *Elaphe*). All these bones are movable, being only loosely attached to the skull. They are not used for mastication, but for holding struggling or slippery prey—the fact that they are recurved prevents prey from escaping. The jaws are only loosely connected at the rear of the skull. In front the two halves of each jaw are united by an elastic ligament, which affords considerable flexibility, as they can be moved independently. A snake can thus swallow prey larger in girth than itself. If necessary the jaws can open to an angle exceeding 90°.

Swallowing is aided by the distensibility of the skin and the flexibility of the ribs, particularly in the fore-part of the snake. The process may take only a few minutes or several hours, depending on the size of the prey. Breathing continues without interruption during long periods of swallowing, as the glottis can be extended beyond the mouth. Very long-bodied prey remains protruding from the mouth, until the part of it in the stomach has been digested. Some snakes have been known to eat others as long as, or longer than, themselves.

Tortoises Whereas the land tortoises are predominantly vegetarian, the terrapins are almost exclusively carnivorous.

These reptiles do not possess teeth. Instead there is a sharp horny beak present both on the upper and lower jaws. Terrapins eat mainly aquatic animals, both vertebrates and invertebrates.

Drinking
Most reptiles drink freely and often. Even reptiles, particularly snakes, that refuse all food in captivity, usually continue to drink. Most lizards lap up water with their tongues, whereas snakes and tortoises submerge the tips of their jaws and suck it up. Thirsty reptiles can drink for several minutes, and snakes often raise their heads intermittently to aid swallowing.

Excretion
In the lizards, snakes and land tortoises, urine, for which little water is required, is excreted largely as uric acid along with the faeces in a solid form. According to Bellairs and Attridge (1975), lizards and snakes may also produce a considerable amount of urea, and this may even predominate in some lizards.

The urino-genital organs lead via ducts into the cloaca. There is normally one defecation after each meal, though there are more frequent kidney discharges, which consist mainly of uric acid. The terrapins excrete mainly urea and ammonia, and comparatively little uric acid. When about to excrete snakes lift up the base of their tails.

Reproduction

For most European reptiles, mating is an annual event, taking place every spring. Rivalry may occur among the males during this period, often involving fierce fighting in which severe, sometimes even permanent, wounds may result. Male snakes however do not inflict such serious injuries on one another. It is at this time that rival male adders perform their spectacular 'dance' (p. 202). Copulation is often preceded by courtship displays.

The male snake, aroused by a scent exuded from the female, tries to stimulate her by rubbing his chin along her back, with his tongue constantly flickering upon her in an agitated manner. The male tortoise knocks his shell against that of the female; he may bite her throat, legs and tail in his efforts to arouse her.

Copulation in reptiles may require anything from a few minutes to several hours. It is usually a silent, often almost immobile affair. It may take place more than once between two individuals. The role of the female is usually completely passive, though there are a few records of female lizards taking the initiative in approaching a reluctant male. Mating may subsequently take place with other partners. Some species may mate at other times of the year, especially in the autumn.

In lizards and snakes the cloacal opening is transverse and the copulatory organ is paired, while in the tortoises the former is either round or longitudinal, and the copulatory organ is single. The paired organs of male lizards and snakes are known as the *hemipenes*. They are each lodged in a cavity in the base of the tail as is the penis of the tortoise. Although female lizards and snakes have two egg tubes, only one of the *hemipenes* is engaged at any one time.

The male organ is a tube of erectile tissue, which is turned inside out, and projected from the side of the cloaca. It is erected by the action of muscles and blood vessels, which causes it to swell. Blood is pumped in by one of the main arteries. It is withdrawn by a special muscle, the *retractor penis*, which extends from the organ to the caudal vertebrae. The *hemipenes* are much shorter in lizards than in snakes. In order to prevent withdrawal during copulation, the males of many species of snakes are provided with special spines, which protrude from the cloaca and are also inserted into the female. After copulation the spermatozoa progress along the oviducts where ripe ova have either recently arrived or are shortly to arrive. In snakes the right oviduct is longer than the left and normally produces more eggs.

After fertilization, the young develop in foetal membranes (*amnion*, *chorion* and *allantois*), and remain in the oviduct for the rest of their development within the female. They feed mainly upon the yolk, of which, in most species, there is an abundant supply. The snake embryo is coiled up in a spiral.

Most reptiles, including all tortoises, lay eggs, and are thus known as *oviparous*. The eggs, which are laid in fairly quick succession, are protected by a tough, elastic, but porous shell. Water necessary for their development is thus easily absorbed, and causes them to swell a little. In shape they are spherical or elongate, and their usual colour is whitish or creamish. They are buried or hidden by the female in some suitably warm and humid spot.

The development of the egg has often begun before the eggs are laid. Little parental care is shown by the mother in most cases; having deposited her eggs, she moves off and forgets all about them, leaving them to develop on their own. When their development is complete the young lizards and snakes emerge from the shell with the aid of a specially provided egg-tooth, which is situated in front of the upper jaw as an appendage to the snout. With this the young reptile cuts one or more slits. The base of the tooth is an impression in the pre-maxillary bone. Shortly after use, the egg-tooth is shed. Young tortoises free themselves from the egg by means of a horny knob or *caruncle* on the tip of the snout.

In some lizards and snakes the complete development of the young takes place inside the mother's oviduct. As in oviparous species the young are nourished by their own yolk sac, though moisture necessary to their development is provided by the mother.

The young are born in a transparent, albuminous sac from which they usually almost immediately emerge. Such species are termed *ovo-viviparous*. The egg-tooth, though present, is vestigial, and is apparently non-functional.

Ovo-viviparity has a definite advantage over the previous method, since the developing embryo is no longer directly dependent on external sources for warmth, this being provided by the mother's body, which acts as an incubator. Pregnant females of such species therefore spend much time basking. In general ovo-viviparous species like the common lizard, slow worm and adder have been able to extend their range further north than the oviparous species. They also extend to higher altitudes.

Ovo-viviparity is a transitional stage between oviparity and true *viviparity*. Only a few reptiles can be regarded as being truly viviparous, these including the three toed skink (*Chalcides chalcides*), where placentation is relatively well developed, and there is a reduction in the size of the yolk-sac.

The number of young varies according to the species, but depends also on the size, age and condition of the mother. Thus large, older females produce the most. There are occasional reports of a second, even third, egg-laying taking place a month or two after the first laying—without a subsequent mating. Such instances are however unknown in lizards.

Young reptiles usually hatch or are born from mid-summer to autumn, though these processes may be delayed until the following spring if it has been unusually cold.

Newly-emerged reptiles are more or less exact replicas of their parents, and are quite able to fend for themselves. Young vipers at this stage are fully equipped with fangs and venom, and so are dangerous. The umbilicus of lizards and snakes can be seen as a little slit, occupying some two or three ventral scales in front of the vent. The scar may remain visible for a few months, after which it disappears.

Occasionally two-headed (*dicephalus*) snakes have been born, as in certain cases of the grass snake, smooth snake, adder and aspic viper. Boulenger (1913) refers to the case of a three-headed snake seen at Lake Ontario. Such specimens do not survive for long however. Hybrid reptiles, that is offspring produced as a result of a mating of two closely related species, are rarely found in the wild state. A number of successful experiments in hybridization have been achieved in captivity however. A few cases of *parthenogenesis* (the ability of a female to reproduce without being fertilized by a male) are known in reptiles. Various lizard populations living in the Caucasus (eg. *Lacerta unisexualis*) are composed exclusively of females.

Growth and life span

Growth in reptiles is usually most rapid during the first four or five years of life, after which it becomes much slower, although it never ceases completely. Often an increase in girth rather than in length is conspicuous after sexual maturity is attained. This is reached by the lacertids at about two or three years, and they may survive for up to six or even twelve years. A slow worm is known to have attained an age of at least 35 years. Colubrids become mature after three or four years and are thought to live up to fifteen years. A captive grass snake lived for 20 years, and the south European colubrid, a leopard snake (*Elaphe situla*), lived for 23 years. There is a record of a black and white-lipped cobra (*Naja melanoleuca*) and an anaconda (*Eunectes murinus*) surviving for 30 and 32 years respectively. Given suitable conditions, specimens in captivity, protected from their usual enemies, stand a better chance of reaching a great age.

Some tortoises have been known to exceed an age of 150 years—the longest ages known to have been attained by vertebrates. These reptiles are of course helped by having relatively few enemies.

Habitat

Reptiles have been remarkable in adapting to a wide variety of conditions, some being exclusively territorial, even fossorial (burrowing) while others are partly or wholly aquatic, some mainly arboreal (tree-dwelling). Thickly forested regions are avoided by all but a few species however, and in Europe only the Aesculapian snake on rare occasions penetrates into densely wooded country. All reptiles are inhabitants of relatively undisturbed areas, being absent from completely urbanised districts and areas of intensive agriculture. A large number of species however lives in close proximity to human habitation, near houses, farms and gardens. Some even occur in towns and in cities, provided ecological conditions are favourable.

Some species are confined to arid districts, while others are only found where it is marshy. Certain species are restricted to flat low-lying areas, while other kinds are associated with higher altitudes. Certain ecological conditions will often provide a habitat for several species of reptiles. Thus in a few localities of southern England, for example, all six of the native British species may be found living in the same area. In some parts of central and especially southern Europe, even larger numbers of species may co-habit.

Many reptiles are present only in areas with particular types of soil or vegetation. There are species however, which have adapted to a wide variety of habitats. Frequently such species (as for example the sand lizard, the green lizard and the smooth snake) require more specialized conditions in the fringe areas of their range. The warm vine-growing regions of the middle Rhine district are favourable to several species more extensively distributed further south. Localities with a sandy soil, easily warmed by the sun, are sometimes similarly inhabited by species whose general range is more southerly, for example, the eyed lizard and the southern smooth snake in south-western France, and the green lizard in eastern Germany.

Behaviour

Compared with more advanced vertebrates, reptiles spend a lot of time being inactive. Their principal activities are those concerned with feeding and breeding, and sloughing the skin. Most of the remainder of the time is spent either basking or hiding in retreat; their basking spots are situated close to their hiding places. Basking takes place most regularly in the spring months. Since the majority of reptiles are unable to provide their own bodily warmth, it is necessary for them to seek warm situations in order that their body functions normally. Most species of reptiles in Europe are diurnal, and those that are active at night may spend much time basking during the day while they sleep.

Diurnal species bask in the early morning prior to such activities as feeding and breeding. They may often retire during the warmer parts of the day, re-emerging in the late afternoon. Cold, windy and rainy weather keeps reptiles inside their retreat and their metabolic rate is reduced. During the prolonged winter months their metabolic rate is drastically lowered. Some species appear to dislike direct exposure to the sun, preferring to hide under vegetation, stones and rubble, where they are able to obtain the necessary warmth. In northern Europe reptiles may be found in hiding beneath discarded pieces of scrap metal. Further south however reptiles tend to avoid contact with metallic objects as these can quickly absorb a great deal of heat.

Comparatively little research has so far been done on the migratory habits of reptiles, and it is not fully understood to what extent their movements are arbitrary or instinctive. Their retreats and basking places can be quite frequently changed. Available evidence however suggests that certain species of lizards spend their entire lives within a comparatively confined area, whereas it is now established that some snakes may travel annually several kilometres from their hibernation and breeding area, to the main summer feeding area.

Some reptiles are sociable by nature, and are frequently found living in colonies. The wall lizard in particular is often observed in large numbers. Other reptiles disperse after hibernation and mating, and are most often found living alone.

Hibernation

In cool weather the metabolic rate of reptiles is reduced and they become less active. In most of Europe, temperature conditions become so unfavourable between late autumn and spring that bodily functions are suspended or greatly reduced, and a prolonged period is spent in hibernation. A substantial reserve of fat, acquired in the preceding months, is stored in the tissues. Normally only relatively little body weight is lost over the winter period. The amount lost by the common lizard during this time, for example varies, according to Hvass (1972), from 2 to 10 per cent.

With the exception of the terrapins, which may hibernate in the mud at the bottom of a pond or stream, the reptiles of Europe hibernate in cavities beneath the roots of trees and thick vegetation, holes in banks and in the ground, and always in well sheltered and well drained areas.

Some specimens hibernate singly, others collectively. Often members of different species may share the same retreat, including species that do not normally consort closely together during the active months of the year. It is thus not unusual for example for a suitable refuge to contain common lizards, slow worms and adders. These lizards do not thereby expose themselves to danger during the winter months, because their potential enemies have no desire to eat during this time. The young are normally the last to be seen about in late autumn, whereas the adult males are usually the first to emerge in spring.

The time of disappearance and emergence is dependent upon the weather conditions, latitude, altitude, and of course varies according to the species. In central and southern Europe it is frequently those species that have shown themselves to be capable of adapting themselves to conditions in northern Europe, that have the shortest period of inactivity. The usual time of hibernation extends from about mid-October to mid-March or early April, though further north, at higher altitudes, and in an abnormally long winter, the inactive period is prolonged. In the Arctic region, hibernation may last for some eight or nine months, while in southern Europe it is of short duration, and in suitably mild localities may not occur at all. Occasionally, even in northern Europe, including Britain, individual reptiles have been found about in mid-winter, during a spell of mild, sunny weather. It is not unusual to find a large number of snakes congregating together in early spring in the vicinity of their hibernation den.

Reptiles living in tropical regions do not hibernate, though a prolonged period of intense heat may force them into retirement. Even in temperate Europe, a week or two of very hot weather will cause the disappearance of many reptiles. The retreat of animals during the summer is known as *aestivation*.

Defence
The reptiles described in this book are by no means aggressive by nature. Their instinct, when approached by a potential aggressor, is to disappear quickly and unobtrusively into the undergrowth, and they often return as soon as all danger appears to have receded. Some vipers may emit a loud and prolonged warning hiss before making off. If cornered however, some reptiles put on threatening displays. Lacertids, if trapped within a confined space, may dash around wildly, and if approached, may hiss with the mouth wide open. Slow worms by contrast may show little reaction on being found.

Lizards   Many lizards, such as the lacertids, geckos, skinks and anguids, as well as the tuatera, have the ability to shed their tail voluntarily, when this is seized by an enemy. This device is known as *autotomy*, and is brought about by a sudden contraction of the muscles. The newly-shed tail jerks excitedly to and fro for several minutes, and these movements can be sufficient to distract a hungry snake, while the lizard is able to escape. Rival males often lose their tails while fighting during the mating season. The tail is composed of a series of many small segments, and it can be severed at the junction of any two of these. The fracture takes place across the corresponding vertebra at a point of incomplete ossification. Such points occur on all vertebrae from the sixth onwards. The severed portion is replaced during the course of a few months, though the vertebrae are not restored, but substituted by a rod of cartilage. The scales of the regenerated part are less deeply pigmented than those of the original tail, and the continuation of the original pattern is not maintained. Consequently a substitute tail is always recognisable, except when it has been regenerated in the very young. The base of the tail is never severed. Quite a high proportion of lizards have a regenerated tail. Sometimes when a tail has been only partially severed, a new tail will grow from the site of the wound and the lizard will eventually possess two tails. According to Frommhold (1965) lizards have been found with as many as five tails.

Most lizards on being picked up struggle and try to bite. The bite of the larger lizards such as the green lizard, and especially the eyed lizard, can be painful, and many lizards fasten their jaws firmly until they are released. By contrast, a few species, such as the common lizard, may behave quite docilely even when first handled. Many lizards may defecate because of nervousness.

Snakes Many snakes when cornered contract into a tight writhing coil, and the head is usually flattened, giving a broad and somewhat sinister appearance. They frequently hiss, this being brought about by the forceful expulsion of air from the lungs, through the glottis and the notch in the upper lip, the mouth being kept closed. At the same time the body is alternately inflated and deflated. The tongue flickers continuously, and the grass snake sometimes holds it out erect as though it were a sting. This and allied species frequently strike, usually however with the mouth closed, seldom biting. If picked up they writhe and usually release a foul smelling fluid from the vent. The grass snake in particular is also noted for its ability to feign death, a habit frequently resorted to when caught. Some snakes may remain immobile in the hope of avoiding detection.

COLUBRIDS Whip snakes, if cornered, may leap forward with great force, savagely trying to bite. If seized they struggle violently, and furiously lash their tails. Having fastened their jaws on to their captor, they tend to cling on, making chewing movements, as a result of which, one can find one's hand covered with blood. Though usually reacting in a more docile manner, the smooth snakes may often without warning slowly open their jaws and secure them around any available finger. The teeth of harmless snakes leave a horseshoe-shaped row of perforations, which usually start to bleed, but there are normally no further complications, except in tropical countries where secondary infection may set in.

VIPERS Vipers attack their enemies by making a sudden, lightning strike, in the same manner as when biting their prey (p. 28). They withdraw immediately, never clinging on in the manner of the whip snakes. If molestation continues they will strike repeatedly, though in this way the supply of venom is rapidly exhausted, and a period of recuperation is required. Though the fangs normally return to the recumbent position straight away, they may remain hanging downwards for some while after repeated use.

Treatment of snake bite

Venomous snakes appear to be fairly resistant to the bites of other members of their own species, though they may succumb to the effects of the poison of other species (Bellairs and Carrington, 1966). Some harmless species are immune to the venom of certain venomous snakes. The adder's venom for example is reported to have no effect on the grass snake.

Accidents involving man are not infrequent, especially in some parts of Europe. Fatal cases of adder bite are rare, and the most frequent victims are children. Elderly people and those in ill health are also more especially vulnerable. Fatal accidents involving the aspic and horned vipers are somewhat more common. The number of deaths due to adder bite recorded in Britain to date this century amount to about ten. Lanceau (1974) states that two people died in France as a result of snake bite in 1969, but contrasts this figure with nearly 9000 deaths resulting from road accidents there during the same year. An estimated 50 people die each year in all of Europe as a result of snake bite.

The bite   In most cases it is the limbs that are involved. In a viper bite, the flesh is punctured in only one or two places, depending on whether one or both of the fangs have penetrated. These tiny wounds bleed at first, and there may be a slight tingling sensation in the immediate area. Within ten minutes the surrounding tissues start to swell, and this may cause the bleeding to cease.

Treatment   Bleeding however should be encouraged by pressure but not by cutting with a razor, since this will usually do more harm than good. It is however advisable to disinfect the wound in order to prevent secondary infection caused by bacteria from the snake's mouth. Ideally the affected limb should be immobilized, and medical attention obtained as quickly as possible, to avert the possibility of permanent injury or even death.

Venom is rapidly absorbed by the blood stream and quickly circulates around the body. Unfortunately panic and quick movements only serve to stimulate the circulation, thereby accelerating the dispersal of the venom. Where possible the patient should be laid down to prevent unconsciousness. Some of the venom may be removed by sucking the wound. Though venom is normally ineffective when swallowed, it can prove hazardous if there are any abrasions in the mouth or alimentary tract.

Treatment by use of a tourniquet, tied between the wound and the heart, can delay the absorption of venom, but its use by unskilled people can result in gangrene. If applied, a tourniquet should be released for one minute out of every fifteen. Former methods of treatment, such as cauterizing the wound with a red hot iron, or disinfecting with alcohol or ammonia must never be done. Hot drinks and even caffeine injections can be used to combat shock, though alcohol should be avoided as this hinders the action of the antiserum.

The subsequent symptoms are extremely variable, depending on the amount of venom received, as well as on the body weight, age and general health of the victim. The quantity of venom produced seems to be influenced by the environmental temperature, and according to Fretey (1975) there is an increase in its toxicity from March to October. At best the effects may be trivial, little worse than a bee sting, while at worst, death may ensue, after a period ranging from 2 to 60 hours. In some snakes the venom is predominantly neurotoxic in effect, acting upon the heart and lungs, and causing paralysis in fatal cases.

The venom of vipers however is mainly haemolytic. It destroys the red corpuscles, and causes haemorrhage of the blood vessels, as well as extensive damage to the tissues. It can also induce intravascular thrombosis. In fatal cases death ensues as a result of cardiac failure. The venom of the Balkan adder (*Vipera berus bosniensis*) has a relatively high neurotoxic action, and cannot be neutralized with antiserum that is normally effective in cases of adder bite. According to Bolkay (1929), the poison is very similar to that of the Indian cobra, and this snake has been considered to be the most poisonous of European snakes. According to Lombardi and Bianco (1974), the adder is less dangerous than the aspic viper. The average amount of venom injected per bite by the adder and aspic viper is, they state, 3.5 milligrammes and 5 milligrammes respectively (dry weight). The horned viper is apparently able to inject up to 7 milligrammes.

After the initial swelling, a burning sensation develops at the site of injection, and in severe cases the swelling quickly progresses up the entire limb, extending onto the body, added to which such general symptoms as giddiness, vomiting, diarrhoea, prostration as well as a feeble pulse, cold, clammy perspiration and general restlessness may develop. These effects are certainly aggravated by shock, and the patient may eventually pass into a coma. Severe swelling may continue for up to 24 hours or longer, though it normally subsides within three days. A heavy, aching sensation is subsequently felt around the bitten area, and the surrounding tissues show discolouration, reddish in mild cases, blackish or purple when the condition is more severe.

At one time an antiserum was given to all patients as a matter of hospital routine. Within recent years however doubts have arisen concerning the wisdom of this procedure, since some people are hypersensitive to its effects. At least 3 deaths in Britain resulted from antiserum reaction. In mild cases antiserum may not be administered at all, though in serious cases it is the only reliable form of treatment. In order to be effective it should be given within four hours after an accident. Nowadays antihistamine drugs are frequently injected first of all, thereby reducing the possibility of an adverse reaction.

The antiserum is available in ampoules of 10cc, and should be injected as soon as possible, either under the skin of the thigh, or near the wound. It should be injected slowly and carefully, and it is advisable for 1 cc only to be injected at first in case of extreme sensitivity. Normally the full amount should be given to both children and adults, and if there is no rapid improvement, the dosage should be repeated, several times if necessary. As a last resort a blood transfusion can be given, and this can bring about a sudden improvement.

Antiserums are prepared by immunizing horses with a certain type of venom in regulated and increasing doses. Samples of the horses' lymph are subsequently taken, sterilized and prepared for inoculation. The antiserum known as 'ER' produced by the Pasteur Institute in Paris, is effective in neutralizing the venom of *Vipera berus berus* and *Vipera aspis*, while 'EO' is used in cases involving *Vipera aspis* and *Vipera ammodytes*. Behringwerke AG of Marburg now produce a polyvalent serum known as 'Europa', for use in the treatment of accidents with European and Mediterranean vipers. Recently it has been made effective also against the venom of *Vipera berus bosniensis*.

Tortoises   Tortoises have hardly any means of defence, apart from their hard, bony shell, into which they can quickly withdraw their head, limbs and tail. This gives ample protection from would-be predators. If picked up, they remain in this position for some while. Some species of tortoise, such as the European pond tortoise, may use their sharp claws, in an effort to free themselves. The same species may also release a jet of water from the anal sacs, mixed with excreta, a foul-smelling combination. Only very rarely do tortoises bite. Young tortoises are more vulnerable to predators however because of their soft shell.

Parasites
The parasites of reptiles are of three kinds: protozoa, worms, and the ticks and mites, particularly the latter. Protozoa are primitive unicellular animals, all of which are very tiny, only the largest being visible to the naked eye. Most of them live in the soil and in water, but some inhabit the internal organs of higher forms of life, especially the digestive tract and the blood. All reptiles act as hosts to a number of species of such parasites at any given time, without any

adverse effects, though nourishment is gained at the expense of the host. Several types of parasitic worm, *Cestoda* (tape worms), *Nematoda* (thread worms), *Trematoda* (flukes) and *Acanthocephala* (thorny-headed worms), inhabit the internal organs of reptiles, especially the alimentary canal. Both kinds of parasite may eventually be passed on to a new host, being transferred via the excrement of the original host.

Ticks and mites are fairly close relatives of the spiders, and these are external parasites, attaching themselves to the skin of their host in order to feed on their blood. They frequently lodge themselves under the belly plates of snakes as well as under the scales. They are most usually found on captive reptiles, seldom on specimens in the wild. If left to multiply unchecked, these parasites can reduce the host to an emaciated state. One snake mite is the carrier of the harmful bacteria *Proteus hydrophilus* whose presence can rapidly prove fatal for the host.

Relationship with man

There is no doubt that, in the past, many European reptiles have been aided by the activities of man, especially by the clearance of thick forest land, and the reclamation of water-logged areas. The establishment of country paths, ditches and hedgerows, and the building of stone walls have provided good habitats where reptiles have settled and subsequently thrived. Even quarries and dumps have become favourite haunts for certain species.

More recently however reptile populations have become reduced because of intensive agricultural development, urbanization and afforestation. Furthermore, greater mobility has given large numbers of people access to many areas previously safe from intrusion. The establishment of seaside resorts has also proven detrimental. The pollution of ponds and rivers and the use of pesticides have certainly contributed to a decline in the number of reptiles. Fires have similarly played a negative role. In addition fear and prejudice have led to the indiscriminate killing of reptiles, especially snakes and slow worms. Even the innocuous three toed skink is frequently regarded as venomous, and killed. The killing of poisonous snakes is more understandable. In some areas they are abundant, despite intensive efforts to reduce their numbers, and they are therefore a potential hazard to man. In other areas however, campaigns to get rid of snakes have been effective.

Unfortunately the harm done to reptilian populations has not been solely perpetrated by those wilfully intent on their destruction. The reduction of reptiles in some areas is certainly due to over-zealous collectors, people who are contributing to the decline of the very species whose survival they would like to see ensured. From a conservation viewpoint little harm can be done by keeping individual reptiles in captivity for study purposes, provided that such specimens have been obtained from localities where the species occurs in abundance. Regrettably in some parts of the European mainland, whole areas have been plundered by professional and semi-professional collectors who supply pet shops with large numbers of reptiles, many of which die before they can be sold because of inadequate conditions and overcrowding while in transit. In some European countries the harmless reptiles are protected by law. In Switzerland, Hungary and East Germany all species—including the poisonous vipers—are protected. Because of its rarity, the meadow viper is protected in both Austria and France. In Romania land tortoises are protected throughout the country; other reptiles only in nature reserves. In Britain protection has been given only to the two species most threatened with extinction: the sand lizard and the smooth snake. On 1 August 1975 the Conservation of Wild Creatures and Wild Plants Act came into effect, making it illegal to take, touch, kill, injure, sell or offer for sale either of these reptiles without a special licence from the Nature Conservancy Council. Particularly constructive has been the establishment of nature reserves, where suitable habitat is set aside, and subsequently maintained.

Though of little direct commercial value to man, reptiles are of considerable economic value, since they destroy a wide range of pests, such as slugs, insects and rodents. Within recent years snake venoms have played an increasingly important part in medicine, and have been adapted for use as pain-killers, and as blood coagulants (in haemophilia). They have also been employed in the treatment of rheumatism, sciatica, arthritis, neuralgia, convulsions and epilepsy.

The severe flooding of Hamburg in 1962 has been attributed to the failure of the dykes to resist the incoming torrents, because of extensive burrowing in them by voles. These rodents were apparently able to breed unchecked, after the adder population there had been drastically reduced.

Reptiles in captivity Within recent years reptiles have become increasingly popular in captivity and all too frequently one witnesses unhappy captives constantly struggling in vain to escape cramped, inhospitable cages. Furthermore the keeping of wild animals in captivity might be objected to in principle. However, many species adapt well to life in captivity, when adequate living quarters and a suitable diet are provided, giving us the opportunity to learn much about their behaviour.

Ideal conditions are those which closely resemble the native habitat, and therefore the outdoor garden reptilary is most suitable to native species. This however is insufficient for reptiles used to a higher temperature than that offered by the British climate. In this case the use of a greenhouse or heated vivarium is preferable, though glass has the effect of filtering important ultra-violet rays. This can be remedied by the use of an ultra-violet lamp.

If good health is to be maintained, it is important to provide a regular supply of food and fresh water. The diet should resemble as far as possible that preferred in the wild state, and should be varied from time to time. Such items as mealworms and gentles are usually easy to obtain and are readily accepted by most lizards. It is essential that reptiles should not be over-fed, especially shortly before hibernation, as their ability to digest becomes drastically reduced. Excreta should be promptly removed, as should fragments of shed skin.

Reptiles should never be kept in cramped or over-crowded surroundings, for they quickly succumb to disease. Those given a fairly natural environment tend to live in a similar manner to those in the wild.

Reptiles can be kept active throughout the hibernation period by providing some artificial source of warmth. Normally however these reptiles do not survive as long as those which have been allowed to hibernate. During the winter months the vivarium should be kept in a dark, dry and cool, but frost-free condition. A constant temperature of about 5°C is ideal. Care should be taken to ensure that their winter quarters are not accessible to rats and mice.

It is possible to rear eggs laid in captivity, provided a suitable degree of warmth and humidity is provided. The success rate varies according to the species however. If kept insufficiently moist reptile eggs shrivel, whereas they grow a mould if allowed to become too wet.

Many reptiles will in time allow themselves to be picked up, and show no alarm when handled. Non-poisonous snakes are often best tamed by regular handling; lizards by being tempted with items of food offered in the hand. The response can vary from one specimen to another. Some individuals refuse to be tamed, and ignore all food. It is inadvisable for inexperienced people to force-feed snakes, since their mouths are delicate, and are easily damaged.

Snakes should never be pinned down by the throat with a forked stick, when about to pick them up or transfer them from place to place, as this can inflict damage to the gullet.

Caution should always be exercised when dealing with poisonous snakes. Since the Dangerous Wild Animals Bill became law in Britain in 1976, those wishing to keep them must first apply for a local authority licence, which is granted only exceptionally, after a thorough scrutiny of the available facilities.

Disease

Reptiles, if exposed to cold or draught, may succumb to pneumonia or tuberculosis. Pneumonia can also develop in overcrowded or inadequately ventilated cages. Captive snakes occasionally suffer from canker, a disease which involves the mouth and digestive tract, and if untreated proves fatal.

Those infected with ticks and mites can be cured, in the early stages at least, by being liberally bathed in castor oil, medicinal paraffin or vaseline, and placed in a clean polythene or cloth bag for a period of about 24 hours, preferably in a cool, dark place. After this they can be returned to their quarters, which in the meantime should be thoroughly cleansed.

Distribution

It was in the Carboniferous period, some 310 million years ago, that the first reptiles evolved from the early amphibians. They developed rapidly in the Permian period and reached their zenith in the Mesozoic era. Most of the groups of reptiles that flourished at that time eventually became extinct, and today only six orders survive, having become reconciled to the domination of mammalian forms. The SAURIA and SERPENTES (lizards and snakes) are of comparatively recent origin, and evidence of their success is shown by the great variety and number of their forms. By contrast the TESTUDINES are a very ancient order and have changed little since they first appeared. They are in fact older than some long extinct forms. Today four orders of reptiles are found in Europe: the SAURIA, AMPHISBAENIA (with a single species), SERPENTES and the TESTUDINES. None of the families of reptiles occurring in Europe are confined to this region, and in fact all of them are better represented elsewhere.

Two factors influence distribution of species and numbers: geological history and climate. The species living in northern and central Europe today have descended from those which recolonized this area after the last Ice Age. At its maximum extent, the ice shield covered most of Ireland, most of Britain (to about as far south as 52°N.), and much of continental Europe, extending approximately as far south as Cologne, Cracow and Kiev. In addition many of the mountainous districts of central Europe were extensively glaciated. The zone lying between these areas was a region of loess, with a tundra climate and vegetation with perhaps scattered conifers, thus being totally unsuited to reptile life. The spread of the glaciers during this time inevitably resulted in a slow southward migration of reptiles, though this was severely limited by the high mountain ranges, which in Europe, unlike those of North America, run from west to east, rather than from north to south. A further obstacle was the Mediterranean Sea. These factors may largely account for the small number of species inhabiting Europe today, compared with the numbers inhabiting North America. From time to time land bridges were formed between southern Europe and Africa as a result of the general drop in sea-level, which accompanied the glaciation further north. The mild climate of the Sahara at that time was an ideal retreat for those species able to reach it. As the glaciers started slowly to withdraw, there was a gradual migration north of fauna and flora from the south and south-east. Many species were assisted to a great extent by the removal of large tracts of forest land, first by mesolithic, and later by neolithic man.

Britain remained attached to the continent until the opening of the straits of Dover, about 7000 years ago. It was prior to this that Britain's present species of reptiles arrived. Britain's separation from the continent, like Ireland's from Britain, was brought about by a general rise in the sea level due to the melting ice, and resultant subsidence of the land.

As climatic conditions improved, Europe's connections with Africa became severed, and the subsequent development of desert conditions in the Sahara region forced many species to retreat further south, another reason why Europe's fauna today is not as rich as it might have been.

The other major factor influencing reptilian distribution is climatic, the number of species being fewer further north. A continental climate is more favourable to reptiles, because of the warmer summers which aid the development of the eggs of oviparous species, and also because of the winters which are more consistently cold, offering better prospects for an uninterrupted hibernation. Up to some 10,000 years ago, the general climate in Europe was warmer and dryer than that of today, and as a result, many species had wider ranges than at present. The European pond tortoise occurred in eastern Britain, Denmark and southern Sweden, but has since become extinct in these regions. Other species may survive only as isolated relics in warm localities in the more northern parts of their range, as for example the wall lizard, green lizard, dice snake and Aesculapian snake which are all found in Germany.

In southern Europe the Mediterranean islands are rich in endemic races, but the reptiles of northern Europe's islands merely reflect the mainland fauna, there being no known endemic races. It should be remembered that the former islands have been habitable for a much longer time, so that more time has elapsed during which variations were able to evolve. In addition they have longer and more favourable summer seasons, and consequently a higher reproductive rate.

The total absence of reptiles from Iceland is probably due to its isolation since the last Ice Age rather than present climatic conditions. A few species occur at a similar latitude in Scandinavia. The paucity of reptiles in Ireland is attributable to the fact that this island probably became severed from Britain before south-eastern England broke its ties with the continent and reptiles had not reached further than southern Britain. Climatic reasons are likely to account for the small numbers of reptiles in Britain and Scandinavia, and significantly it is the same six species which occur in both areas.

Despite man's ceaseless activity in Europe since the last Ice Age, reptiles—especially the much-persecuted snakes—have shown themselves remarkably resilient. Some reptiles, due to climatic or ecological changes, or to man's interference, are at present retreating. They are particularly vulnerable on the edge of their ranges where fragmentation occurs. Many species, historically common, have become rare. Although man is the greatest threat to reptilian life, there is no immediate danger of the complete extinction for any of the species described here.

At last there are now more hopeful signs that man may at last be developing a more responsible attitude towards his environment. Life on this planet has taken millions of years to evolve. It would be an irreversible tragedy to destroy it in a few decades through sheer greed and thoughtlessness.

Numerous attempts have been made to transfer reptiles from one locality to another, with the aim of establishing breeding colonies. They are usually released in some more northerly land, where they were not known to occur previously, or have become extinct. Efforts to establish the European pond tortoise, green lizard and wall lizard in Britain have mostly proved futile, though there are a few successful breeding colonies of the wall lizard in southern England. Such attempts can succeed only where conditions approximate to those in the species' native land, offering a suitable climate, plenty of cover, and an adequate food supply, relatively few predators and competitors, as well as good conditions for the incubation of the eggs and for hibernation. The introduction of a totally new species could unbalance the present ecosystem and should not be advocated.

THE
LIZARDS

The Common Lizard
Lacerta vivipara **Jacquin** 1787

Terra typica: Schneeberg, near Vienna, Austria
Plate 1

The common lizard has a fairly slender body and a shortish head. The comparatively short and thick tail is, from the base, fairly uniform in size for about half of its length. In males the tail is swollen at the base and constitutes a little under two-thirds, while in the females it forms up to about three-fifths, of the total length. In the very young however, it is only a little longer than the head and body together. This species normally grows to a length of about 14 centimetres though some specimens have been known to reach up to 18 centimetres. The largest specimen mentioned by Smith (1969) from the British Isles was a female from County Meath, (Ireland), which measured 17.8 centimetres.

Scalation

Dorsals: 25–37 oval or hexagonal scales around middle of body, keeled, more or less imbricate; tail scales strongly keeled above & pointed backwards, smooth underneath. 6 or 8 longitudinal (23–33 transverse) rows of *ventrals*. *Anal* preceded by 2 (rarely 1) rows of small plates; 5–15 *femoral* pores on each thigh. Nostril at junction of 2 or 3 plates, not bordering *rostral*; 1 (rarely 2) *postnasals*; 1 anterior *loreal* bordering *internasal*; 2–4 *temporals* bordering each *parietal*; 3 or 4 (rarely 5) upper *labials* anterior to *subocular*; *gular* fold indistinct or absent; collar comprising 7–10 (usually 8–10) strongly serrated plates.

Colouration

Dorsal region   The ground colour of the common lizard is quite variable, being yellowish, reddish, bronze, brown, grey-brown or dark greenish. Males are usually darker than females. A row of whitish or pale yellow spots, which may link to form a longitudinal stripe, is present on either side of the back and along each flank, and each row may continue more or less distinctly for some way along the tail. In addition a more or less continuous dark brown or black stripe extends along the vertebral region, particularly in females. This stripe soon disintegrates on the tail. A few scattered dark, light or mixed flecks may be present on either side of the vertebral stripe, and these may form longitudinal rows. Similar markings frequently occur on the flanks. In males these flecks are often more densely distributed and the vertebral stripe may be obscure or even non-existent. Sometimes the light flecks are bordered with black. The flanks are generally darker than the top of the back.

Sporadic black, white or rusty-coloured spots may be present on the limbs and tail which are otherwise similar to the dorsal colouration. The head is usually light, dark or olive-brown above, sometimes with irregular dark spots, and the upper lip shields are usually a dirty white. I have occasionally found individuals, usually females, whose basic colour was an attractive light turquoise. The chin and throat are whitish, sometimes with a bluish tinge, and a few tiny black dots may be present.

Ventral region   There is a marked contrast between the two sexes in the colouration of the belly. That of the male is orange or bright red, and there are numerous black spots. In the female it is a mustard colour, yellow or whitish, sometimes with a bluish or even greenish tinge on either side of the belly. It is usually unspotted, though in some cases a few light or dark brown spots may be present. I once found a female in Hampshire, whose belly was thickly flecked with dark blue spots. The underside of the tail is a dirty white, sometimes with black flecks.

Juvenile colouration   The ground colour of the young is black, blackish bronze or dark brown, though the adult pattern is already faintly visible as a golden or dirty yellowish outline. The underside is a uniform dirty white or even bluish silver.

Varieties   Melanic specimens (var. *nigra*) are occasionally found, even in England. Those that I found had faint tints of orange or yellow on the belly, which acted as a guide as to their sexes. A variety, formerly known as var. *carniolica* is distinguished by being almost uniformly brown.

Habitat
This species avoids the hotter parts of Europe and Asia. In southern Europe it favours higher altitudes, rarely being met with below 500 metres, except in certain humid districts, such as rice fields and marshy meadows. North of the Alps, as well as in Britain and in Scandinavia, it has adapted itself to a wide range of conditions. It is at home on commons, moorlands, heaths, meadows, boglands, hedgerows, grassy banks, the borders of woods, forest clearings and in sunny glades. It does not avoid damp regions, frequently occurring near water. In coastal regions it inhabits marshes, sand dunes and rocky or chalk cliffs. It is found beside country paths and roads, beside old walls and fences, on railway embankments, in stone quarries and in rubbish dumps. Unlike the wall lizard it does not penetrate far into villages and towns. It is apparently absent from the steppeland districts of southern Russia.

Altitude The common lizard is found up to 3000 metres in Austria and the French Alps, even exceeding this altitude in Switzerland and Italy.

Co-habiting species The common lizard is frequently found living in the same localities as the sand lizard, the slow worm, the grass snake, the smooth snake and the adder. I have also come across it in areas favoured by the meadow viper (in Austria), and the aspic viper (in Switzerland).

Behaviour

The common lizard is very much a sun-lover, and when completely relaxed likes to spend much of the day basking with its body flattened out and tilted towards the sun, with its limbs extended. In addition it may turn up the soles of its feet. It is however easily alerted and is quite agile in its movements, though less so than the wall lizard. When disturbed it makes its way off into the undergrowth by an alternating series of abrupt dashes and brief pauses, but usually returns to its original basking spot or one nearby, when all danger seems to have disappeared. It will often return on successive days to some favourite sun-trap, such as a pile of brushwood, a log, stone or clearing amid thick vegetation. It sometimes basks on tree stumps and on the low branches and trunks of trees. Prior to leaving its retreat first thing in the morning, it cautiously protrudes its snout for some while before emerging.

Though a sunlover, it none the less dislikes a strong heat and in hot weather is most usually found in some shady retreat. During a continuous hot spell it may prove difficult to find. After the sun has set and in cool weather I have frequently found it curled up under flat stones, logs, pieces of bark or discarded scrap metal. According to Avery and McArdle (1973) the preferred body temperature of this species in the west of England is about 30°C., a temperature which, they state can be achieved very rapidly in summer. The earliest time this species was observed in March was 9.15 a.m., the earliest time in June, 7.54 a.m.

Compared to the sand lizard it is quite a good climber, although it is rather less accomplished than the wall lizard. It is an excellent swimmer and has been known to enter water in search of food, as well as in times of emergency. In the latter circumstances it has been known to submerge itself for up to nine minutes (Smith, 1969).

It is most often found alone, except during early spring, in the mating season and during hibernation. I have sometimes found it in hiding under the same piece of rubble as the slow worm, with which it gets on well. The common lizard appears to spend its entire life within a comparatively small area. Its territorial routes are, according to Simms (1971), less defined than those of the sand lizard.

Food

The common lizard's diet consists chiefly of spiders, harvestmen, and such insects as bugs, aphides, flies and small beetles. Other insects and their larvae are sometimes taken, though large beetles and hairy caterpillars are ignored. Centipedes, earthworms and slugs are occasionally devoured; in my experience woodlice are frequently rejected, though I have known an isolated specimen in captivity to accept them with relish. According to Smith (1969) ants (*Formica fusca*) are sometimes eaten as well as their eggs and larvae. This species appears to be insensitive to *Hymenoptera* venom. Large or struggling prey is secured in the jaws, and well shaken until it is stunned, before being swallowed.

Detailed accounts of this species' feeding habits are given by Avery (1962) and Simms (1971).

Enemies

In various parts of its range the common lizard is preyed upon by the adder and the meadow viper. Doubtless the smooth snake also accounts for large numbers of common lizards. Apart from snakes its enemies include flesh-eating mammals as well as predatory birds.

Reproduction

Mating   The usual time for mating is late April or May. Fights between rival males over a female are frequent at this time. This fighting however is not as fierce as it is between rival male sand lizards. The successful contestant seizes the female's head or flank firmly in his jaws, and copulation proceeds straight away. During this act the male continues to hold his mate in his jaws, and this may leave a bluish scar visible for several months. Smith (1969) states that mating may vary from five to thirty minutes, and that it may take place more than once between the same partners.

Birth of young   Despite its scientific name *vivipara*, this species is really ovo-viviparous in most of its range. In this respect it is unique for its genus, since the remaining species are all oviparous. The young are born from late June until early September, usually at the end of July. The females frequently resort to the same area to have their young, normally somewhere fairly damp, and subsequently quite large numbers of young can be seen within the same vicinity for several weeks. The usual number of young varies from five to eight, and ten is frequently stated to be the maximum. Angel (1946) however states that from 3 to 15 are produced. A specimen found near Bournemouth, Dorset, was given to me, and subsequently (in July 1956) brought forth a litter of 15. The young are usually laid in quick succession, though there is sometimes an interval of several days before laying is complete. The female shows no interest in her newly-born offspring. Hatching from the membrane often takes place almost immediately, though this can be delayed for several hours; or according to Smith (1969), even days. The egg-membranes measure approximately 11 millimetres by 8–9 millimetres, and when hatched the young measure from 35 to 50 millimetres.

The poorly developed egg-tooth is non-functional and the lizard frees itself from the membrane mainly by stabbing movements of the head. In rare cases this membrane is already punctured within the oviduct. During the first 24 hours the egg-tooth is shed. The little yolk sac protruding from the belly soon becomes detached as the creature starts its independent life.

Growth and maturity   The young grow somewhat during the late summer and autumn before their first hibernation. A year later the sexes have developed their distinctive colouration, and the males by then possess the swelling at the tail base. According to Simms (1971) the males are able to breed after 22 to 23 months, the females after 32 to 36 months.

Oviparity   The common lizard apparently becomes an oviparous species in the Pyrenees. In 1924 Lantz discovered a cluster of some sixty eggs with parchment-like shells under a stone, near the village of Gerde (Haute-Pyrénées). The eggs measured about 11.5 by 9 millimetres, and the embryos were apparently in very different stages of development. The egg-tooth was much more developed than is normal in this species.

Hibernation
The common lizard generally disappears into its winter retreat about the middle of October, selecting suitable holes in the ground and crevices amid the roots of vegetation. The adults are the first to disappear while the young may still be active up to the end of the month, or even into November. The latest date I found one in western Hampshire was on 30 October (1954). This species usually hibernates in groups. I once knew a disused railway track which was a favourite haunt of these lizards. During January 1955 the track and sleepers were removed, revealing several groups of hibernating common lizards. The number of specimens in each group varied from four to a dozen. In the same area on 27 December (1954) I found two baby specimens curled up together under a half buried piece of coke. Mild, sunny weather has been known to attract this species out for a short spell in the middle of winter.

The common lizard usually emerges from hibernation in March, though if it is sufficiently warm and sunny, it may leave its winter quarters early in

February. The earliest I have seen it in west Hampshire was on 12 February (1957). Towards the Arctic Circle the hibernation period becomes progressively longer. According to Terent'ev and Cernov (1949), it awakens in late March or the beginning of April in Russia, though in the north of its Russian range it does not appear until the middle of June. In the north of Scandinavia it is active for a maximum of only three or four months, spending the rest of the year in hibernation.

Male common lizards are normally the first to leave their winter quarters; these are followed by the young, and then finally the females.

Ecdysis
The adult common lizard sheds its skin up to four times a year. Simms (1971) reports that immature specimens shed some six times during the active season, this being the time of the most rapid growth. He states that baby specimens shed their skins some two or three times before their first hibernation.

General response
The rapidity with which it darts through the undergrowth when alarmed makes it quite a difficult species to catch. Although it may repeatedly return to the same spot after having been frightened off, it does not usually reappear if its tail has been severed or even if it has been touched in an unsuccessful attempt to catch it. I have frequently been able to coax a basking specimen to come nearer towards me by deliberately and carefully casting a shadow over it, and over the area behind it, at the same time ensuring that the area before it is well exposed to the sun. When found in retreat however it is much more sluggish in its movements, and is far more easy to catch.

The newly-caught common lizard frequently shows little fear if carefully handled. I have known it to sit on my hand quite freely a few minutes after capture, showing no desire to escape, though it may suddenly make a dash for freedom. This species rarely bites, but I have known the occasional pregnant female do so.

This species does well in captivity. Food may be refused for a day or two after capture, but is normally readily taken. It can become very tame, and will learn to take food offered to it from the hand. I have known common lizards to rush towards me and carefully search each finger in turn in the hope of finding some tit-bit. It lives well with other members of its species, though tug-of-war battles usually develop when food is presented. I have experienced no difficulty in keeping it with other species of lizards of similar size, and I have also kept it safely with slow worms and even grass snakes. Unless given ample space in which to pursue its activities, captive specimens frequently lose some of their agility. It has been known to survive for five years in captivity.

Distribution

The common lizard has an immensely wide range, extending across most of northern and central Europe, as well as temperate Asia. It is in fact the world's most widely distributed reptile.

British Isles   In Britain it occurs more or less throughout, though it becomes rare around the Scottish lakes and in the highlands. The off-shore islands where it is found include the Inner Hebrides (Skye, Mull, Jura, Islay and Arran among them), the Isle of Man, Anglesey, and some of the smaller Welsh islands: Bardsey, Ramsey and Skomer (Lockley, 1970). It also occurs on the Isle of Wight.

Ireland   It is the only species of reptile to inhabit Ireland, where it has a fairly extensive range, although it does not yet appear to be on record from certain counties. Its apparent absence from some areas is probably due to lack of observations. I have found it near the town of Tipperary, though I know of no other records of its occurrence from any part of that county. In some parts of Ireland it appears to be quite a common species. Hecht (1928) mentions it from the island of Scariff, off the south-western coast of County Kerry. It is also known from Cape Clear island.

Scandinavia   It is found throughout most of Scandinavia and Finland, including Lapland, and reaches about 70°N. In Sweden it is common in the southern and central parts while in the north it has been found as far north as Karesuando (68° 30 N) near the Finnish border (Gislén and Kauri, 1959). It also occurs on Gotland and Öland, as well as the Ahvenanmaa islands. According to Hecht (1928), it is absent from Gottska Sandön. In many parts of Norway it is quite abundant.

France, Spain and Benelux   In France it is widespread though local, often occurring in places where the wall lizard is absent. It is rare in much of the south-west, while in the south it is associated with high altitudes. In neighbouring Spain it is confined to the north-western Pyrenees and the Cantabrian mountains. In Belgium it is the only reptile to occur in all provinces; it is also present in Luxembourg. It inhabits Holland – mainly the eastern and southern parts, being locally distributed in the central region, and in addition it reappears on the island of Schouwen-Duiveland in the south and on Terschelling in the north.

Central Europe   It is well represented in Germany, inhabiting also the islands of Fehmarn, Rügen and Usedom. It appears to have been introduced to all of the East Frisian islands, with the exception of Wangerooge (Rühmekorf,

1970). It is also widespread in Denmark and many of its islands, including Bornholm, as well as in Poland where it ranges almost throughout, but is most common in the foothills and mountains of the south, though it avoids the very high mountainous regions (Berger, Jaskowska and Młynarski, 1969). It is known from all parts of Switzerland, though according to Stemmler (1971) it occurs only locally below 1000m. Capocaccia (1968) states that it is common in the Alpine districts of Italy. It is also known from the Adige and Po valleys, as well as the provinces of Lombardy and Venetia. For Austria Eiselt (1961) lists it from the northern and eastern Tirol, as well as the provinces of Vorarlberg, Salzburg, Upper and Lower Austria, Styria, Carinthia and finally north-eastern Burgenland, east of Neusiedler Lake. In Lower Austria it is absent to the north of the Danube (Werner, 1897).

Eastern central Europe   In Czechoslovakia it is found mainly in mountainous regions and foothills. Its range in Hungary is quite limited, being known from a few places in the north-west near the Austrian border, and on the Great Plain south-east of Budapest. It is also associated with the mountains of the north-east, as well as with the lowlands near the Russian and Romanian borders. In Romania it appears to be restricted to Transylvania and the Carpathian regions.

Balkans   On the Balkan peninsula it is represented mainly at higher altitudes, occurring in Slovenia, Croatia (Velebit, Kapela and Papuk), Bosnia, south eastern Montenegro, eastern Serbia and western Macedonia, but it is apparently absent from Hercegovina, Istria and the Adriatic region. It also inhabits the higher altitudes of western Bulgaria (Beškov and Beron, 1964).

Eastern range   Its range in eastern Europe includes the Baltic states, the islands of Hiiumaa and Saaremaa (Kauri, 1946) and much of Russia, where it is found as far north as Archangel and the Kola peninsula. It seldom extends further south than 50 to 51°N in Russia. It is absent from the Crimean peninsula, as well as from the Caucasus. To the south of the tundra zone it extends across Siberia to the Altai mountains, northern Mongolia, the Kolyma region, the Sea of Okhotsk, and the coastal region of Manchuria, as well as the island of Sachalin, north of Japan. Terent' ev and Cernov (1949) mention it from the Ussuri region to the south of Lake Khanka.

   Despite its vast range and the varied types of habitat to which it has adapted itself, this species is often considered to be monotypic, though the far eastern form has been regarded as a distinct race: *Lacerta vivipara sachalinensis* **Terent' ev.**

Nomenclature *for northern and central Europe*

English   Common lizard, Viviparous lizard
Dutch   Levendbare hagedis
German   Waldeidechse, Bergeidechse
Danish   Levendefødende Firben, Skovfirben
Norwegian   Firfisle
Swedish   Skogs-ödla
French   Lézard vivipare
Italian   Lucertola vivipara
Romanian Sopîrla de munte
Hungarian Elevenszülő gyík, Fialló gyík
Finnish   Sisilisko
Czech   Ještěrka živorodá
Slovakian   Jašterica živorodá
Polish   Jaszczurka żyworodna
Serbo-Croatian   Močvarna gušterica
Russian   Живородящая Ящерица

The Pontic Lizard
Lacerta praticola

Sub-species found in eastern central Europe:
Lacerta praticola pontica **Lantz & Cyrén** 1919
Terra typica restricta: Gagry, in the western Caucasus
Plate 2

Rather similar in appearance to the common lizard is the little-known Pontic lizard. This species is one of the smallest of the European lacertids, seldom reaching a length of 15 centimetres. The maximum recorded length so far appears to have been 15.4 centimetres. It has a narrow body and a moderate-sized head, which is markedly broader than high, but is somewhat narrower and longer than that of the common lizard. In the male the tail is barely twice the length of the rest of the body, while in the female it is not more than one and a third times as long.

Scalation
Dorsals: 32–43 hexagonal or rhomboid scales around middle of body, juxtaposed or subimbricate and diagonally keeled. 6 longitudinal rows of *ventrals* (25–28 transverse rows in males, 28–31 in females). *Anal* preceded by 1

row of small plates; 9–13 *femoral* pores on each thigh. Nostril at junction of 3 (rarely 4) plates, not bordering *rostral*; usually 1 *postnasal*; 1 anterior *loreal*; 2–4 upper *temporals*; 4 upper *labials* anterior to *subocular*; *gular* fold absent or indistinct; collar comprising 5–9 more or less serrated plates.

Colouration
The basic colouration on top of the back and tail is light or olive brown, and along the spinal region is a thick stripe composed of small and irregular dark brown patches. This stripe extends from the nape along the body to the tail, where it then quickly disintegrates. I have frequently observed a greenish sheen on top of the back. The sides are a darker brown and there is a narrow, longitudinal stripe composed of a row of whitish spots, which continues for a short distance along the side of the tail. Above the head is uniformly brown. The sides of the head are also brown but the upper labials are a dirty white, and the throat is white. The legs are brown and have occasional whitish spots. In the male the belly is pea-green, light green or greenish yellow, while that of the female is sulphur or light yellow. The ventral colouration persists for a while along the underside of the tail, and this then fades into a dirty white.

The young are similar to the adults in colour, but are uniformly brown, a feature which may sometimes be maintained throughout adult life.

Habitat
This species inhabits the borders of woods and forests, as well as sunny glades. According to Nikol'skii (1915), in Russia it avoids treeless localities and areas devoid of bushy vegetation. It is, he states, an inhabitant of dense broadleaf forests and virgin forest thickets. The localities familiar to me are invariably hilly, warm, dry and well sheltered. Schreiber (1912) states that it has been found at a height of 569 metres in the hills near Orșova in Romania, while Beškov and Beron (1964) report that it extends to 700–800 metres in Bulgaria. According to Cyrén (1933) in the Black Sea coastal regions of Bulgaria it even inhabits marshy territory.

Co-habiting species   In eastern Yugoslavia I have observed the Pontic lizard living in the same habitat as the Balkan skink, as well as with wall and green lizards. Stugren (1961) says that in Romania he found it living alongside the green lizard and slow worm, but not with the wall lizard.

Behaviour
The Pontic lizard is a sun lover which enjoys basking on piles of wood, on brushwood and in clearings in the undergrowth. It is easily overlooked because of its brown colouration, but when disturbed, it makes a dash for cover,

thereby drawing attention to itself. I have noticed that it normally returns to resume its basking when all appears to be safe again. Unlike the wall lizard it is not particularly agile in its movements, and is thus not too difficult to catch. Sometimes it may be found in hiding under rocks. It is a reasonably good climber and is able to run up tree trunks. I have found it a rather docile species, nothing like so timid as the wall lizard, but neither so responsive nor so tamable as the common lizard.

Food
According to Terent' ev and Cernov (1949) beetles constitute about 50 per cent of its diet. Cicadas, Orthoptera—especially grasshoppers are taken, and other insects such as flies, small butterflies and caterpillars—if not too hairy—are also devoured. Spiders are accepted, but Schreiber (1912) states that earthworms and slugs are rejected. He also says that this species drinks comparatively little. Those that I kept in captivity fed readily upon spiders and mealworms. I was not able to persuade them to come and collect food offered in my fingers.

Reproduction
This lizard, unlike its near relative the common lizard, is oviparous. Mating takes place in May, and the female lays from four to six pure-white eggs at the end of June or July. They measure approximately 6.5 to 7 by 10 to 12 millimetres. The newly hatched have a total length of about 5 centimetres.

Hibernation
The Pontic lizard is active from April until October in Romania. In Russia, near Krasnodar it appears at the beginning of April, and Terent' ev and Cernov (1949) state that active life similarly continues until October, the adults being the first to disappear.

Distribution
The Pontic lizard was apparently not discovered in the Danubian region until as recently as 1894, when Méhely found it living in large numbers near Baïle Herculane in the Cerna valley in Romania. Elsewhere in Romania it is known to occur in the mountainous districts in the south of the Banat, in the Iron Gate area, and in the regions of Oltenia and Bucharest. In Yugoslavia it is found in the eastern part: near Bela Crkva, Belgrade, in the Iron Gate region south of the Danube, in the Timok valley near the Bulgarian border and near Vranje in southern Serbia. In Bulgaria it is found near Belogradčik in the north west, but otherwise appears to be restricted to the eastern part, extending as far west as Ruse, Kotel and Malko Târnovo (Beškov and Beron, 1964), the last locality

being situated near the Turkish border. It has recently been discovered in the Istranca mountains on the Turkish side of the border (Eiselt, 1970). In the Caucasus region it is confined to the north-western part, in the coastal districts of the Black Sea, and its range terminates approximately in the region of Krasnodar.

Other sub-species

An attempt has been made to subdivide this sub-species into two further sub-species, based on minor differences in the scalation of the head (see Stugren, 1961). If this classification is valid the west Romanian form would be known as *Lacerta praticola hungarica* **Sobolewsky.**

Most of the Caucasus region, as well as north-western Iran is inhabited by the sub-species known as *Lacerta praticola praticola* **Eversmann**.

Nomenclature *for northern and central Europe*
German   Wieseneidechse
Italian   Lucertola dei prati
Romanian   Șopîrla de pădure
Russian   Луговая Ящерица

The Sand Lizard
Lacerta agilis
Sub-species found in northern and central Europe:
Lacerta agilis agilis **Linnaeus** 1758
Terra typica restricta: Southern Sweden

Lacerta agilis bosnica **Schreiber** 1912
Terra typica: Bosnia
Plates 3, 4, 5, see also colour plate

This species of lizard has quite a plump body, in contrast to the rather flattened bodies of the common lizard and Pontic lizard. The shortish head is distinctly larger in male specimens, and the snout is short and fairly blunt. The tail is thick but comparatively short, often being less than one and a half times the length of the body. Proportionally speaking the legs are quite short. The sand lizard attains a length of 18 centimetres, although specimens up to 25 centimetres have occasionally been reported from the continent. Female specimens grow slightly longer than males.

Scalation

Lacerta agilis agilis   Dorsals: 32–52 (usually 36–40) scales around middle of body, strongly keeled, elliptical or hexagonal and very narrow on top of back; tail scales strongly keeled above and on sides. 6 or 8 longitudinal rows of *ventrals* (24–29 transverse rows in males, 27–31 in females). *Anal* preceded by 1 (rarely 2) rows of small plates; 10–17 *femoral* pores on each thigh. Nostril at junction of 3 or 4 (rarely 2) plates, not bordering *rostral*; 1 (rarely 2) *postnasals*; 2 superposed anterior *loreals*; 1–3 (usually 2) upper *temporals* bordering each *parietal*; 4 (rarely 3 or 5) upper *labials* anterior to subocular; *gular* fold usually indistinct or absent; collar comprising 7–12 (usually 8–10) strongly serrated plates.

Lacerta agilis bosnica   Below average number of *dorsals*; *dorso-lateral* series less clearly differenciated from those on top of back. 1 (occasionally 2) *postnasals*; 1 anterior *loreal* (occasionally 2 or even none); 11–13 *femoral* pores. Scalation otherwise as above.

Colouration

Dorsal region   The sand lizard is certainly one of the most beautiful species of lizard inhabiting Europe. On top of the back the ground colour is pale grey or light brown, but along the centre of the back is a wide band composed of a series of irregular dark brown blotches, each of which contains a small whitish fleck. Occasionally some or all of these blotches are connected, and a thick vertebral stripe is formed. More usually the blotches are divided by light brown shadowy patches.

Female colouration   The pattern on the flanks is most clearly defined in the female. As on top of the back there is a longitudinal row of brownish blotches, likewise with whitish flecks. These blotches do not completely interconnect as they sometimes do on top of the back however. On many specimens a second series of brown blotches, sometimes devoid of the central white flecks, is present on the lower part of the flank. The underside of the female is whitish, dullish cream or yellow, either uniform or stippled with small black dots.

Male colouration   The flanks of the male are similar in pattern to the female but far less distinct. The ground colour of the flanks and also of the side of the head is yellowish green, grass-green, emerald- or dark green, giving a most striking appearance, particularly during the mating season when this colouration is at its most intense. Many observers have been deceived into believing that they have seen a green lizard (*Lacerta viridis*). The throat and belly of the male are pale green, and there is a small spot or two on almost every scale. Sometimes each spot may have a dark green centre.

Head, tail and limbs   In both sexes the top of the head is greyish or brownish with irregular darker mottlings. The tail is greyish above, although traces of the dorsal and lateral brown blotches are present, particularly in the upper part. The underside of the tail is a dirty white, sometimes with tiny dark spots.

All the limbs of the female are brownish with occasional whitish and dark brown spots. The fore-limbs of the male are usually green and flecked with black. The hind-limbs are more similar to those of the female.

Juvenile colouration   Very young males and females are slender in build and almost identical in appearance. In colour they are grey brown with longitudinal rows of white ocellations, each of which is bordered with black. They resemble the adult female, but are somewhat darker, and the pattern is less distinct. The underside is a uniform dirty-white, cream or sometimes even a very light greenish white. At this stage the tail constitutes little more than a half of the total length.

Variations   According to Sternfeld and Steiner (1952) in some old adult males from south-western Germany the brilliant colouration of the flanks is more or less extended on top of the back and even on top of the head. Specimens may sometimes be found with stippled flanks, being devoid of the usual blotches. I once found a pregnant female near Örkény in Hungary with light green flanks and belly which, at a glance, could easily have passed for a male.

VAR ERYTHRONOTUS   The red-backed sand lizard, formerly known as var. *erythronotus* or var. *rubra*, has not been recorded from Britain but is known from France, Germany, Austria, Hungary, Czechoslovakia, the Carpathian region of Romania and Poland. In some districts, notably in Transylvania, it has replaced the normal form. In certain areas of Czechoslovakia some 90 per cent or more of specimens are referable to this variety. Typical examples are apparently rare in Germany however (Sternfeld and Steiner, 1952). I know a locality in southern Slovakia where the two forms co-habit, and intermediate stages are quite common.

The distinguishing feature of this variety is the top of its back which is uniformly brown or brick red with no hint of the usual pattern, although this is present on the flanks. Sporadic dark spots may occur on top of the back of some specimens. I have seen a male of this form whose ground colour on the flanks and belly was pale white.

MELANISM   Melanistic specimens are rare. In 1972 one was found at Rahnsdorf near East Berlin (Petzold, 1972). They have not yet been reported from Britain.

Lacerta agilis bosnica   The Balkan race *bosnica* is similar in pattern to the typical form. The small whitish flecks on the vertebral region tend to connect however, and a more or less continuous narrow vertebral stripe is formed.

Habitat
In Britain the sand lizard is an inhabitant of dry and warm regions, being confined to a few coastal dune areas and the heathlands of the south. In the latter areas it often shares its habitat with the smooth snake—perhaps its chief predator. Both species prefer thick, dry heathland, although during high summer I have sometimes known the sand lizard to gravitate to nearby marshy areas where coarse grass predominates.

In much of Europe however it is far more generally distributed. It occurs in hedgerows, beside bushes, in sunny meadows and on the borders of agricultural land, fields and woods. It inhabits sunny glades, verges beside paths and roads, and grassy and bushy slopes—railway embankments often being favoured. Stony regions are not avoided, and it is sometimes found in stone as well as sand quarries. It can also be observed in gardens, parks, cemeteries and in the vicinity of vineyards. It appears to have some capacity for survival even in urban districts. For example I once found a number of young specimens inhabiting a small piece of derelict land in Bratislava. The surrounding areas were completely built up. Rühmekorf (1970) states that it inhabits sandy soil almost exclusively on the north German plain.

Altitude The sand lizard is at home both in flat and hilly regions. In Switzerland it ascends to 1650 metres (Stemmler, 1971). In western Bulgaria the Balkan race *bosnica* attains 2000 metres (Beškov and Beron, 1964).

Co-habiting species I have frequently come across it living in close proximity to other species of lizards. In places as far apart as Berlin and Bournemouth I have found it sharing its habitat with the common lizard, and on occasions I have seen an individual of each species basking no more than 50 centimetres apart from one another. (One such locality in Bournemouth was Horseshoe Common, right in the heart of the town, where both species survived into the mid-fifties. This small habitat has subsequently succumbed to urban development.) In the northern parts of its range I have often observed it living near the slow worm, while in Hungary I have sometimes seen it in the same localities as the green lizard. I once discovered a baby specimen in hiding under a large sheet of scrap metal. Two adult grass snakes were coiled up nearby, one only 4 centimetres from the lizard. In fact on the continent I have found the sand lizard sharing its habitat with the grass snake more frequently than with other species of reptile.

Behaviour

The sand lizard is fond of basking in the sun, either beside clumps of heather or other suitably low bushes which offer a retreat in times of danger. Although a sun lover it dislikes great heat, spending any hot periods of the day under cover. Sometimes during the hottest parts of the summer it can prove difficult to find. During cool weather and in the evening I have sometimes found it in hiding under rubble or a piece of rusty metal. Normally it retires into cavities amid the roots of bushy vegetation or in holes in the ground. These holes may sometimes be excavated by the lizard itself, this species being rather fond of digging, at least in areas with loose soil. Sometimes however it will adopt the deserted burrows of voles, mice and moles. I once found a baby specimen beneath a pile of stony debris. It had made its home there inside a thickly spun funnel-shaped but abandoned cobweb. It seldom ascends far up onto vegetation in order to bask, being rather clumsy and inexpert at climbing by comparison with the other lacertids. However one that I pursued in southern Hungary ran for a distance of about 1m. up the bark of a birch tree. It does not enter water voluntarily, although it is able to swim in times of emergency. Despite its name it is not a particularly agile lizard.

The sand lizard shows a strong attachment to its chosen terrain especially during the spring, and male specimens will savagely attack and try to drive off rival males. Smith (1969) states that it is more socially inclined than the common lizard and that it often lives in colonies. Most frequently I have found it basking alone outside of the mating season, though one August in Hampshire I saw three basking together. During early spring most specimens encountered are males, but by mid-summer the situation is reversed, and the males may appear to be quite rare. Sand lizards sometimes signal to one another by raising and shaking one of their fore-feet. The exact significance of this action is not really understood, as isolated individuals sometimes do it.

Food

This species devours a wide variety of insects, including flies, various orthoptera (especially grasshoppers), beetles, butterflies, moths and caterpillars if not too hairy, as well as flying ants. In addition, earthworms, slugs, spiders and centipedes are also taken, and some that I kept showed a particular fondness for woodlice, one individual eating fourteen in succession. Another time I was amazed to see one of them supplementing his usual diet of spiders and woodlice with small pieces of dried moss. Before being eaten all living prey is held in the jaws and briskly shaken until it is stunned. The sand lizard is known for its occasional cannibalistic tendencies. I have known captive specimens devour their own young and also very young common lizards and slow worms. Some specimens in captivity have been known to

Female (left) and male sand lizards *(Lacerta agilis agilis)*. The two sexes are easily identifiable by their colouration, the green flanks of the male being particularly well marked during the spring months.

The eyed lizard *(Lacerta lepida lepida)* is a very quick and alert species. If seized it is able to inflict a very painful bite.

Blue spotted slow worm *(Anguis fragilis fragilis)*. Specimens of this colour variety are almost always males.

Viperine snakes *(Natrix maura)* are seldom found far from the vicinity of water, particularly during the summer months. The form shown is a striped variety.

accept raw meat when chopped up and even honey, which is licked up with the tongue.

Enemies

Its principal enemies are snakes, birds, martens, weasels and domestic cats. Apart from the smooth snake, the meadow viper in particular is a regular predator of the sand lizard. Among the birds known to devour them on occasion are jays, ravens, blackbirds, buzzards, falcons and storks, as well as ducks, chicken and turkeys.

Reproduction

Male rivalry and mating Mating takes place from April until June but normally occurs in May, as soon as the males have shed their skins. They are then particularly conspicuous, being clad in their brilliant green colouration. They are also extremely aggressive at this time, and once an individual has selected his mate he will remain basking with her for days and drive off all other male intruders, unless one of them happens to be larger and stronger, in which case the weaker male will be driven off himself, and have to find a new mate. Battles between rival males are fierce and blood is sometimes shed. During these skirmishes each male faces his opponent with back highly arched, neck puffed well out and mouth wide open. Raised high on all fours and with lowered heads they then charge, and seize one another in their jaws which become firmly interlocked. The rivals then roll over and over, sometimes shaking one another violently until eventually one of them has had enough and runs off, pursued for a little way by his opponent.

In the spring of 1956 I kept a number of males and females in captivity. Fights between the males were frequent, and I decided to try an experiment. I isolated one of the males and placed him before a mirror. On seeing his own reflection he angrily charged forward in the characteristic manner and proceeded to attack his own reflection! The same experiment worked successfully with the remaining males, none of whom at this stage had shown any apparent interest in the females.

Copulation During copulation, which may take place several times over a period of a few days, the male holds the female's flank firmly in his jaws, his body being bent in a semi-circle, and the two lizards remain fairly static until they separate.

Abnormal behaviour In the spring of 1965 I found three specimens near Berlin which I kept in captivity for several weeks. The group consisted of an adult female and two adult males, one rather small, the other fully grown. Mating took place on several occasions, both males being involved, though I never observed any fighting. One day the female was mated by both of the males. Sometimes, both during and after copulation, the larger male while holding the female in his jaws would make nervous jerking movements in a persistent regular rhythm, often accompanied by a repeated, short staccato hiss. One day on hearing this hissing I went to investigate and to my surprise I found the large male holding the smaller one in his jaws. He continued to make these jerking movements for some while until the smaller one snapped aggressively, whereupon he was instantly released. The female was basking impassively nearby.

Egg laying   As the female's state of pregnancy becomes more advanced the outline of the eggs in her body becomes quite distinct. They are normally laid between the end of May and July, and the size of the litter varies from 3 to 14 according to the size and age of the female. In size the eggs are not much bigger than a pea but are more elliptical. They vary from 12 to 15 millimetres in length by 7 to 10 millimetres in diameter. In colour they are whitish with a slight pinkish tinge. When laid they are buried in a hole specially excavated in sand or loose soil by the mother using her fore-limbs, and who afterwards carefully covers them over. They have also been found hidden in wall crevices, under stones and in compost heaps.

One afternoon in western Hampshire I found a female in the middle of a sandy path preoccupied with the laying of her eggs. She was fully exposed on a fairly wide patch of loose white sand with little nearby vegetation into which to retreat. She completely ignored my presence, busily attending to the burial of her most recently laid egg. Once concealed the female shows no more interest in her offspring. Females that have already laid their eggs in May may shortly afterwards mate again. According to Smith (1969) there is no record in England of a subsequent laying.

During the period of incubation, which may vary from 40 to 60 days or in a cool summer even up to three months, the size of the eggs increases a little.

Hatching   Hatching takes place from the end of June until September. The shell is punctured by means of the well-developed egg-tooth. The young measure from about 45 to 60 millimetres, and they grow somewhat before disappearing into hibernation.

Maturity   At the age of two the males are already able to mate, though the females apparently reach maturity a year later (Angel, 1946).

Hybrids   Mertens (1956) refers to some successful experiments made by Drzewicki in mating specimens of the typical form with those of the red-backed variety. In the resultant offspring the characteristics of the latter form were dominant. He also reports on the discovery of a female lizard from Maria Taferl in Lower Austria, which showed characteristics of both the sand and the green lizard and appears to have been a hybrid.

Hibernation

The sand lizard usually disappears into hibernation between the end of September and the beginning of October. The very young however retire a little later. In western Hampshire I have seen them about in suitable weather in mid-October, and in 1965 I found several basking in the afternoon sun as late as 17 October. On the continent at least the sand lizard has been known to emerge during the middle of winter when the weather has been sufficiently mild. The males are the first to leave their winter quarters in spring. They sometimes appear up to three weeks before the females, the time of their emergence depending both on the weather and on the locality. In southern England I have seen males about as early as 23 February (1974), and 10 March (1956). It is not unusual for them to emerge there in mid-March provided it is suitably warm. Angel (1946) states that in the southern parts of its range it may be found as early as February. In eastern Europe it is seldom seen before the end of March but is normally active by mid-April. Terent' ev and Cernov (1949) state that in the USSR it awakens in April.

Ecdysis

According to Frommhold (1956) this species sheds its skin about every four to six weeks. The pattern on the sloughed skin fragments is dark brown and shows up very clearly.

General response

In the wild state it is rather timid by nature, and it can be quite difficult to catch as it persistently darts off into nearby undergrowth when any attempt is made to seize it. It is far more excitable than the common lizard, and when freshly caught it bites readily and fiercely. If placed in a cage it will charge around wildly and when cornered will adopt a threatening posture: the mouth is kept wide open, and there is frequent hissing. The sand lizard bites with considerable force and sometimes shows a reluctance to release its grip. It will even allow itself to be suspended in mid air, supported only by its jaws.

It is however quickly and easily tamed, although it is now illegal to keep it in captivity in Britain. It is perhaps the most tamable of all European lizards. Food may sometimes be refused at first, but soon after it is seized readily. I have known one specimen to eat within half an hour of being caught. Sand lizards will soon learn to come and take food from the hand. Some that I kept would investigate each of my fingers carefully in the hope of finding a tasty meal. One female specimen would run towards me and settle on my hand and bask in the sun. Occasionally she liked to climb up my arm to sit on my shoulder, and when I moved this into the shade would then climb onto my head to resume basking, making absolutely no attempt to escape. Rollinat (1934) devoted much of his time to making experiments in the taming of this species and was of the opinion that it was the most intelligent of all the French reptiles.

Distribution

Britain   The sand lizard is by far the rarest species of lizard inhabiting Britain. Its limited choice of habitat has inevitably proven detrimental to its survival, and its numbers are continuing to decline. It is still to be found in the heathland regions of eastern Dorset and western Hampshire, though even here its numbers have been substantially reduced in recent years because of urban development, afforestation, military manoeuvres and heath fires. Private collectors have also contributed to this decrease. Its decline in the heathlands of the Hampshire-Surrey-Sussex border region, has been even more drastic for much of the same reasons, and in many localities it has become extinct there. The development of seaside amentities has similarly had an adverse effect on its occurrence in the coastal dune areas, the most well-known being that situated between Crosby and Southport in Lancashire. Fortunately, as from 1 August 1975, this species has obtained legal protection in Britain under the Conservation of Wild Creatures and Wild Plants Act.

Scandinavia   In Sweden it occurs in the south and has been reported from over 100 localities. Only in Scania is it reasonably common. It extends north-eastwards to Uppland, Viggbyholm (approx. 61° N.) (Gislén and Kauri, 1959). It is absent from Finland and Norway but has been found at Strömstad-Drivnäs near the Norwegian border in south-western Sweden.

France, Spain and Benelux   In France it occurs mainly in the northern, central and eastern parts and extends westwards to the département of Vienne, though it is rare there. According to Fretey (1975), it is absent from Normandy to the west of Bagnoles-de-l'Orne. It has been recorded from the département of Charente-Maritime, but is otherwise apparently absent from the extreme west. South of the latitude of Bordeaux it is either very rare or, as in the département of Landes and in Provence, absent; but it has been reported from Ariège, Pyrénées-Orientales and Hérault. In Spain it is confined to the high valleys of the Pyrénées (Salvador, 1974b). Somewhat rare in Belgium it is restricted to the Campine-Anvers district and the Jurassic region of Luxembourg province. It also occurs in Luxembourg itself as well as in Holland, where its range comprises the dune and diluvial sand areas, and the islands of Vlieland, Terschelling and Schiermonnikoog, but not Texel however (Bund, 1964).

Germany and Denmark   In Germany it is found almost throughout, and is the commonest species of reptile there. It also inhabits the islands of Rügen, Usedom and Wolin, while Rühmekorf (1970) states that it has been introduced to Juist and Wangerooge. It is fairly common in Denmark. The islands where it is present include Bornholm and Anholt in the Kattegat.

Central Europe   In central Europe it is found throughout Austria, Hungary and Switzerland (north of the Alps). In Czechoslovakia it is common, especially in low lying areas, while similarly in Poland it becomes rare only at higher altitudes. It has not been recorded from Italy (Lanza, 1968) and appears to be absent south of the Alps.

Yugoslavia, Bulgaria, Hungary and Romania   In Yugoslavia it inhabits parts of Slovenia and Croatia, being replaced elsewhere by *Lacerta agilis bosnica* **Schreiber**. The exact range of the latter sub-species is uncertain, but according to Karaman (1921) it occurs to the south of a line extending from Rijeka to Karlovac. It is known mainly from Bosnia, Hercegovina, western Croatia, southern Serbia and Macedonia. It is also on record from Nikšić in Montenegro, and from Promina and Crkvice in Dalmatia, while I have recorded it from the Sava valley near Slavonski Brod (Street, 1976). It also occurs in western Bulgaria.

Among a population of apparently typical sand lizards which I observed south of Siklós (County Baranya) in southern Hungary, near the Yugoslav border, one female which I captured closely resembled *bosnica* in appearance. It possessed an almost continuous white vertebral stripe; a single anterior *loreal* and single *nasal* on the left side of the head, and a single anterior *loreal* but two *postnasals* on the right side. The number of *femoral* pores for the right and left thighs were 12 and 14 respectively. The scales around the body numbered from 38 to 40. The *dorsals* were however fairly distinct from the *dorso-laterals*. This could suggest that the vicinity might be on the fringe of an area of intergradation between the two sub-species.

In Romania *Lacerta agilis agilis* is confined to the Banat region, Transylvania and the Carpathians. *Lacerta agilis euxinica* **Fuhn & Vancea** is endemic to the Dobruja and the Danube delta districts.

Eastern range   The region to the south and east of the Carpathians, extending into European Russia about as far as the river Dnieper and northwards to Leningrad and Petrozavodsk (between lakes Ladoga and Onega), is the home of *Lacerta agilis chersonensis* **Andrzejowski**. The north-western part of European Russia as well as the Baltic states and perhaps the island of Saaremaa (but not Hiiumaa) are inhabited by *Lacerta agilis agilis*, but in the central and southern parts of the USSR east of the river Dnieper, this form is replaced by *Lacerta agilis exigua* **Eichwald**, a sub-species which is also found in central Asia, though it is absent from the desert regions. According to Peters (1962a) there is a broad transition zone between *chersonensis* and *exigua* in the northern Ukraine and in the adjoining Russian region. The range of *exigua* extends as far east as the Altai mountains, the river Yenisey, southern Transbaikalia, northern Mongolia and the Tien Shan range. Finally there are three further sub-species associated with the Caucasus region. *Lacerta agilis boemica* **Suchow** is restricted to the north-eastern part and Daghestan, while *Lacerta agilis grusinica* **Peters** inhabits western Georgia, extending a little way into Turkey. The remaining sub-species is *Lacerta agilis brevicaudata* **Peters** which occurs in Armenia, north-eastern Turkey and north-western Iran.

Nomenclature *in northern and central Europe*
Dutch Zandhagedis
German Zauneidechse
Danish Markfirben
Norwegian Markfirfisle
Swedish Sandödla
French Lézard des souches
Italian Lucertola dei ceppi
Romanian Șopîrla de cîmp
Hungarian Fürge gyík
Czech Ještěrka obecná západní
Slovakian Jašterica obyčajná
Polish Jaszczurka zwinka
Serbo-Croatian Gorska gušterica
Russian Прыткая Ящерица

The Green Lizard
Lacerta viridis
Sub-species found in northern and central Europe:
Lacerta viridis viridis (**Laurenti**) 1768
Terra typica designata: Vienna, Austria
Plate 6

This lacertid is the largest species of lizard occurring to the north of the Alpine region. It has a strong, fairly thick-set body, which is not flattened as is that of the common or wall lizards, for example. The head, which is distinctly larger and wider in male specimens, is moderately long and pointed, and the snout, though fairly long, is obtuse. The tail, which forms about two-thirds of the total length and sometimes even more in specimens from the southern parts of its range, gradually tapers to a very fine point. In male specimens the hind limbs are markedly stouter, and the tail root is thicker. In the south of its range the green lizard may reach a maximum length of 40 centimetres. Further north however, it seldom exceeds a length of 30 centimetres. Males are usually a little longer than females.

Scalation
Dorsals: 40–56 strongly keeled rhombic or hexagonal scales around middle of body, juxtaposed or subimbricate; tail scales keeled, pointing backwards. 6 or 8 longitudinal (26–32 transverse) rows of *ventrals*. *Anal* preceded by 2 (rarely 1) rows of small plates; 13–21 *femoral* pores on each thigh. Nostril normally borders *rostral*; 2 (rarely 3) *postnasals*; 1 anterior *loreal* (rarely divided); 2 large *temporals* (sometimes fused) bordering each *parietal*; almost always 4 upper *labials* anterior to *subocular*; *gular* fold distinct; collar comprising 7–12 (usually 7–10) strongly serrated plates.

Colouration
Male colouration   The male and female are easily distinguishable. The upper surface of the male's body is grass-green or yellowy green and is finely stippled with black. On top the head is also green and is spotted with yellow. The forepart of the tail is bright green above, usually with black flecks, but the hind part is a dull brownish. The throat is normally light blue in young males, becoming a darker shade in older specimens. A bluish tinge may also be present on the sides of the head and neck. This colouration is particularly marked during the mating season, fading somewhat afterwards. Some individuals by the autumn may exhibit no trace of blue, being instead lightly stained with brown. Occasional specimens do not acquire any blue colouration. According to Peters (1970) some males have already acquired their blue chin and throat before their second period of hibernation, though the majority develop this feature during the following spring and summer. The belly is a pale yellow, and there may be a greenish tinge towards the flanks. The underside of the tail is a dirty white.

Female colouration   Female specimens are more variable than males. The green is often less pronounced, and brown colouration may be more or less prominent. Occasionally the ground colour may be entirely brown, particularly in specimens from south-eastern Europe, though such individuals have been found as far west as the Atlantic coast of France. Whitish or yellowish dorso-lateral stripes, often present on the young, are sometimes retained throughout the female's life. These stripes often extend for some way along the length of the tail. The black spots are fewer but frequently larger than those of the male. They may occur all over the top of the back, sometimes being quite thickly crowded. In some cases however they may form rows or even continuous stripes on either side of the back, adjacent to the dorso-lateral stripes. Such rows of black spots may occur on either side of these stripes. A longitudinal row of whitish spots is sometimes present on the lower part of the flanks, and these may also link up to form a continuous stripe which extends along most of the length of the tail. The head is often uniformly brown or olive above, although irregular black flecks may be present. Some females have a blue throat, similar to that of the males. This develops about a year later than in males. The female's belly is normally yellow or lime green. The colouration of the adults is most vivid in spring, after the first shedding. By late summer and autumn, the colours have faded somewhat.

Juvenile colouration   The ground colouration of the young is bronze, leathery-brown, greyish, rusty-brown or olive-brown, or greenish grey. The upper surface of the back is flecked with black or brownish spots, and there are frequently two dorso-lateral stripes or rows of spots, whitish or pale yellow in colour. There is also a similar stripe or row on each flank. The top of the head is olive-brown. The underside is a dirty or creamy white or greenish yellow, the throat usually being pale yellow. At this stage the tail is only a little longer than the head and body together.

Colour variations   A few rare cases of albinism and melanism have been reported for this species.

Habitat

The green lizard inhabits a wide variety of conditions. It occurs on grassy, bushy and lightly wooded slopes, sunny glades, the borders of forests, the edges of paths, roadsides and river banks. It is also found in stone quarries, vineyards, on rough common land, and beside cultivated fields. In some areas, as in Brandenburg and in south-western France, it is associated with sandy heathlands and pine forests. According to Peters (1970), in the Ukraine it avoids the steppe regions, living in river valleys, on the borders of woods, and in bushy ravines. In the north of its range it is recorded mainly in dry and fairly low altitudes as well as undulating country, rarely being met with over 600 metres. Further south however, as in Spain, Yugoslavia and Greece, it is more frequently encountered in damper regions and at higher altitudes. Arid districts are avoided.

Altitude   The green lizard extends to 1300 metres in Austria (Eiselt, 1961) and Switzerland (Stemmler, 1971), and 1700 metres in the Alpes-Maritimes (Angel, 1946).

Co-habiting species   Because of its adaptability to such diverse types of country, it occurs in the same localities as a wide variety of lizards and snakes. In Hungary I have quite often observed it living near the sand lizard, while in Romania I have found it in the same localities as the Greek tortoise. In the region of Brandenburg it has been noted sharing its habitat with the common lizard, sand lizard, slow worm, grass snake and smooth snake. In some parts of the Balkans it shares its territory with the closely related three lined lizard *Lacerta trilineata trilineata*. Zapf (1969) has recorded this species in Carinthia sunning itself on a wall together with an Aesculapian snake, throughout an entire summer.

Behaviour
This species is diurnal in its habits, spending much of the day basking. Although it enjoys a warm atmosphere, it avoids a strong midday sun, even in the north of its range, and retreats under grass and other thick vegetation. It likes to sun itself on stones, low bushes, and sunny clearings amid thick vegetation. It is, however, less tolerant of strong heat than the eyed lizard, and during hot summer spells may spend the day in retreat or in the shade. Usually as evening approaches it retires into cavities in the soil or in crevices amid the roots of vegetation, and I have not infrequently found it under a flat stone, or a pile of rocks, or beneath strewn pieces of broken bark. In such conditions it can sometimes be found in dull weather. Referring to specimens from Lieberose in Brandenburg, Peters (1970) remarks that the hollow roots of pine stumps are the preferred retreat of the adults, and are also used almost exclusively for hibernation. The burrows of voles are inhabited mainly by year old specimens and juveniles. Although adults sometimes occupy them in summer, it is only for short periods.

The green lizard is very timid by nature, and very agile in its movements, much more so than the sand lizard. An excellent climber, it frequently ascends low vegetation and stony walls in order to reach a suitable place for basking. It does not hesitate to cross roads, especially when being pursued. It has even been known to plunge into water, concealing itself in the mud (Angel, 1946). During hot spells it may enter shallow water in order to bathe. The green lizard frequently excavates its own burrow, which, according to Terent' ev and Cernov (1949), may be up to a metre in depth.

It usually spends its entire life within a comparatively small locality. Peters (1970) observed that many specimens which he surveyed in Brandenburg spent almost their whole lives within an area whose greatest diameter was sometimes less than 30, and at the most 50 metres. It is quite a solitary species, usually found basking alone outside of the mating season, even though other specimens are not infrequently found in the same vicinity.

Food

The green lizard has a very varied diet, eating a wide range of insects, among them grasshoppers, beetles, flies, bees, butterflies and their larvae; as well as slugs, earthworms, woodlice and, especially, spiders. It is a voracious creature, often devouring many of its favourite food items in succession. Werner records a specimen which, within ten months, consumed no less than 3000 items, among them 2040 mealworms. In addition it is known to eat young slow worms, small lacertids and on rare occasions even their eggs. Peters (1970) once observed a specimen with an ant in its mouth. An equally unusual item of diet referred to by him were dung beetles (*Geotrupes*). Captive green lizards are quarrelsome over food, and readily try to snatch prey from the mouths of other specimens. An occasional individual, having done so, may then bite its companion on the head and flanks. Such behaviour was not observed by Peters with wild specimens, however. The green lizard drinks quite frequently.

Enemies

The adult green lizard's size and strength enable it to put up considerable resistance to many would-be predators. Though it can defend itself against some snakes, it is unable to protect itself against a hungry, full grown whip snake. Apart from snakes, this lizard falls prey to many species of bird, among them poultry. Potential enemies listed by Peters are thrushes, hoopoes, crows, magpies, jays, buzzards, kites, harriers and red-backed shrikes. Flesh-eating mammals such as weasels, badgers, polecats, hedgehogs, shrews, foxes and wild boar are known to devour them. The very young are frequently eaten by smooth snakes, occasionally by adult sand lizards, and even by the adults of their own species. As Peters has pointed out, it is to the advantage of the young that during their first autumn, the adults have already disappeared into hibernation.

Reproduction

Male rivalry and mating   Depending on latitude and temperature, the green lizard mates from late March to May, or, exceptionally in June. This normally, though not invariably, occurs after the first ecdysis. In Switzerland the usual time is March or April, while in the southern Ukraine, near Odessa, they mate in April or at the beginning of May (Terent' ev and Cernov, 1949). During this time there is fierce fighting among rival males for the possession of a female. According to Peters (1970), one-and-a-half-year olds suffer bloody head wounds and even fractures, which however subsequently heal. Fretey (1975) states that fights between rival males may even result in death. Though the female normally plays an entirely passive role, Peters refers to the case of a female which pursued an unwilling male, biting him on the root of the tail, on the hind legs, and also on the flanks.

While copulating the male holds the female firmly in his jaws. This often results in scars which are clearly visible until the skin is shed again. Green lizards copulate several times, usually with different partners. In exceptional cases however, according to Peters, a relatively isolated pair may remain together throughout the mating season. During the spring and early summer pairs may often be seen basking together.

Egg laying Some four to six weeks after mating, usually in May or June, depending on the weather, the female lays from 4 to 21 yellowish white eggs; 13 being the maximum for specimens in the north of its range. They measure from 15 to 18 millimetres by 8 to 11 millimetres. When laid they are carefully placed in a hole in the soil specially excavated by the female using her front feet. Subsequently she replaces the soil to conceal them. According to Lanceau and Lanceau (1974) this hole measures between 15 and 30 centimetres in depth. She may first of all dig a few trial holes. If disturbed in the process, she is likely to dig a new hole elsewhere. Peters (1970) did not observe any case of a female in Brandenburg becoming pregnant twice within one year.

Abnormal behaviour Interesting and unusual behaviour was recently observed in a pair of pregnant female specimens by Race (1971). These were kept in a greenhouse, and on the evening of 30 June 1968, after a very hot day when the temperature there was still 26°C, the more dominant of the females, in the presence of a nearby basking male, seized the tail of the other female, which made no effort to escape. Her jaws worked their way up until the shoulder region where she strengthened her hold. She then adjusted her position to bring the cloacas into apposition, her own being distended for about half a minute as if in preparation to take a male's penis. The lizards then parted.

Hatching Hatching usually occurs between mid-August and mid-September. A cold summer will delay incubation, and if the summer offers too little sun the embryos may even perish. At the time of emergence the young measure some 8 to 9.8 centimetres. The egg-tooth is shed from one to five days after hatching (Angel, 1946). The females at this stage already have a relatively longer body and a smaller, narrower head. For several days after hatching green lizards can be seen living in groups.

Growth Growth is very intensive during the first two years of life, after which it gradually slows down. Peters states that the young are able to mate at the age of just over one and a half years, that is after their second hibernation. Their first young thus hatch when they themselves are two years old. One-and-a-half- year old specimens lay their eggs later than those of two-and-a-half years or more. The length of the tail continues to increase quite substantially for some years after body growth has slowed down.

A case of hermaphroditism in this species is on record.

Hybrids In captivity offspring were produced as a result of a successful mating of a male green lizard and a female Schreiber's lizard (*Lacerta schreiberi*). Sixteen hybrids, the result of a mating between this species and *Lacerta trilineata trilineata*, were hatched in July 1974 (Nettmann and Rykene, 1974). An apparent hybrid from these two species was found at Dubrovnik (Mertens, 1964).

Hibernation

In northern and central Europe the green lizard disappears into hibernation between late August and early November, depending on latitude, and also on weather conditions. Referring to Brandenburg specimens, Peters remarks that after a normal warm summer there is a gradual reduction in the number of active adults in the latter part of August, and that they almost completely disappear during the first half of September. The very young, and isolated one-year old specimens, are still about on mild days at the beginning of October. After a poor summer however when insufficient food has been taken, the adult specimens are still about in September in order to build up their reserve supplies (fat-bodies). In such summers the young will have largely failed to hatch.

To the south of the Alps the green lizard can remain active until November, and according to Angel (1946), in central France it disappears at the beginning of November until February, March or April, depending again on the temperature. It is, he adds, never seen about on warm winter days. It hibernates in holes in the ground, in cavities under the roots of shrubs and trees, as well as in rocky crevices. In Germany it usually emerges from its winter sleep in mid or late April. In the Swiss canton of Tessin and in the south Tirol it usually reappears in March. In 1964 I found a young specimen near Budapest on 3 April. It appeared to have just emerged from hibernation, as dried mud was encrusted on its limbs and digits. In the southern parts of its range, as in Spain and southern Greece, it may be active all the year or may disappear for only a very short period, and may still be seen about in mild weather during the middle of winter. The males are the first to emerge in spring. The young are the last to appear.

General response
When pursued it can show itself a fast, skilful climber. I once observed a large adult male climb rapidly up into a tree near Belgrade, swiftly disappearing out of my reach. Such behaviour is more frequently associated with the eyed lizard. Unless found curled up in its retreat, it is normally a very difficult lizard to catch. When freshly caught it behaves wildly, struggling violently. It has a powerful bite which can be quite painful, and usually it keeps its jaws firmly fastened on until it is released.

It tames fairly well in captivity, but needs a great deal of living space. It has long been a favourite of vivarium keepers. It none the less retains some of its nervous disposition, being quickly alarmed by any abrupt movements. In my opinion it is the most easily tamed *Lacerta* after the common and sand lizards, and will soon learn to accept food from the hand. Its diet should be varied in order to maintain good health. It can be fed with mealworms and cockroaches, and may come to accept raw, chopped-up meat and even soft fruit, such as sweet grapes. It appears to have survived for ten years as a captive.

Distribution
Owing to its popularity as a pet, this species has been over-collected in some areas, and as a result has become rarer.

France and Channel Islands It ranges over most of France, but is absent however to the north of a line extending from Rouen, through Paris to Mulhouse. It inhabits the Atlantic île d'Oléron, and I have also seen it on Noirmoutier. Off the Mediterranean coast it is indigenous to the île de Jarre. It occurs on two of the Channel islands, Jersey and Guernsey, where it is fairly rare, but it is absent from the British Isles, and all attempts to introduce it have so far been abortive.

Germany It is absent from Belgium, Luxembourg and Holland, but occurs in Germany where it is however the rarest species of lizard. In the middle Rhine valley it occurred until recently in a few localities on the eastern bank between Braubach and Rüdesheim, while in the adjoining Nahe valley it was known between Bingen and Kreuznach. These areas are also associated with the wall lizard and the dice snake, likewise southerly species, represented in this area by small, isolated populations. It is now rare in the Mosel valley. Elsewhere in the Rhine valley it is known from Worms and Kaiserstuhl, and formerly at least from near Freiburg and Wylen Efringen near Basle.

In the German Danube region it is known only from near Passau, not far from the Austrian border. In eastern Germany it survives with certainty only near Lieberose in the upper Spree region, and appears to have become extinct at Oderberg, Beelitz and other localities in the Brandenburg region within the last six decades. This decline has been discussed by Peters (1970), who attributed it to a deterioration in climatic conditions, and believes that remaining northern populations are similarly threatened, and that a future series of unfavourable summers could soon prove fatal. Sunshine is of paramount importance for the incubation of the eggs, and Peters notes that even an extremely cool, but sunny, summer (as in 1962) is better for their development than an average warm, but cloudy summer. That the Lieberose specimens have been able to survive the bad breeding summers is due to the relatively advanced age attained in these populations, on account of the small number of predators.

Poland   Although the green lizard formerly occurred in Poland in the Vistula valley between Warsaw and Toruń, and near Kielce, it now appears to be extinct in that country, there being no reports of its having been sighted for about 50 years (Berger, Jaskowska and Młynarski, 1969).

Alpine lands   In Switzerland it is found around Geneva, in Valais and south of the Alps. According to Stemmler (1971) it was still found on the banks of the Rhine near Basle in 1940, but is probably extinct there now. In Austria it occurs in the Danube valley, both in Upper and Lower Austria, and in the latter province it also inhabits the lower Kamp valley, two localities (Hardegg and Retz) near the Czech border, the region of Vienna and the Leitha hills. The provinces of southern Styria, southern Carinthia and Burgenland are included in its range, but its presence in the eastern Tirol requires confirmation (Eiselt, 1961). It appears to be most abundant in Carinthia.

Eastern central Europe   Štěpánek (1949) reports that in Czechoslovakia it is found in a few localities in Bohemia (near Prague, Beroun, Rakovník, Zvíkov and in the Sázava district), as well as in Moravia and Slovakia, where it is common in some places. According to Ponec (1965) it is frequently seen in central and southern, sometimes even in northern Slovakia, and extends as far east as Vihorlat and the Carpathian slopes. It is widely distributed in Hungary and Romania and is often found in mountainous districts as well as in the plains.

Russia   In the USSR it is confined to the Ukraine where, according to Peters, it is never found further north than 50°, except for one isolated population which occurs just south of Kiev (50° 24 N). Its range in the Ukraine terminates a little to the east of the river Dnieper.

Southern Europe   In southern Europe it is found in northern Spain, extending as far west as Asturias (where the fairly closely related *Lacerta schreiberi* also occurs), and as far south as the Iberian mountains and the provinces of Leon and Burgos (Salvador, 1974b). It also lives in northern and central Italy, Corsica, and almost the entire Balkan peninsula, as far south as the Greek island of Euboea.

Other sub-species   Four other sub-species of green lizard are at present recognized. *Lacerta viridis fejervaryi* **Vasvári** inhabits the southern Italian provinces of Campania and Apulia as well as the island of Elba, while *Lacerta viridis chloronata* **Rafinesque** replaces it in Calabria and Sicily. *Lacerta viridis meridionalis* **Cyrén** is an inhabitant of southern Romania, eastern Bulgaria—mainly the Dobruja and Black Sea littoral (Beškov and Beron, 1964), European Turkey and Asia Minor. The final sub-species *Lacerta viridis citrovittata* **Werner** is endemic to the island of Tinos in the Cyclades.

Nomenclature *in northern and central Europe*
  Dutch   Smaragdhagedis
  German   Smaragdeidechse
  French   Lézard vert
  Italian   Ramarro
  Romanian   Guster
  Hungarian   Zöld gyík
  Czech   Ještěrka zelená středoevropská
  Slovakian   Jašterica zelená
  Polish   Jaszczurka zielona
  Serbo-Croation   Zelembač
  Russian   Зеленая Ящерица

The Eyed Lizard
Lacerta lepida

Sub-species found in western Europe:
Lacerta lepida lepida **Daudin** 1802
(formerly *Lacerta ocellata*)
Terra typica restricta: Montpellier, southern France
Plate 7, see also colour plate

The eyed or ocellated lizard is the largest and most impressive of all European lizards, and is also the largest of all surviving lacertids. It has a large, thick-set body and a large head. Males are even more strongly built than females. In adult specimens, particularly in males, the cheeks are very swollen, and the head shields are divided by deep furrows. The long tail comprises about two-thirds of the total length. The limbs, especially the hind pair, are powerfully built, notably in the male. Males may occasionally reach a maximum length of 60 or even 70 centimetres, while females may attain 50 centimetres or more. Some individuals referred to by Angel (1946) from the Pyrénées-Orientales (southern France), presumably males, have been reported with a length of 90 centimetres. The largest specimen recorded by Peters (1962a) from this region weighed nearly 300 grams.

Scalation
Dorsals: 63–80 very feebly keeled granular scales around middle of body; tail scales strongly keeled. 8–10 longitudinal (28–34 transverse) rows of *ventrals*. *Anal* preceded by 2–4 rows of small plates; 11–16 *femoral* pores on each thigh. Nostril at junction of 5 plates, normally bordering *rostral*. *Occipital* larger than *interparietal*, at least as long as *frontal* in adults. 2 superposed *postnasals*; 1 anterior *loreal* (rarely divided); 2 large *temporals* bordering each *parietal*; 4 upper *labials* anterior to *subocular*; *gular* fold distinct or absent; collar comprising 9–14 (usually 10–13) strongly serrated plates.

Elderly specimens sometimes develop a few scale-covered warts on their back, which may grow up to 5 millimetres in length.

Colouration
This species is one of the most strikingly beautiful of all the reptiles living in Europe. In the adult the top of the head is green, brownish or yellowish green, becoming darker on the rear part. The sides of the head are green or yellowish-green. The colouration of the back is variable. Many of the tiny bead-like scales, particularly those on top of the back, are black, but these are interspersed with other scales which are green, yellow, yellowish green, greenish- or reddish brown. These may form either a network of short radiating lines, or more or less distinct hexagonal shapes, or transverse rows of ocellations. On each side there are from 13 to 24 large blue spots or patches, each often, though not invariably, bordered with a black margin. These spots are arranged in three or four rows. The pattern on top of the back is continued for a little way along the tail, then disintegrates.

In the neck region the colouration appears rather faded by comparison with the rest of the dorsal pattern. The lower surface, including the underside of the tail, is a dirty cream, greenish white, yellow or greenish yellow, and is devoid of markings, while the chin is similar in colour to the sides of the head. The

The dark green whip snake *(Coluber viridiflavus viridiflavus)*. Adult specimen about to shed its skin, as indicated by the blue appearance of its eyes.

Juvenile dark green whip snakes are, like the adults, always ready to bite when captured.

Male (upper) and female adders *(Vipera berus berus)*. The two sexes of this race of adder are usually easily distinguishable by their colouration.

Aspic viper *(Vipera aspis francisciredi)* with her newly-born young. The female soon leaves the young to fend for themselves. Even at this stage the young possess poisonous fangs.

colouration of the upper surface of the limbs resembles that of the body, though without any trace of blue spots; the lower surface of the limbs is coloured rather like the belly.

Juvenile colouration   Young eyed lizards are quite different in appearance. Their general colouration is grey or olive, later becoming green, olive-green, or yellowish green. The top of the back and the upper part of the flanks have fairly large yellowish, white, or whitish green spots, each being surrounded by a black margin. Similar, though less distinct spots are present on the upper surface of the limbs, and sometimes also on top of the green or olive-green head, towards the neck region. As in the adult, the sides are lightest, and the rows of blue spots with black or whitish borders are already present. In some young individuals the black margins surrounding the dorsal spots link up forming a transverse series of chains, creating a pattern which is reminiscent of that of some adults. The tail is dull brown with occasional whitish and black flecks. The chin and throat are pale yellow or greenish white; the belly is uniformly greenish- or yellowish white, and the underside of the tail is a dirty white.

Habitat
This species lives mainly on the ground, though it does like to climb onto low bushes or piles of rocks and boulders in order to bask. It particularly favours rocky slopes well exposed to the sun. Sometimes it may be found basking on old walls. It often lives at roadsides, and though timid by disposition, does not appear to mind constant traffic. It does not hesitate to cross roads, as occasional crushed specimens testify. I have also found it on railway embankments and near farms. It always lives in conditions where it can rapidly conceal itself when necessary, and if no rocks are available it lives beside thick bushes or thick grass. In the north of its range it tends to prefer dry scrubby land in rocky or sandy areas. In Spain I have found it near rivers, and I once found a small specimen living on a tiny island, less than one metre square in the middle of a rather shallow river. Compared with the green lizard, it seems less able to adapt itself to man's interference with the environment, but it is able to survive on the borders of cultivated land, and even in gardens. The development of tourist amenities in coastal districts has inevitably forced it to retreat to less disturbed areas. Normally adult specimens at least are, according to Peters (1962a), faithful to their chosen territory.

Altitude   According to Lanza (1968), it ascends to an altitude of about 1500 metres in the Alps. The sub-species *Lacerta lepida pater* is found up to 2500 metres in the mountainous regions of Morocco (Pasteur and Bons, 1960).

Co-habiting species   In some parts of its range it is found in the same areas as the green lizard, though the two species avoid sharing the same territory. In grassy localities I have found it living near the three toed skink. The other species of reptiles which I have found sharing its habitat are: the Spanish sand racer (*Psammodromus hispanicus*), the Montpellier snake (*Malpolon monspessulanus*), the hooded snake (*Macroprotodon cucullatus*), the ladder snake (*Elaphe scalaris*), the horseshoe whip snake (*Coluber hippocrepis*), as well as the southern smooth snake.

I once found a small specimen in southern Spain living in a hole about 1.5 metres deep. The area of the base was about 1 square metre, and the hole had vertical sides which were too steep for climbing. The lizard was thus trapped, but had made its retreat amid rubble there, next to a small pool of water, which was inhabited by three similarly stranded Spanish terrapins (*Mauremys caspica leprosa*).

Behaviour

Like all the previous species of lizard, the eyed lizard is diurnal, spending much of its time basking, often with its eyes closed. It appears to enjoy quite a hot sun. It retires in the evening as the sun is setting, and subsequently may sometimes be found in retreat under flat stones or rocks. During the early summer period in the Pyrénées-Orientales, Peters (1962a) found that they emerged about 8 a.m., disappearing around 5 p.m. By disposition it is very shy and nervous. It is also very agile. As soon as any attempt is made to get near it, it at once disappears into thick vegetation, in fissures between boulders or rocky crevices, tree hollows or holes in the ground. In my experience, when pursued it avoids running off for long distances where possible, preferring to take cover in the nearest suitable retreat. Before returning to its basking spot, it first of all projects its head out of the hide-out in order to survey the scene. Any hint of danger will send it scurrying back to safety. If suitable cover is not immediately available, it may sometimes scale the trunk of a nearby tree, from which it has been said to leap to the ground from a height of up to 5 metres. One that I found did not hesitate to cross a small pool of water to a favourite retreat, repeatingly doing so each time I approached. The eyed lizard is able to leap horizontally for distances of a metre or more. I have found it to be a little less alert in the early morning while the sun is comparatively weak, otherwise it is a very difficult species to approach.

Hvass (1972) states that it can sometimes be found living in pairs, even after mating has occurred. Peters on the other hand found that the shortest distance between two adults during a summer period was about 150 metres.

Food

Its diet is very varied. It eats a wide variety of insects, enjoying grasshoppers, cockroaches and cockchafers in particular. It will devour earthworms, snails, lacertids, geckos, even amphisbaenians (*Blanus cinereus*)—according to Salvador (1974b), small snakes, reptiles' eggs, young rodents and small birds and their eggs. It readily climbs into bushes and trees in order to plunder nests. One adult in my possession accepted a young three toed skink without hesitation, while some adults have been known to devour the very young of their own species. In captivity this species has been observed eating up to 65 grasshoppers or 50 mealworms at a single meal, the latter often being seized three or four at a time. I have sometimes fed the young with ant pupae. This species has also been known to eat raw meat as well as honey and fresh, juicy fruits such as figs, grapes and cherries.

Enemies

The adult has few enemies apart from the Montpellier snake, whose range in western Europe is very similar to that of this species. Some of the larger birds such as buzzards and eagles will devour it, while the young are eaten by various mammals and also by snakes. Doubtless the southern smooth snake will eat the very young, though it is likely that the adults will take the young of this snake. It can defend itself against many of its enemies by using its sharply pointed claws. It has even been known to put up a successful fight against dogs and cats, grasping them firmly by the throat until released.

Reproduction

The eyed lizard mates at the end of April or beginning of May. Much rivalry occurs among the males at this time, and they are then clad in their most brilliant colouration. They pursue one another and engage in fierce fights. Their cat-like aggressive postures resemble those of rival male sand lizards. It is said that they are fond of attacking one another's tails, and that these may even be lost in the process. After a preliminary courtship display, the male seizes the female's flank in his jaws—sometimes so powerfully that blood is drawn, and deep, even permanent, wounds are inflicted. The body and tail are twisted into an S-shape, and a hind foot is placed on the anterior part of the female's tail. The cloacas are then brought into apposition, and copulation can take place. Angel (1946) states that copulation takes about half an hour, and that it can be repeated once daily for several days. The female lays some six to ten, at most sixteen elliptical, whitish eggs, often in tree hollows. Lydekker (1896) remarks that olive trees are generally favoured as incubation sites.

About 40 days elapse between mating and laying, and apparently some 90 days are required for the incubation of the eggs, when the temperature is suitably warm. Peters (1962a) states that there is only one laying per year. According to Angel, (1946) the male is sexually mature at about 18 months, and the female at 3½ years.

The successful mating of a female of this sub-species with a male of the north African form *Lacerta lepida pater* has been achieved. The offspring died of pneumonia shortly after hatching however (Mertens, 1956).

Longevity

The average life span of the eyed lizard is six or seven years, the maximum duration being fourteen years (Fretey, 1975).

Hibernation

The eyed lizard disappears from active life in October, seldom reappearing before mid-April. It has apparently not been observed about in mild spells during the winter months. Peters (1962a) states that the food stored in the fat-bodies (masses of fat tissue) is used mainly for their sexual development, rather than for hibernation.

General response

When found in hiding under a rock, it dashes back and forth, eventually darting off to find refuge under the next convenient rock. If no cover is available it will dash off for some 5–10 metres before pausing. It is an excellent dodger, but if cornered, hisses menacingly with jaws wide open, a habit which may persist for some while in captivity. When freshly caught it struggles violently and tries to bite. The massive jaws of the adult are forbidding enough in appearance, and a bite can be very painful. In my experience however it usually releases its grip when suspended in the air, seldom holding on for as long as some lizards. Its well-developed claws can scratch vigorously and easily cause bleeding. When catching a specimen with bare hands, I try to seize it with my right hand, simultaneously offering it some convenient object—I have even used my wallet—with the left hand. Any object is readily seized in the lizard's jaws, and an unpleasant bite is thereby prevented. I then hold the lizard carefully but firmly to the ground, so that the claws have less freedom to scratch, and then as quickly as possible I open out a dark bag with the left hand, placing it over the lizard's head. If released, it is the instinct of this species to make a dash for cover—straight into the bag! At first it remains very much on the alert, always being ready to make a sudden getaway.

After a while it becomes comparatively tame, though not to the extent that the sand lizard does, for example. Some specimens may eventually come to accept food from the hand, others keep their distance and quickly become excitable and nervous when approached. Certain old individuals may refuse to be tamed and even ignore any food offered. Specimens confined to cages may refuse to eat. According to Gadow (1901) it has survived captive life for 13 years.

Distribution

Lacerta lepida lepida   This sub-species is chiefly an inhabitant of the Iberian peninsula. Its range in France is somewhat fragmentary, particularly north of the Mediterranean region. It is on record from as far north as the south of the département of Côte-d'Or, Jura, Charente-Maritime, Haute-Vienne (near Limoges), and the southern part of the île d'Oléron. It is also known from the départements of Gironde, southern Cantal, Gers and Vaucluse, besides the Cevennes and most of the départements which border the southern coast: Pyrénées-Orientales, Hérault, Bouches-du-Rhône, Var and Alpes-Maritimes. Finally it is known from the îles d'Hyères (Porquerolles) and the tiny island of Ratonneau off the coast of Marseilles.

As regards Spain, Salvador (1974b) reports that it is absent only from the provinces of Asturias, Santander, the Basque Country and the high Pyrenees, while in the regions of Almeria, Murcia and Alicante it is replaced by *Lacerta lepida nevadensis* **Buchholz**, a new sub-species whose exact range is not yet fully known. In Italy it is restricted to Liguria.

Other sub-species   *Lacerta lepida pater* (**Lataste**) is confined to north-western Africa, north of the Sahara, thus occurring in Morocco, where it extends as far south as the High Atlas, Algeria and Tunisia.

Nomenclature *for northern and central Europe*
  English   Eyed lizard, Ocellated lizard
  German   Perleidechse
  French   Lézard ocellé
  Italian   Lucertola occhiata, Lucertola ocellata.

The Wall Lizard
Podarcis muralis
(formerly *Lacerta muralis*)
Sub-species found in northern and central Europe:
Podarcis muralis muralis (**Laurenti**) 1768
Terra typica restricta: Vienna, Austria

Podarcis muralis maculiventris **Werner** 1891
Patria restricta: Bassovica, near Trieste, Italy

Podarcis muralis oyensis **Blanchard** 1891
Terra typica: île d'Yeu, France
Plates 8, 9, 10

This species has a very slender and flat body and a long and pointed head, which is slightly larger in the male, and a very long, finely tapering tail, which constitutes about two-thirds of the total length. The male reaches a length of 18 or 19 centimetres in the north of its range, and 20 centimetres (exceptionally 23 centimetres) further south. The female attains a maximum length of 17 or 18 centimetres.

Scalation

Dorsals: 40–65 tiny juxtaposed scales around middle of body, more or less distinctly keeled, sometimes smooth; tail scales narrow, obtusely keeled above. 6 longitudinal rows of *ventrals* (23–28 transverse rows in males, 25–32 in females). *Anal* preceded by 1 (rarely 2) rows of small plates; 13–27 *femoral* pores on each thigh. Nostril at junction of 3 (rarely 4) plates, not normally bordering *rostral*; usually 1 *postnasal*; 1 anterior *loreal*; upper *temporals* variable in number; 4 (rarely 3 or 5) upper *labials* anterior to *subocular*; *gular* fold normally distinct; collar comprising 7–13 (usually 8–11) plates—hardly or not serrated.

Colouration

Podarcis muralis muralis   Even within the typical form *Podarcis muralis muralis* there is considerable variation in colour and pattern between different specimens, often within the same area. The back of the male tends to be greyish, brown or brownish red, and is normally fairly densely covered with small black patches or streaks, which often join up to form a network. Sometimes there is also a more or less distinct vertebral stripe. The sides are similarly dark and are well spotted with whitish flecks, which may often form a central, longitudinal band. The belly is whitish, yellowish, orange or brick-red, and is bordered on each side by a row of flecks, which may be pale or bright blue, black, rust, or mixed.

The back of the female is generally lighter than that of the male, usually light brown, and there is often, though not invariably, a longitudinal row of dark brown or black streaks along the middle of the back, which may join up to form a continuous vertebral stripe. A whitish or yellowish stripe may often be present on either side of the back. In addition, rather indistinct dark flecks may be irregularly scattered on top of the back, and frequently a row of more pronounced dark flecks may occur on each side of the back, adjoining the whitish stripes. The flanks are much darker, but have whitish spots, which can form a central longitudinal stripe as in some males, extending from the lip shields along each side of the body. In general the throat and belly are whitish or yellowish, and are sometimes tinged with rust or red. In some cases the throat may be orange. The belly is normally unspotted, though a few black flecks may be present. As in the male a row of blue or black spots can occur on each side.

There is usually a black fleck on the anal shield, a feature I have noticed on *oyensis*, and on *maculiventris*, besides the principal form. The head is dark brown or greyish brown above, sometimes with faint, darker, irregular markings. The limbs are brown above, and have light spots, often with a black border. Underneath they are usually yellowy white. The tail is brown above, and each segment frequently has white and black flecks on the sides. Underneath it is a dirty white, sometimes with reddish marks towards the cloaca. Green colouration does not occur in either sex in this sub-species, although some specimens may display a greenish sheen while basking in the sun.

As regards pattern, newly-hatched wall lizards resemble their parents. Their tails are proportionally shorter however. Specimens uniformly black both above and on the ventral side are not uncommon in some areas, and such melanism appears to be a prominent feature of many wall lizards which live on the islands of Lake Maggiore in northern Italy.

Podarcis muralis maculiventris   This sub-species is very similar to the typical form. Above its pattern is very clearly defined, and the colouration varies from light or dark greyish brown to nut-brown, often with a strong greenish tinge. In the shoulder region there is usually a white or blue fleck which is superimposed on a dark background. It is most readily distinguished by its underside, which is well flecked with black spots, these occurring on the throat, neck, belly and on the underside of the tail.

Podarcis muralis oyensis   The form known as *Podarcis muralis oyensis* is characterized by its larger build and dark, somewhat drab colouration. Klemmer (1964) also refers to the red colouration of the belly in this sub-species. In September 1969 I paid a visit to the île d'Yeu (Vendée) and examined over a score of adult specimens, both males and females, all of which had a whitish or yellowish belly. Some of the males had the black network on top of the back superimposed upon a bluish ground colour, which sometimes had a distinct yellowish or turquoise tinge, and there was frequently a blue or more rarely yellow spot above the shoulder. The throats of both sexes were spotted with black, and there was sometimes a row of black spots on either side of the belly, and also on the belly plates near the throat region. Klemmer has suggested (*in litt.*) that the males may lose their red colouration by late summer and autumn. The females are similar in appearance to those of *Podarcis muralis muralis*.

As Klemmer had remarked that the nearby island of Noirmoutier did not appear to have been investigated regarding its wall lizard population, I visited this island while en route to the île d'Yeu. The lizards of Noirmoutier are similar to those of the latter island, and seem to be referable to *oyensis*, an opinion shared by Klemmer on seeing photographs of the lizards I found there. He remarked however that the variability of these lizards is wider than that of the Yeu population. None of the lizards I examined on Noirmoutier had a red belly. It seems likely that the lizards of Belle Île (Brittany) would also belong to this sub-species, but this requires confirmation.

Podarcis muralis calbia   The stature of *Podarcis muralis calbia* **Blanchard** as a distinct sub-species has been questioned by Klemmer (1964), who regards it as a form of *oyensis*. It is distinguished by its smaller build and lighter colouration. There is a prominent greenish sheen on the back, especially on the supraciliary stripes.

Habitat

The wall lizard is at home in a wide variety of conditions where it is sufficiently dry and sunny. As its name indicates, it is a frequent inhabitant of walls—garden walls, the outer walls of village houses, the rocky walls surrounding plots of agricultural land and vineyards, and also ruins and piles of rocks. It can often be found within urban areas where there is sufficient vegetation and cover, and may even be found on derelict land well into cities. Cemeteries are frequently favoured. In addition it can be found on bushy or grassy slopes, in quarries, and in dry, thinly-wooded districts. I have frequently observed it on railway embankments. It is also found beside country paths and roads and in hedgerows. It often lives on cliffs in coastal regions.

An interesting observation was made by Kramer and Mertens (1938), concerning the wall lizards of Istria. *Podarcis muralis maculiventris* is confined to the western part of the peninsula, where it is associated with areas of human habitation, whereas *Podarcis muralis muralis* is found more in the central and eastern parts, including areas which are far from human dwellings. Between these populations intermediate forms have been observed.

Altitude   It seems equally at home in flat, hilly and mountainous districts. It attains 1700 metres in Switzerland (Stemmler, 1971), and approximately 2000 metres in the Taygetos Mountains in Greece.

Co-habiting species   As a result of its adaptation to a wide variety of habitats, it may be found living in the same localities as many other species of reptile. Its geographical range is fairly similar to that of the green lizard, and in both eastern and western Europe I have frequently found the two species living in fairly close proximity to one another.

Behaviour

This sun-lover likes to spend much of its available time basking and is able to enjoy quite a hot sun, though very hot weather will force it into retreat. It retires in the evening as the sun is setting, and earlier in hilly localities that receive no sun during the latter part of the day. When the weather is very hot it retreats into the shade, or may dig a hole with its snout and feet in sand or soft earth. By disposition it is a very shy and nervous creature, extremely agile and graceful in its movements, and is constantly on the alert. It basks where plenty of rocks, crevices or thick vegetation are available into which it can disappear at the slightest hint of danger. Before re-emerging from cover, it will cautiously peep around to survey the scene, and if all appears to be safe will come out to resume basking. It has a remarkable climbing ability, and is well able to dart up and down vertical walls. I have sometimes found it basking on the bark of trees, which it has little difficulty in scaling.

At one time I lived on the fourth floor of a large building. In my room I kept some wall lizards, one of which managed to escape from its cage which stood on the window-sill. Unfortunately the window was slightly open, and it dashed out. Before I could reach it, it had proceeded to climb up the outside wall, past the fifth floor to the roof. It was about to climb from the wall onto the roof when it fell down into the garden below, which was in an enclosed courtyard. I immediately hurried down to find it, and soon discovered it, apparently unharmed, and still very active. It had fallen a distance of some 20 metres and never subsequently showed itself to be any the worse for its experience.

The wall lizard is very much a gregarious species. It is frequently found living in quite large colonies, even within towns. In the evening and in cool weather it can often be found in retreat under a pile of rocks, a suitable stone or flat piece of metal. In such circumstances it is most easily caught. Its sluggishness is only temporary however and it soon becomes active.

Food

The diet of this species consists of spiders, insects including flies, bees, butterflies and beetles, and insect larvae. Earthworms are also sometimes devoured, as are small molluscs. The young similarly eat spiders and tiny insects. In consequence this species renders a valuable service to agriculture, especially in areas where it is particularly abundant. There is a record of wall lizards living by the coast, entering the water in order to catch sandhoppers, little crabs and shrimps (Angel, 1946). Even fleshy, succulent plants are sometimes devoured, particularly in hotter localities where water has become scarce.

Enemies

Despite its alertness, it is not free from enemies, falling a prey to flesh-eating mammals—weasels and shrews, birds and also snakes, which can most easily catch the lizards after they have settled in their retreat and are no longer alert.

Reproduction

Mating   Mating takes place shortly after emergence from hibernation. This may already occur in February in the south of its range. In such cases the eggs are laid quite early, and a second mating and laying may take place. There may even be three matings and layings during the course of the spring months. Throughout the mating season, which may extend until June, there is rivalry among the males over the possession of a nearby female. The victor, having fought off his opponent, turns to the female, whom he seizes in his jaws, and copulation ensues. I once observed a pair copulating on the side of a vertical wall, some 60 centimetres above the ground. When they became aware of my presence, they leapt to the ground, separated, and sped off in different directions.

Egg laying   An early mating will result in the eggs being laid in April. The usual time for egg laying is late April, May and June.

From 2 to 10 pale white eggs are laid, and these are carefully buried in a hole some 20 centimetres in depth, specially excavated by the female. The eggs measure from 10–12 by 5–6 millimetres, though during the incubation period they enlarge somewhat to 14–15 by 11–12 millimetres.

Hatching   Hatching usually takes place between the end of July and the beginning of September, most often in August. The newly hatched measure from 56 to 65 millimetres. The egg-tooth is sometimes shed shortly after hatching, though this can be delayed for up to a week.

Growth   The males reach a total length of 14 to 14.5 centimetres at the end of their first year, females measure about 13.5 centimetres (Angel, 1946). The females apparently breed from the age of about two.

Regeneration   The wall lizard is not only able to regenerate a broken tail, but has been known to partially replace lost limbs and digits.

Hybrids In captivity hybrids have been produced as a result of the mating between a male *maculiventris* and a female of the typical form. Similar success has been achieved in obtaining hybrids from a male Karst lizard (*Podarcis melisellensis fiumana*) and a female *Podarcis muralis muralis*, and also from these two species with the sexes reversed. There is also the record of the crossing of a male *Podarcis tiliguerta* with a female *Podarcis muralis muralis* (Mertens, 1950).

Longevity
According to Fretey (1975), this species has a maximum life-span of ten years, but on average survives some four to six years.

Hibernation
Hibernation varies considerably, according to latitude, altitude and climate. Despite this species' love of warmth, the period of winter sleep is nowhere very prolonged, and in some southern regions it may not occur at all. In Germany it can still be found in November on sufficiently mild days, and it can be seen about again at the beginning of March or April, but isolated specimens may sometimes be found even earlier. In the south Tirol its normal period of hibernation is from December to mid-February. It may sometimes remain active throughout the winter in the south of France. Even in the north of its range it can occasionally be seen about during a mild frost-free spell in mid-winter.

General response
In warm weather considerable skill and patience are required to catch this species, which is even more agile than the common lizard. From a relaxed sedentary position it can flee at lightning speed when any attempt is made to grab it. It appears to settle in a new position almost instantaneously, as if nothing had happened. When seized it will try to bite, though its teeth are too tiny to do harm or even to hurt.

One evening I observed a wall lizard's tail which was slightly protruding from a narrow hole in a large boulder. I eased the tail very gently towards me until the body emerged, and I then grabbed this quickly. My success in catching the lizard with its tail completely intact was, I believe, partly due to the narrowness of the hole, which prevented the lizard from wriggling, and also due to its lack of alertness in the cool evening temperature. On a sunny day it would I think be impossible to catch this species by the tail.

It is inadvisable to hold a newly-caught specimen for long in the hand, since it usually makes abrupt struggling movements which cause it to shed its tail. When first placed in a cage it usually dashes about wildly, and if cornered will open its mouth and threaten to strike. On one occasion I witnessed a freshly-caught wall lizard disgorge an earthworm.

In captivity it soon settles down, taking food readily. It never becomes completely tame in the same way as the common or sand lizard. It is difficult to induce it to feed from the hand, though this can be done with perseverance. It cannot be held freely in the hand as can the other two species, without the risk of it making a sudden leap for freedom.

Distribution

Podarcis muralis muralis This sub-species is by far the most widely distributed.

FRANCE AND CHANNEL ISLANDS   It is the commonest species of reptile to occur in France, where it extends right up to the northern coast of Brittany and the island of Chausey, southwards to the Mediterranean zone, including the island of Riou. Most of the Atlantic islands are inhabited by another sub-species (*oyensis*), though the typical form lives on the île d'Oléron. It is also present on Jersey, occurring on the north-eastern coast (Frazer, 1949). At present there appear to be no data regarding Herm or Sark (Klemmer, 1964).

ENGLAND   Two breeding colonies have been established in Surrey, one of which has derived from twelve specimens released in 1932 (Frazer, 1964). Two colonies have also been introduced on the Isle of Wight, although their racial identity awaits confirmation.

BENELUX   In Belgium it is found in the Jurassic and Calcareous regions of the south, particularly in the Meuse valley. In Luxembourg it is the commonest species of lizard. In Holland however it survives only in one locality near Maastricht, where according to Bund (1964), it is threatened with extinction due to the restoration of the old walls.

GERMANY   A century ago in Germany it was apparently found almost everywhere in the region of vineyards (Grzimek, 1971), but has now become extinct in many places. Even since the Second World War it has decreased considerably, again due to the replacement of old walls. It occurs in the middle Rhine valley, on the eastern bank between Bingen and Koblenz, and also between Bingen and Wiesbaden on the northern bank. In addition it penetrates into the Lahn and Nahe valleys. In these regions it appears to be confined to the river valleys and does not extend into the surrounding hills. It is also found near Worms and in the Neckar valley near the Odenwald district in Hessen. It has an extensive but localised range in Baden-Württemberg. Finally it is isolated in parts of Upper Bavaria.

Its status as an indigenous species in Poland has never been confirmed (Berger, Jaskowska and Młynarski, 1969).

ALPINE LANDS   It is fairly widespread in Switzerland to the north of the Alps, though it is absent from certain areas of the central and eastern regions

(Stemmler, 1971). South of the Alps it is mainly replaced by *Podarcis muralis maculiventris*. In Austria it is found in the northern Tirol (in and around Innsbruck, and in the Inn valley), in the eastern Tirol, in Lower Austria (from Vienna to Adlitzgräben, and in the Pielach valley), near Güssing in southern Burgenland, central and southern Styria and in Carinthia. It has also been introduced near Linz (Eiselt, 1961). It does not appear to occur to the north of the Danube in Austria.

EASTERN CENTRAL EUROPE   According to Štěpánek (1949), in Czechoslovakia it is very rare, being confined to a few localities in southern and eastern Slovakia. It has a very restricted range in Hungary, being found around Budapest, and extending from the Buda and Pilis hills north-eastwards over the Borzsöny, Matra, Bükk and Zemplén mountain ranges. It is also known from the hilly region west of the Danube in southern Hungary. In Romania it is confined to Transylvania and the Carpathian regions, though in these areas it appears to be quite widespread.

SOUTHERN EUROPE   In northern Spain it extends from Galicia to the Pyrenees, and it recurs at higher altitudes in the Iberian and Castilian mountains, being elsewhere replaced by the Spanish wall lizard (*Podarcis hispanica*), while in Italy it occurs in Liguria, parts of Piedmont, Lombardy and Trentino-Alto-Adige. It extends over much of the Balkan peninsula and reaches as far south as the Taygetos mountains. In Yugoslavia it is absent from the south Adriatic coast. According to Cyrén (1933) it extends from the mountainous regions of Bulgaria to the Black Sea coast. In southern Bulgaria however, it is replaced by *Podarcis erhardii*. In Greece it appears to be confined to the mountainous regions. Outside of Europe it is known only from north-western Asia Minor.

Podarcis muralis maculiventris   This sub-species is an inhabitant of Switzerland south of the Alps (Tessin), north-eastern Italy, Yugoslavia and Romania. In Italy it is confined to the plains and hills of Piedmont, Lombardy, Venetia and parts of Emilia. In Yugoslavia its range extends from southern Slovenia and the Istrian coast, along the south-eastern borders of the Velebit range, and in the Adriatic region to northern Dalmatia. Finally, in Romania it occurs in the southern Banat, in the province of Oltenia and in the Dobruja.

Podarcis muralis oyensis   This sub-species is found along the western and southern coasts of Brittany. Its range includes the île d'Ouessant, the Pointe du Raz, the Archipel des Glénans, and the islands of Cigogne, Penfret, Noirmoutier and d'Yeu (Vendée).

Other sub-species   *Podarcis muralis brueggemanni* **Bedriaga** is indigenous to

Italy where it extends from Genoa in Liguria to Tuscany and Rome province, its eastern limits being Bologna and Florence.

Many varieties of lizard in the Mediterranean, Adriatic and Aegean regions were formerly classified as forms of wall lizard, but are now considered to belong to other species. The following forms are recognised as being further sub-species of wall lizard. *Podarcis muralis rasquinetii* **Bedriaga** lives on a few islands near Gijón in the province of Asturias in north-western Spain. *Podarcis muralis sebastiani* **Klemmer** inhabits Monte Urgull and the Isla Santa Clara, near San Sebastian. *Podarcis muralis occidentalis* **Knoepffler** has recently been described from the Pyrénées-Orientales in France, and the Spanish massif of Portolas. *Podarcis muralis merremia* **Risso** is confined to the French *département* of Bouches-du-Rhône on the south coast.

Podarcis muralis tinettoi **Taddei** is found on Tinetto island, and *Podarcis muralis vinciguerrai* **Mertens** inhabits Gorgona island, both these islands being situated in the Ligurian Sea. *Podarcis muralis colosii* **Taddei** occurs on Elba, Palmajola and possibly Monte Massoncello. *Podarcis muralis insulanica* **Bedriaga** inhabits the nearby island of Pianosa and its smaller neighbouring islands, though La Scuola island has its own endemic sub-species: *Podarcis muralis muellerlorenzi* **Taddei**. *Podarcis muralis paulini* **Taddei** is a native of Monte Argentario, while *Podarcis muralis beccarii* **Lanza** inhabits the nearby Isolotto di Port' Ercole.

Podarcis muralis marcucci **Lanza** and *Podarcis muralis corsica* **Lanza** are endemic to the Tuscan island of Argentarolo and to Corsica respectively. Two other forms are found on the Italian mainland. These are *Podarcis muralis nigriventris* (**Bonaparte**) from the Rome area, and *Podarcis muralis breviceps* **Boulenger,** an inhabitant of Calabria, which is found above an altitude of 700 metres. Finally there is *Podarcis muralis albanica* **Bolkay**, which occurs in southern Yugoslavia, Albania and Greece, including the Peloponnese.

Nomenclature *in northern and central Europe*
  Dutch   Muur-Hagedis
  German   Mauereidechse
  French   Lézard des murailles
  Italian   Lucertola delle muraglie
  Romanian   Şopîrla de ziduri
  Hungarian   Fali gyík
  Czech   Ještěrka zední
  Slovakian   Jašterica múrová
  Polish   Jaszczurka murowa
  Serbo-Croatian   Zidna gušterica

The Ruin Lizard
Podarcis sicula
(formerly *Lacerta serpa*)
Sub-species found in central Europe:
Podarcis sicula campestris (**De Betta**) 1857
Terra typica restricta: Verona, Italy
Plate 11

Of those species sometimes grouped together under the general heading of
'wall lizards', this is one of the longest and most strongly built. The flattish
head is very pointed, the body is fairly depressed, and the long, finely tapering
tail comprises about two-thirds of the total length, which averages about 17
centimetres. Males attain a greater length than females and 23 centimetres is
the maximum length attained.

Scalation
Dorsals: 50–67 (usually 53–62) tiny, roundish or hexagonal scales around
middle of body, often sharply keeled, becoming weakly keeled or smooth on
lower laterals; tail scales more or less keeled—upper scales obtusely pointed
posteriorly. 6 longitudinal rows of *ventrals* (23–29 transverse rows in males,
27–31 in females). *Anal* preceded by 2 or 3 rows of small plates (1 row when
anal is large); 15–24 (usually 17–22) *femoral* pores on each thigh. Nostril
borders *rostral*, or is narrowly separated from it; 1 *postnasal*; almost always 4
upper *labials* anterior to *subocular*; *gular* fold distinct; collar comprising 9–11
(rarely 7 or 8) more or less distinctly serrated plates.

Colouration
Dorsal region The general colouration on top of the back, for about two-thirds
of its length, is yellow green, grass-green or light olive green. There is a thick
brown vertebral stripe flecked with irregular black spots. These spots, which
are more numerous in females, may sometimes be arranged in two parallel
longitudinal rows. As in the meadow lizard, towards the tail region the general
colouration of the back is brown, and the black flecks continue to about as far
as the beginning of the tail. The sides are light brownish and are flecked with
black and dirty yellow or white spots. Some of the lighter spots, which may be
edged with brown, may form a more or less continuous dorso-lateral as well as a
lateral stripe. Black flecks may occur on top of the back, adjacent to the
dorso-lateral stripes. Above the fore-limbs there is a black spot or ocellus, with
a bluish or greenish centre. In some cases this spot may be uniformly light
blue. Between this spot and the head I have sometimes observed a black
blotch.

Ventral region   The throat and belly are uniformly white, pale greenish white, mother of pearl or exceptionally pink. The belly may become darker towards the edges, and on each side there is normally a longitudinal row of blue, bluish green, brown or sometimes black spots.

Limbs   The fore-limbs are brown with obscure black flecks, while the hind limbs, also brown, have white spots, and these are bordered with black. The undersurface of each limb is similar to the belly, and is unspotted.

Head and tail   The top of the head is usually bright green or olive brown in adult males and light brown in females. Sporadic black flecks may also be present. The lip shields are a dirty white. Above, the tail is a light grey brown with an indistinct whitish stripe on either side, while below it is a dirty white.

Juvenile colouration   The pattern of the young is similar to that of the adults, though no trace of green is present, the general colouration being brown.

This species is not unlike the meadow lizard (p. 99) in appearance. It is most easily distinguished by its stronger build, and by the dark vertebral stripe.

Habitat

The ruin lizard has adapted itself to a wide variety of conditions, though its range of habitat is not quite as varied as that of the wall lizard. As its scientific name *campestris* indicates, it is an inhabitant of fields and meadows. I have found it on sunny banks, grassy verges, bushy country, beside copses, country paths and roadsides sometimes with continually passing traffic. I have also seen it living quite abundantly amid piles of refuse. It often favours coastal regions, and can be met with on sandy beaches, and at the bottoms of cliffs. It is often found living in the vicinity of human habitation, not only in villages but sometimes even in the less densely urbanized parts of cities.

This is predominantly a lowland species. In Provence it extends to only 300 metres. In Italy however it is still found at 1260 metres at the Lago di Barrea region of the Abruzzi (Müller, 1974), and according to Stemmler (1971), it is on rare occasions found above 1300 metres in Italy.

I have most commonly encountered it living in the same localities as the wall lizard, especially with *Podarcis muralis brueggemanni*. In various parts of Italy I have found it inhabiting the same territory as the green lizard, the three toed skink (Italian race), the slow worm, the dark green whip snake and the aspic viper.

Behaviour
The ruin lizard is a great sun-worshipper, and loves to bask beside thick vegetation, and at the foot of walls and ruins. Although its habits are similar to those of the wall lizard it is less adept at climbing, and is usually seen basking on the ground. Occasionally however I have observed it sunning itself on the trunks of trees, which it seems to scale more easily than walls, and it is able to dash at lightning speed into a convenient crevice in the bark. Having been frightened away from its basking spot, it frequently returns a short while later when all danger appears to have vanished. On the ground it appears no less agile than the wall lizard. I have sometimes found quite large numbers of this species living within the same vicinity.

Food
Its diet consists mainly of insects and their larvae, together with spiders. Worms, slugs and little snails are also devoured, as are certain fruits and berries (Stemmler, 1971). In general this species is of great benefit to agriculture, especially in areas where it occurs in abundance. In Dalmatia, Bolkay observed this species eating ripe black nightshade berries (*Solanum nigrum*). All those he caught at a Dubrovnik locality were stuffed with them.

Reproduction
Mating takes place shortly after hibernation, and may be extended into the summer months. According to Stemmler the female may lay eggs from two to five times between early and late summer. The broods normally vary from four to seven, though as many as twelve have been reported. Hatching, he states, requires from four to seven weeks according to the temperature. Maturity is reached after one or two years. Hybrids have been reared as the result of the mating of a male specimen with a female Karst lizard (*Podarcis melisellensis fiumana*) (Mertens, 1950).

General response
This species is if anything more shy and nervous than the wall lizard, and just as difficult to catch. In my opinion it is more savage by nature, and when seized it struggles wildly and tries to bite. Frequently when first caught it discharges the contents of the cloaca.

Although it is an attractive lizard, and lives well in captivity, usually feeding regularly, I have not yet known it to become really tame. Even after months of captive life it may still become alarmed when approached, bite, and discharge its excrement on being picked up. It has some ability to leap when trying to scale the walls around its enclosure. It usually cannot be held freely in the hand without risk of it making a jump for freedom, and it loses little of its rapidity through closer confinement. I have kept this species living quite happily along with other lacertids of similar size, as well as with three toed skinks and slow worms. In Britain ruin lizards are not infrequently displayed as 'wall lizards' in pet shops.

Distribution
The ruin lizard is confined to Europe, and is found mainly in Italy and its islands, as well as on the islands and Adriatic coastal region of Yugoslavia. The tremendous variety of its sub-species—over fifty now recognised—have given it an almost notorious reputation among taxonomists. Many islands have their own endemic race, and no other European species of reptile is represented by such a wide diversity of forms.

The present sub-species *campestris* is mainly a continental form and occurs principally in northern Italy, Istria and northern Dalmatia. Its extensive range in the Po plain begins west of Turin, and, as has recently been established, it extends northwards as far as Chiasso, thus it just enters Swiss territory in the province of Tessin (Stemmler, 1971). In the Trentino region I have found it near Rovereto, not in the Adige valley, as might be expected, but in the low mountainous country not far from the village of Spino. In Liguria it reaches at least as far west as Portofino (Lanza, 1968).

On the Apennine peninsula it ranges southwards as far as the region of Rome, where it merges imperceptibly with the south Italian race *Podarcis sicula sicula*; and south-eastwards through the Abruzzi mountains to Monte Gargano and the province of Apulia. In addition it inhabits the islands of Elba and Corsica, and various islands in the Venetian gulf.

According to Knoepffler (1961) it is found in all five of the départements of Provence. Mourgue has reported it from the île du Château d'If, off the coast of Marseilles. Such occurrences in France may be the result of introductions. In Yugoslavia it lives in Istria and along the Dalmatian coast, approximately as far south as Split. Between Istria and Dalmatia it inhabits the islands almost exclusively, rarely the mainland (Karaman, 1921). Its presence in central and eastern Istria was first confirmed by Kramer and Mertens (1938). It also occurs on the island of Krk.

According to Stemmler (1971), this species is from time to time introduced to various other parts of Switzerland, amid consignments of vegetables, though it does not appear to be able to establish itself for long north of the Alps. A thriving colony however apparently exists in Philadelphia (U.S.A.), and at Almeria in Spain.

Other sub-species The southern parts of Italy, Sicily and the nearby Egadi islands, as well as Pantelleria, are inhabited by *Podarcis sicula sicula*

Rafinesque. The other known mainland forms are *Podarcis sicula mertensi* **Wettstein** from Paestum, Giunganico and Capaccio in the Gulf of Salerno; *Podarcis sicula ragusae* **Wettstein** from southern Dalmatia, and *Podarcis sicula hieroglyphica* **Berthold**, which is found isolatedly around Istanbul, both on the shores of the sea of Marmara and on the islands. *Podarcis sicula cettii* **Cara** occurs on Sardinia (and has been introduced to Corsica and Menorca). The remaining races—about 50 at present recognised—are endemic to many of the small islands off the coasts of Italy and Yugoslavia.

Nomenclature *for northern and central Europe*
  German   Ruineneidechse
  French   Lézard des ruines, Lézard sicilien
  Italian   Lucertola campestre

The Meadow Lizard
Podarcis taurica
Sub-species found in central Europe:
Podarcis taurica taurica **Pallas** 1814
(formerly *Lacerta taurica taurica*)
Terra typica: Crimean peninsula, Ukraine
Plate 12

The meadow lizard is a particularly pretty species. It is not unlike the wall lizard in build, but is a little smaller. It has a short, smallish body, a fairly long and pointed head, which is a little larger in the male, and a long, tapering tail which comprises about two-thirds of its total length. Its usual maximum length varies between 14 and 18 centimetres, though in Romania at least it has been known to reach 20 centimetres (Fuhn, 1969). As a rule the male of this species is slightly longer than the female.

Scalation
Dorsals: 42–62 tiny more or less diagonally keeled scales around middle of body. 6 (rarely 8) longitudinal (25–32 transverse) rows of *ventrals*. *Anal* preceded by 2 or 3 rows of small plates; 14–21 *femoral* pores on each thigh. Nostril at junction of 3 plates (including *rostral*); usually 1 *postnasal*; 1 anterior *loreal*; usually 2 or 3 upper *temporals*; 4 (rarely 3 or 5) upper *labials* anterior to *subocular*; *gular* fold well defined; collar comprising 8–12 (usually 9–11) more or less distinctly serrated plates.

Colouration
Dorsal region　For about two-thirds of its length the top of the back is normally bright green, but sometimes dark green. On each side of the back there is a whitish, yellowish or yellowish-green dorso-lateral stripe, which is separated from the green colouration by a light brown or cinnamon-coloured band. The latter is flecked with a row of irregular dark brown or black spots which, like the dorso-lateral stripes extend for a short way along the tail. Occasionally the spots may occur on the green colouration however. The flanks, the lower third of the dorsal region, and the upper surface of the tail are light brown or cinnamon-coloured. A longitudinal stripe similar in colour to the dorso-lateral stripes extends from the upper labials along the flanks, above and sometimes below, or even across which is a further row of irregular dark brown or black spots. The lateral markings are continued for a short distance along the side of the tail. The tail is greyish brown above, with occasional black spots. An attractive blue spot may sometimes occur above each fore-limb joint. The top of the head is dark green, greenish brown or grey-brown, and there may be a few isolated black spots. Similar spots may also occur on the nape.

Ventral region　The throat of both sexes is a dirty white. The male has an orange, yellowish or sometimes brick-red belly. That of the female is pearly white or a dirty cream, although towards the sides the belly may become darker or display a greenish tinge. The sides of the belly are often flecked with a row of light blue or a mixture of blue, black and sometimes purple spots. Underneath the tail is uniformly cream or whitish.

Juvenile colouration　The pattern of the young is similar to that of the adults, but the top of the head and back are brown. I have seen adult specimens from Hungary and Bulgaria similarly devoid of green colouration. One such specimen however, showed a distinct greenish tinge on top of the back after having shed its skin.

Habitat
The meadow lizard is chiefly an inhabitant of grassy meadows and hills. In my experience it avoids barren, rocky and scrubby areas, except where there is plenty of thick grass. It may be found on grassy patches near human dwellings, in gardens, at the edges of paths, and in fields and vineyards. I have sometimes come across it beside roads with persistent traffic. In Romania it inhabits loess regions. In Hungary it is particularly associated with sandy localities, occurring in the steppeland district in the central part of the country. The Hungarian name *Homoki gyík* means in fact 'sand lizard'. In parts of its range it becomes a mountain dweller, and it derives its name from the Yaila (i.e.

Taurican) mountains in the south of the Crimean peninsula. Terent' ev and
Cernov (1949) state that in this region it prefers areas which are more or less
stony. The southern form *Podarcis taurica ionica* has been reported from a
height of 2375 metres at the peak of Mt. Killene (Wettstein, 1953).

Co-habiting species   Its habitat in Hungary is sometimes associated with that
of the meadow viper, while elsewhere I have also found it living in the same
localities as the striped grass snake, the Caspian whip snake, the green lizard
and the Greek tortoise. In Yugoslavia and Greece it often shares its habitat with
the wall lizard and with Erhard's wall lizard (*Podarcis erhardii*).

Behaviour

Few observations so far appear to have been made on the behaviour of this
species. I have found it a very shy and retiring lizard, fond of basking, and
sometimes enjoying a very hot sun. It is a less socially inclined species than the
ruin or wall lizards, for although I know areas where it is quite common, I have
most frequently found it alone. Normally it likes to bask in a suitable sunny
clearing amid grass and low shrubbery. I have seldom found it sunning itself
upon rocks, even though these may have been abundant. In time of danger
however it does not hesitate to retreat into any available pile of rocks. Like
other reptiles it may often return to its original basking site when all danger is
past. I have never found it scaling walls; in fact it is not a particularly good
climber. The statement sometimes made that this species is easy to catch on
account of its fondness for a grassy environment is I feel misleading, since it is a
very agile and alert little lizard, and when alarmed will dart off for surprisingly
long distances before pausing. Furthermore the combination of green and
brown in its colouration enables it to camouflage well with its surroundings.

Food

It is generally believed that grasshoppers form the principal item of the
meadow lizard's diet. However in an analysis of the prey of 32 specimens from
open meadows in the Black Sea region of Bulgaria, Kabisch and Engelmann
(1970) reported that bugs constituted 22.7 per cent of their diet, beetles 17.2
per cent, various Hymenoptera 14.1 per cent, spiders 11.0 per cent, flies 8.7
per cent, woodlice 8 per cent, various Homoptera 4.9 per cent, butterflies 4.3
per cent, while grasshoppers, although abundant, formed only 2.5 per cent.
Insect larvae are readily taken. Those that I kept in captivity accepted small
butterflies and mealworms without hesitation.

Reproduction

Mating occurs in May, and the eggs are laid in June. The brood is small, varying from two to five. The eggs are buried by the female in sand or loose soil, and measure approximately 13 to 15 by 7 millimetres. The young hatch in September and then measure from about 28 to 30 millimetres.

Hibernation

The meadow lizard generally emerges from hibernation in April, and active life continues until October, or sometimes even until November. In southern Serbia (near Vranje) I once found it basking within an hour after a brief snow storm. This was on 8 April, 1964. According to Vásárhelyi (1965) this species in Hungary spends the winter months in suitable holes in the sand. The winter quarters may sometimes be excavated by the lizard itself.

General response

When freshly caught this species behaves wildly and tries to bite the hand of its captor. If successful it may cling on, and will allow itself to be suspended in mid-air, supported only by its jaws. Due to its nervous disposition it may defecate, a habit which sometimes persists in captivity whenever it is first picked up. Some nervousness may still be apparent after months of captive life, and care should be taken when it is held in the hand as it may make a sudden dart for freedom, though it is rather more reliable than the wall lizard in this respect. Some specimens may continue to behave quite wildly and try to bite whenever an attempt is made to pick them up, though when actually held, they quickly become more docile. Food is readily accepted in captivity, yet the meadow lizard often proves a somewhat delicate species, and sometimes does not survive for many months.

Distribution

In Hungary the meadow lizard is known from a number of localities in the central region, situated between the rivers Danube and Tisza. It occurs there as far north as Budapest, Szöd and Gödöllő, and as far south as Szeged and Tompa. To the east of the Tisza it is known from Hortobágy and Hajdubagos. In Transdanubia it is now known to occur at Pákozd, north of Lake Velence (Dely, 1965). In Romania it lives in the Banat region from Bazias, to Vîrciorova, and is also found in the Danubian lowlands, where it is uncommon. Its range includes the regions of Oltenia, Bucharest and the Dobruja. In Yugoslavia it is known from Bežanija in Slavonia, the Bǎcka region, two localities in the southern Banat (Pančevo and Deliblato); parts of eastern Serbia, near Studenica west of the river Ibar, and the province of Kosovo Metohija. In addition it is found throughout Macedonia (Radovanović, 1964). Elsewhere it is found in much of Bulgaria, where it avoids the high mountains; in Albania and northern and eastern Greece, including Chalkidike, but it is absent from the Peloponnese. It is present in European Turkey, while further east I have encountered it near Izmit in north-west Asia Minor. In the Ukraine it is found along the western and northern borders of the Black Sea, as well as in the Crimean peninsula. Terent' ev and Cernov (1949) include the Taman peninsula in its range; Shcherbak (1966) however does not.

Other sub-species The two other known sub-species are *Podarcis taurica ionica* **Lehrs**, found in southern Albania, in Greece, from Epirus to the Peloponnese, and the Ionian islands; and *Podarcis taurica thasopulae* **Kattinger** which is endemic to the mountains of the island of Thasopulo in the north Aegean Sea. The exact extent of this species' range does not yet appear to be fully known.

Nomenclature *in northern and central Europe*
  English   Meadow lizard, Taurican lizard
  German   Taurische Eidechse
  Romanian   Sopîrla de Stepă
  Hungarian   Homoki gyík
  Czech   Ještěrka travní severní
  Slovakian   Jašterica trávová
  Russian   Крымская Ящерица

The Balkan Skink
Ablepharus kitaibelii
Sub-species found in central Europe:
Ablepharus kitaibelii fitzingeri **Mertens** 1952
(formerly *Ablepharus pannonicus*)
Terra typica restricta: Ofen, near Budapest, Hungary

Ablepharus kitaibelii stepaneki **Fuhn** 1970
Terra typica: Cernica wood, Bucharest, Romania
Plates 13, 14

The Balkan skink, named after the Hungarian botanist Pál Kitaibel, who first noted it in 1797, is one of Europe's smallest species of lizard. It has a somewhat snake-like, more or less cylindrical body, from which the smallish head and the round, tapering and pointed tail are not distinctly set off. This species thus has no well-defined neck. The tail constitutes about half of the total length, or slightly more in male specimens. According to Fuhn (1970), the males are always smaller than females. Each of the small, thin limbs has five digits with tiny, quite pointed claws. The fore-and hind-limbs are widely spaced. As indicated by the scientific name *Ablepharus*, all members of this genus lack eyelids, the eyes being covered by a transparent disc as in snakes. The ear cavity is small and round. The Balkan skink reaches a maximum length of 9 to 11 centimetres.

Scalation
Scales smooth, shiny and metallic, fairly uniform in size, arranged around circumference of body (20–22 rows in *fitzingeri*, 20 in *stepaneki*), largest in neck region. *Rostral* usually rounded at rear; large *frontal*, longer than broad; 3 pairs of *supraoculars* (first pair tiny and triangular); 4 anterior upper *labials* in *fitzingeri* (third and fourth sometimes fused), 3 in *stepaneki*.

Colouration
The two races being discussed here are similar in colour and pattern. The top of the back is olive, yellowish brown, light brown, reddish- or dark brown, tending towards a grey or granite colour in older specimens. There are usually two or four dark longitudinal stripes, each composed of a row of tiny dots, which continue along the tail, where they may become somewhat indistinct. The stripes which run along the centre of the back are the most clearly defined. Above, the head is slightly darker in shade than the upper surface of the back. The upper labials are whitish in colour, and a dark band runs from the nostril to the eye, and then extends from behind the eye along the side of the body and tail. Towards the belly this lateral band becomes lighter. The tail is similar to the body in colouration, though there is less contrast between the light and dark shades. The belly is lightish blue, whitish grey or silvery green, while the underside of the tail is lead-grey or greyish blue.

Habitat
The Balkan skink is an inhabitant of hilly, limestone regions, as well as flat meadows and steppelands, often on sandy or clay soil. It favours localities where the grass is fairly short, and where scattered bushes may be present. It also inhabits the edges and clearings of oak woods. Damp regions however are avoided. In Bulgaria it ascends to 1200 metres (Beškov and Beron, 1964).

In some parts of the Danube region it shares its territory with the Pontic lizard, and I know of one locality where the green and wall lizards, Aesculapian and Caspian whip snakes also occur.

Behaviour
By nature this species is rather timid. It is not often seen about during the daytime, preferring to stay in its retreat, often under a stone, moss, leaves or some convenient branch lying on the ground. However in southern Slovakia it is said to retreat almost exclusively amid fallen leaves, only exceptionally hiding under a stone or in grass. It is usually in the late afternoon or early evening when it makes its appearance abroad. This species is quite agile in its movements, and although the limbs are small, it uses them far more than the three toed skink. It is able to climb onto rough rocks and walls. The occasional conspicuous breathing palpitations of the flanks, just behind the fore-limbs, are a feature that this species shares with the three toed skink and the lacertids.

Food
Its diet consists of small spiders and earthworms, together with insects and their larvae. It is said to be especially fond of flies. Before being swallowed, such long-bodied prey as mealworms are slowly manoeuvred across the jaws in a manner similar to that of a snake devouring a lizard.

Enemies
This species is preyed upon by a great variety of reptiles, birds and mammals. In Czechoslovakia, though protected by law, it is apparently endangered also by collectors because of its rarity value, and at least one prosecution has taken place (Ponec, 1965).

Reproduction
Mating occurs in April. Many skinks produce fully-developed young. Members of the genus *Ablepharus* are however oviparous, and in June the female produces from two to five elliptical eggs, which are whitish in colour. The young hatch in August or September and then measure about 25 millimetres.

Hibernation
The Balkan skink hibernates among rocky crevices, cavities in the soil, and in dry moss.

Ecdysis
As in snakes, the eye appears to become misty prior to the shedding of the skin, which is shed in fragments, not in one piece as in snakes.

General response
It is most easily caught when found in hiding, for like the slow worm it remains

stationary for a while before trying to escape. Care should be taken when picking up this species as its scales are easily damaged through rough handling. Freshly caught individuals are very ready to shed their tails. According to Schreiber (1912) the tail is more or less replaced in four to six weeks. It survives life well in captivity and soon tames; those that I have kept seemed more nervous than slow worms by disposition, but showed no objection to being handled. Food is readily taken, and I have induced it without difficulty to accept mealworms from the hand, especially when these have first been broken up.

Distribution

Ablepharus kitaibelii fitzingeri   This sub-species reaches its northern limit in Czechoslovakia, where it is the rarest species of lizard, occurring only in a few localities in southern Slovakia, near the Hungarian border. Originally known only from Kováčovske Kopce, an area specially set aside for it as a nature reserve, it has since been found on the dry limestone slopes of the Silická and Plesivecká districts (Ponec, 1965). In 1918 it was known from seven localities in Hungary, but by 1965 it had been reported from 33. The most well-known areas are those centred around Budapest, and in the Danube valley to the north of this region. In western Hungary it is known from near Sárvár, and from the Bakony and Vértes hill districts. North-eastwards from Budapest its range includes Isaszeg, Gödöllő and, as recently discovered, the eastern Cserhát, western Mátra and Bükk ranges, as well as the vicinity of Eger. In central Hungary it is found near Kecskemét.

Ablepharus kitaibelii stepaneki   This sub-species occurs in Romania in the regions of Oltenia, Bucharest and the Dobruja, as well as near Dubova and Orșova in the southern Banat. It is found sporadically throughout Bulgaria, and according to Fuhn (1970), it is probably this sub-species which inhabits Albania and Yugoslavia. In the latter country it is known from the Fruška Gora region in Syrmia, from near Belgrade, and from various localities in eastern Serbia and Macedonia.

Other sub-species   The other recognized sub-species are *Ablepharus kitaibelii kitaibelii* **Bibron & Bory** which inhabits Albania, Attika, the Peloponnese, the Ionian islands, the Cyclades (but not Naxos), the southern Sporades, Rhodes, Asia Minor, Cyprus, Syria, Israel, Jordon, the Sinai peninsula, northern Arabia and possibly Iraq; *Ablepharus kitaibelii fabichi* **Štěpánek** which is found on Karpathos, Mikronisi, Kasos and Armathia (small islands off the coast of Crete) (Fuhn, 1970); and finally *Ablepharus kitaibelii chernovi* **Darevsky**, which is known from Armenia and from near Olty in Turkey.

Nomenclature *in northern and central Europe*
English Balkan skink, Snake-eyed skink
German Johannisechse
French Ablephare de Kitaïbel
Romanian Şopîrliţa de frunzar
Hungarian Pannón gyík, Magyar gyík
Czech Krátkonožka evropská Fitzingerova
Slovakian Krátkonožka európska
Russian Европейский Гологлаз

The Three Toed Skink
Chalcides chalcides
Sub-species found in western Europe:
Chalcides chalcides striatus (**Cuvier**) 1828
(formerly *Chalcides lineatus*)
Terra typica restricta: Algeciras, southern Spain
Plate 15

At a glance this species resembles a slow worm with tiny limbs. It has a similarly long, round and snake-like body, which is somewhat flattened above. Its head is fairly pointed, though the snout is rather blunt and protrudes a little beyond the lower jaw. There is no distinct neck region. The cylindrical tail is about the same length as the head and body together, or sometimes a little longer. It tapers evenly to the tip, terminating with a sharp, horny point. The fore- and hind-limbs are widely spaced apart, the hind-limbs being a little longer than the fore-limbs and reaching a maximum length of about 10 millimetres. The first toe on each limb is the shortest, and the second toe is either as long as, or a little longer than the third. Its minute claws are barely visible. The lower eyelid has a transparent disc. The ear cavity is small, though larger than the nostrils; it is distinct and somewhat elongate, measuring from 1 to 1.5 millimetres in length. It is extended by a narrow, longitudinal and easily-overlooked shallow depression.

The occasional palpitation of the flanks while breathing is one feature which distinguishes this species and the Balkan skink from the slow worm and the snakes.

A maximum length of 42 centimetres is attained by its near relative, *Chalcides chalcides chalcides*, but the present form is not known to exceed 40 centimetres.

Scalation

22–24 longitudinal rows of regular, smooth glossy scales around circumference of body. *Anal* plate divided. *Rostral* broader than deep; *frontal* large, longer than wide; 2 large *parietals*; *internasal* usually broader than long; no *prefrontals* or *frontoparietals*; 4 pairs of *supraoculars*; 1 little *postnasal*; fourth *labial* situated below eye; *temporals* similar to, but larger than *dorsals*.

Colouration

Adult The basic colouration of this species is slate-grey, silvery grey, olive-grey, olive-brown, olive-green, turquoise or sometimes brown. On top of the back extending to the upper parts of the sides, where they quickly become less distinct, are from 9 to 13 greyish-brown, brownish or blackish longitudinal bands. They are as wide as, or a little wider than the spaces which separate them. This general pattern is continued along the length of the tail, though it is frequently absent from regenerated tails. The lower parts of the sides are lighter, being more similar to the belly, which is olive green, bluish-grey, grey or creamy white. The underside of the tail is whitish grey. Many individuals are brown in appearance prior to ecdysis. All the scales on the upper surface have a narrow, dark margin.

Juvenile colouration The young are similar to the adults in colour, though the dorsal stripes are indistinct. The scale margins are quite prominent however.

Habitat

The three toed skink is a frequent inhabitant of grassy meadows. I have normally encountered it on dry grassland, often on sandy soil. In coastal regions it is sometimes associated with flat and even damp meadows. In the neighbourhood of rivers and streams it seems to prefer higher elevations, presumably because of better drainage. I have also found it in dry, stony *garrigue* country. It occurs beside paths through pine forests and in vineyards (Fretey, 1975). Though a shy creature it may often be found close to human dwellings, near farms and on grassy verges beside country lanes and even on roadsides with continually passing traffic. I have sometimes found it on railway embankments. Gadow (1901) reports that in the coastal regions of Portugal and western Galicia he frequently found it close to the sea, basking on gorse bushes. In Morocco it ascends to 2300 metres, according to Pasteur and Bons (1960).

I have discovered it in the same localities as the eyed lizard and the viperine snake, as well as the ladder snake (*Elaphe scalaris*), the horseshoe whip snake (*Coluber hippocrepis*) and the hooded snake (*Macroprotodon cucullatus*).

Behaviour

Like the lacertids this skink is a sun-lover and enjoys basking beside thick grassy vegetation, often in the full glare of the sun. It is not however unusual to find it in retreat under piles of leaves, a suitable flat stone, piece of bark or rusty sheet-metal. I know of a locality in southern Spain where it may frequently be found in hiding under the decaying remains of prickly pear plants. It does not normally retire until sunset. With its legs being so small and inconspicuous, it might easily be mistaken for a slow worm, were it not for its amazing degree of alertness, and for the rapidity with which it disappears into hiding.

When disturbed it retreats briefly into the undergrowth, only to return usually less than a minute later, either at the same spot or somewhere suitable nearby. It often returns repeatedly even after continual disturbance. The tiny legs do not serve to support its body, in fact during quick movements it snakes along holding them backwards close to its body, in a shallow furrow specially provided. The legs however are of some use on uneven ground and during slower movements, when it seems to 'paddle' its way carefully along.

Its rapidity combined with its astonishing ability to conceal itself make it an extremely difficult lizard to catch. It tends to move with sudden spurts for short distances, but is often detected only when it makes its next move, fleeing further into the vegetation. I have known it to disappear rapidly out of sight in very short grass, and despite thorough searching have failed to find it. On one occasion a specimen basking on top of a bush on a hillside leapt downwards through the air at my approach and landed on top of the next bush, into which it then vanished. This species does not appear to be gregarious in the wild state. Even in areas where the species is common I have observed only solitary specimens basking.

Food

Its diet consists of earthworms, slugs, small snails and spiders, as well as insects and their larvae. Flies and grasshoppers are freely devoured. In captivity I found that three toed skinks readily accepted mealworms, eating up to twelve in succession. For a short while the head is held poised above the mealworm, which is then suddenly seized by the middle of its body, and slowly manoeuvred across the skink's jaws until the victim can easily be swallowed lengthwise. As with the Balkan skink, this process is reminiscent of a snake devouring a lizard. Some of my captive specimens occasionally took ant larvae. The young, according to Angel (1946), are fond of aphides. One individual of *Chalcides chalcides chalcides* which I captured in Italy devoured a young, worm-sized, European blind snake (*Typhlops vermicularis*).

Enemies

Among its enemies are martens and doubtless many other flesh-eating mammals. Birds known to prey upon it are ravens, jays, falcons, storks and poultry. Snakes probably account for the loss of considerable numbers of this species. I have known a young specimen to be devoured by an adult *Lacerta lepida* in captivity, and it is not unlikely that the latter species would devour any skink it happened to encounter in the wild.

Reproduction
Mating is preceded by violent fights between rival males, which often result in wounds. During copulation the male seizes his partner by the back of the neck in his jaws. This species is one of the few reptiles which can be termed viviparous, as the female possesses a placenta (Petzold, 1971). She produces from 5 to 15 young. According to Fretey (1975), the female often fails to survive parturition, due to her frailty.

Hibernation
The three toed skink is sensitive to the cold, and disappears at the beginning of October, hibernating deep down in the earth. Active life does not commence until the first really warm days of spring, normally in April.

General response
Many other agile reptiles become quite lethargic after a period spent in hiding, say for example under a flat stone, and are then more easily caught.

This species however becomes instantly alert when discovered, and I have failed to catch the majority of those found under such circumstances. Great care should be taken when attempting to seize it, as the skin is very easily damaged, and a violent effort to secure it may result in the removal of several or many scales. The three toed skink readily sheds its tail if this is seized. It sometimes does this during the excited struggles it makes when first caught, if one does not take great care in handling it. It is best to place it straight away in a container already filled with grass, so that it can quickly conceal itself and calm down. Such wildness usually though not invariably lasts only for a few days after which it settles down and can normally be quite safely handled.

Taming The French specimens I have found bit readily on being seized, while those I captured in Spain made no effort to bite, although one individual bit me for the first time after over a month in captivity. Some become considerably tamer than others, and I have known them to accept mealworms offered from the hand. Others would readily devour mealworms in front of me, but could not be persuaded to take them in this manner. In my experience it loses none of its agility in captivity, still making off rapidly when disturbed. Sometimes when picked up I have known it to emit a brief and faint hissing noise.

It is inadvisable to keep a number of three toed skinks, especially male specimens together in one vivarium, since they will attack one another on sight, biting each other without hesitation. In this way they are able to remove some of the scales of their opponents, thereby inflicting permanent damage.

Distribution

The three toed skink is essentially a western Mediterranean species. Five geographical races have been recognized by some authorities, but this classification is disputed by others (see Müller, 1973; Pasteur and Bons, 1960).

Chalcides chalcides striatus   The present form *striatus* occurs in north-western Africa north of the Sahara, the Iberian peninsula, a number of areas in France—where according to Angel (1946), it is quite common—and in Liguria, extending as far east as the province of Savona. For France Angel lists it from the Gironde, and the following more southerly *départements:* Hérault, Vaucluse and Alpes-Maritimes. He adds that it is found on some of the Mediterranean islands, though he does not specify which. According to Fretey (1975) it is absent from the *département* of Basses-Alpes. It is however known from the *départements* of Gers (near Seissan), Tarn (near Rabastens) and Bouches-du-Rhône, where it occurs in the Camargue, though it is fairly rare there. In addition some specimens from the *département* of Gard are preserved in the Natural History Museum at Nîmes. During the last century it was reported from the littoral region of the Charente-Maritime, and Lataste (1876) records that two specimens were found at Lugeras near Montlieu in the same *département*. Fretey mentions it from Bussac, and in August 1958 an inhabitant of the Royan region assured me of the existence near that area of *'un petit serpent avec des petites pattes'*. Though local reports are not always reliable, the description can only fit this species, and I am inclined to accept its occurrence there as a distinct possibility.

It is found throughout most of the Iberian peninsula (Salvador, 1974b), but in the Spanish province of Catalonia it is known from only a few localities (Mertens, 1925).

Other races   The Italian form *Chalcides chalcides chalcides* (**Linnaeus**) inhabits Liguria, the Apennine peninsula and the islands of Elba and Sicily. The western limit of its range appears to be the extreme south-east of France, where it occurs as far as Nice. Intermediate forms are found in those areas where this form occurs along with *Chalcides chalcides striatus* (Capoccacia, 1966). *Chalcides chalcides concolor* (**Metaxa**) described from the Rome area, is now regarded as synonymous with the principal Italian form (Müller, 1973).

The other disputed forms are *Chalcides chalcides vittatus* (**Leuckart**) which

occurs in Sardinia, and *Chalcides chalcides mertensi* **Klausewitz**, described
from Algeria. The enormous degree of variability in African specimens has
however made their classification difficult, and in Morocco for example,
specimens apparently referable to all the above forms occur, with *striatus*
predominating in the western parts of the country. The overall range of this
species in Morocco extends from the High Atlas to the Atlantic and the
Mediterranean (Pasteur and Bons, 1960). Elsewhere in Africa it is found in
Algeria and Tunisia.

Nomenclature *in western Europe*
  German   Erzschleiche
  French   Seps tridactyle
  Italian   Luscengola

The Slow Worm
Anguis fragilis
Sub-species found in northern and central Europe:
Anguis fragilis fragilis **Linnaeus** 1758
Terra typica restricta: Sweden

Anguis fragilis colchicus (**Nordmann**) 1840
Terra typica: Eastern coastal region of the Black Sea, Russia
Plates 16, 17, see also colour plate

The slow worm is readily distinguishable from the previous lizards. It has a
long, almost cylindrical body, and is devoid of limbs. It thus has a very
snake-like appearance. In fact it was not until 1825 that Pierre Latreille showed
it to be not a snake, but a legless lizard. Externally it differs from a snake in
having movable eyelids, and no ventral shields. The jaws are firmly hinged
together, and therefore are incapable of the independent movement
characteristic of snakes' jaws. In common with many other lizards it has the
ability to shed its tail when this is seized by an aggressor. The severed portion is
replaced by a short stump, for the tail never regains its former length. A
relatively high proportion of slow worms lose their tails eventually. Over 35 per
cent of those examined by Smith (1969) had lost their original tails. The name
Anguis fragilis means 'brittle snake'. Despite the alternative English name
'blind worm' and the German name *Blindschleiche*, it is not blind. Recent
research has however, shown it to be colour-blind.

The small head is not distinctly set off from the body, though that of the male is larger and broader than that of the female. The ear cavity is very seldom visible in the western sub-species, while in *Anguis fragilis colchicus* it is often clearly noticeable. Except in pregnant females, the body does not stand out markedly from the gradually tapering tail, but seen from above, appears to flow imperceptibly into it. The cylindrical tail, when complete, is normally a little longer than the head and body together, and terminates with a short spine. It is slightly larger at the base in male specimens, as well as being relatively longer. Adult slow worms reach a maximum length of from 35 to 54 centimetres. Females generally grow longer than males. The largest specimen I found was a male of 46 centimetres. in western Croatia.

Scalation

Anguis fragilis fragilis   24–26 longitudinal rows of smooth, highly polished scales around circumference of body, fairly uniform but largest on top of back and on middle of body. English specimens have 26 rows (Smith, 1969). Conical snout has very small *rostral*; large *frontal* and *interparietal*, the latter as long as but wider than each *parietal*; *parietals* and *interparietal* succeeded by *occipital*; single *internasal*, usually separated from *frontal* by two adjacent *prefrontals*. 5 or 6 pairs of *supraoculars*. Tiny *nasal* shield contains nostril; numerous small *labials* and *loreals* on side of head.

Anguis fragilis colchicus   Scalation similar to *Anguis fragilis fragilis* but possesses 26–30 longitudinal rows of scales around circumference of body. *Prefrontals* usually either somewhat triangular, meeting only at their apexes, or are widely spaced, in which case the *frontal* borders the *internasal*.

Colouration

Male colouration   When adult the two sexes are often clearly distinguishable from one another in colour. On top of the back the males are grey, lead-grey, grey brown, light brown, dark brown, brick-red, copper or a shiny bronze. The sides are similar to the top of the back, though they are often a little lighter, and become whitish towards the belly. The black or dark brown vertebral stripe, present in the young, usually fades in the adult and even disappears, especially on the tail. The underside is thickly mottled with dark grey, dark blue or black on a dirty white, bluish white or pinkish white background. The dark colouration may break up to form two or four parallel rows of spots beneath the tail.

Female colouration   Females are normally light or dark brown, brick-red, copper or tan on top. The dark vertebral stripe is often though not invariably retained, and can be either relatively thick or thin, and it may even form a very fine zigzag. In some cases two narrow, dark, longitudinal rows of spots may occur on either side of the vertebral stripe, and these often form further more or less distinct continuous stripes. Such markings gradually fade on the tail. Though occasionally also present in males they are generally far more distinct in female specimens. The sides are very dark, being black or dark brown, but become lighter, often interspersed with grey or dirty white, towards the belly and head. The underside is usually black, and most intensely dark along the middle, becoming whitish towards the sides. Otherwise it is similar to that of the male.

Head of both sexes The top of the slow worm's head is similar in colour to the top of the back, though sporadic dark flecks are sometimes present. This species has rather small eyes with round pupils. The iris is light brown or golden in the young, and copper or reddish brown in the adult.

Juvenile colouration The newly-born are cream, light yellow, pale bronze, golden brown, sometimes copper or silvery green on top of the back. On the nape of the neck there is a black fleck or a V-shape, and this is continued as a vertebral stripe along the body and tail. The side of the head, the flanks and the belly are uniformly black or a deep dark brown, and well differentiated from the colour of the back, though with age this contrast becomes far less distinct. The snout, lips, chin and throat are less vividly black, having lighter mottlings. At this stage the sexes are identical in appearance. The distinctive sexual variation becomes apparent at the end of the second or in the third year. On rare occasions young specimens have been found entirely devoid of pattern.

Blue-spotted form The most well known variety of *Anguis fragilis fragilis* is the blue-spotted form, sometimes referred to as var. *incerta* or, more confusingly, var. *colchica* (see colour plate). The spots vary from very pale to dark blue or even bluish black or grey, and are strewn more or less irregularly on top of the back, particularly on the anterior part, though some may be present on top of the tail. They are absent from the flanks however. Some form very tiny flecks, while others may sometimes cover an entire scale. They may be very few in number and sporadically distributed, and can therefore easily be overlooked. On other individuals they can be much more numerous, even forming dense clusters or longitudinal rows. Such a row may occur along the vertebral line, or there may be a pair of dorso-lateral rows. Generally the number of spots increases with age. Although there are rare records of females with blue spots, most blue-spotted slow worms are males. According to Smith (1969) these spots first appear during the third year of life.

Anguis fragilis colchicus Whereas blue spots are far from being a regular characteristic of all males of the western sub-species, and in many parts of its range, as for example in Scandinavia, blue-spotted slow worms are unknown, the males of the eastern sub-species *Anguis fragilis colchicus* are most often blue-spotted. Apart from this feature, the eastern sub-species is, as already mentioned, distinguished by its relatively high number of scale rows, the position of the prefrontal shields, and its normally visible ear cavity. In addition the top of the head is relatively longer and the tail shorter in this sub-species. The racial identity of any given specimen cannot be ascertained on the basis of any of the these features alone however.

I have found occasional blue-spotted males of *Anguis fragilis fragilis* with the prefrontals arranged like those of the eastern race, as in single specimens from Fleet in Hampshire, the Camargue in France, and near Ala (Adige valley) in northern Italy. Out of four male slow worms found at Otočac in north-west Croatia, only one was entirely typical of the western race. The remainder had prefrontal shields characteristic of *colchicus*. Two possessed distinctly visible traces of an ear cavity, one of them being blue-spotted. The fourth specimen, although blue-spotted, displayed no hint of an ear cavity. I have never seen a British specimen with visible ear cavities. Blue spots are often present in other species of the *Anguidae* family.

Melanism and albinism Rare cases of melanism and albinism are on record.

Habitat
The slow worm inhabits many types of countryside, but shows a preference for slightly humid conditions, and is absent from dry, arid regions. It is found on common land, fields, grassy meadows, bushy country and heathlands, and often occurs in areas associated with human activity, such as sand and stone quarries, chalk pits, rubbish dumps, the borders of agricultural land, disused farmland, gardens and cemeteries. Frequently it is found in hedgerows, on the borders of woods, open woodlands, in sunny glades and on railway embankments. I have occasionally found it on marshy heathland and in coastal marshes, at least during the summer, though it is not normally a marshland dweller. In Russia it avoids the steppeland regions (Terent' ev and Cernov, 1949).

The slow worm ascends to 2000 metres in the French Alps (Angel, 1946), exceptionally attaining 2400 metres in Austria (Eiselt, 1961). Those that I found in northern Spain, southern France and Italy were usually in well-wooded hilly or mountainous districts. In the north of its range, notably in Scandinavia, it is principally associated with pine forests, being rarely encountered in the higher altitudes of the birch region.

In various parts of its range the slow worm shares its territory with a number of other reptile species. In southern England it sometimes lives in the same vicinity as the other five species, and on several occasions I have found it in hiding with the common lizard and the grass snake. I once discovered one amid a pile of rocks which also harboured an adult Aesculapian snake. On 11 May 1976 in the Camargue, I found four specimens lying under a large discarded sheet of paper. Three of them were entangled with a young viperine snake. This record is of further interest, since Weber and Hoffmann (1970) do not mention the slow worm in their checklist of reptiles from this area.

Behaviour

In many aspects of its behaviour this species resembles a snake more than typical lizards such as the Lacertids.

Unlike the latter it is not normally seen basking for hours during the day in the sun, being more often found in retreat under a flat stone, pile of rocks, log, piece of bark or under discarded pieces of sheet-metal; conditions to which it may return daily. It is occasionally encountered under piles of leaves. It is often difficult to find during a spell of very hot weather. It frequently emerges after rain. It is sometimes found basking early in the morning however, and is often seen roaming about in the early evening. In late summer pregnant females are not infrequently found sunning themselves at other times of day. While basking, the eyes are often closed. It likes to burrow with its snout in light soil, and is fond of lying in a hole in the earth or cavity in the undergrowth, with just the head protruding. Sometimes it retires into the deserted burrows of fieldmice and voles. It often makes its home amid the roots of low bushes. Occasionally it may be found in anthills, being well protected by its tough skin and the underlying bony plates. It appears to be the only vertebrate capable of surviving such conditions. However in April 1974 I discovered a specimen beneath a sheet of rusty metal, where an ant colony had established itself. A group of ants had clustered around the reptile's eyes, and had caused severe damage.

In its movements the slow worm is far less agile than the other lizards, and its normal serpentine movements are rather slow, and less flexible than in snakes. It is not able to wind its body gracefully into a series of coils as snakes can; often it simply forms its body into a loose ring-shape. During movement the tongue is periodically protruded, but by comparison with snakes, its up and down motion is slow and deliberate. Each time this happens the mouth is opened slightly, there being no specially provided notch in the upper jaw, as in snakes. When pursued through thick undergrowth it is able to disappear with a surprising speed. It is not a climber, nor is it a swimmer by nature, though it is able to swim well in an emergency for short distances, but quickly becomes exhausted.

I have often found the slow worm living alone, though I have quite frequently discovered two or three in hiding together. They seldom seem to object to one another's presence. Quite large numbers of slow worms can sometimes be found within a suitable but often relatively small area.

Food

Being somewhat sluggish in its movements by comparison with the previous species of lizards, its diet is generally restricted to slow moving prey, and as the jaws are firmly hinged, the slow worm, unlike snakes, is incapable of swallowing anything much bulkier than itself. The principal items of its diet are slugs and worms, though spiders and certain insects and their larvae, notably smooth caterpillars, are also devoured. Small snails are taken on occasion, these being gradually tugged out of their shells. The swallowing of an earthworm or slug can require up to half an hour or more, and young slow worms may even suffocate in their attempts to devour a large earthworm. According to Smith (1969) the white slug *Agriolimax agrestis* is particularly relished, and all other slugs are rejected in areas where this species occurs. Although found in ants' nests it does not appear to feed on them. There are in addition records of a slow worm eating an adult common lizard, and of a specimen of 29 centimetres which devoured an 18 centimetre grass snake. One female is reported to have eaten one of her own newly-born offspring (Davies, 1967). Captive specimens can be fed upon mealworms and, according to Petzold (1971), grasshoppers and even woodlice. The slow worm displays no interest in dead or motionless prey.

Living prey is slowly approached, investigated with the snout and tongue, then the upper part of the body is slightly raised over the victim, which is then suddenly seized in the jaws. The slow worm hunts in the evening, after a shower of rain, and sometimes in dull weather. It is regrettable that this completely innocuous lizard, which renders such a useful service to agriculture in getting rid of many pests, should so frequently be mistaken for a snake and killed.

Enemies

The small worm-sized young have many enemies, particularly birds. Frogs and toads will also devour them. In addition Petzold mentions beetles of the genus *Carabus*. The predators of the adults include hedgehogs, foxes, badgers, martens, rats, pigs and cats, such predatory birds as eagles, kites, harriers, hawks and buzzards, as well as owls, shrikes, storks, magpies, even mistle-thrushes, poultry, and of course snakes.

Reproduction

Male rivalry and mating   The slow worm mates in late April, May or early

June, and much rivalry takes place among males during this period. They seize one another in their jaws, and much tussling and writhing ensues. Some may even lose their tails during such battles. The jaw marks are often deep enough to leave a permanent scar.

During copulation, which may last for several hours, the male holds the female's head or the nape of her neck in his jaws, his body is curved in a semi-circle and the tails are entwined. The female is not released until the act is over. Only one of the penes is used at any given time. On a few occasions I have discovered mating pairs hidden in the seclusion of their normal retreats. One pair I picked up showed little reaction to my interference. The male continued to hold his partner in his jaws and their bodies remained entwined. I took them home with me and they stayed in this position until the following morning, when they separated. After this the male showed no further interest in the female.

Birth of young The slow worm is an ovo-viviparous species, and the number of young varies from 3 to 26. Smith (1969) states that the average size of the litter varies from 6 to 12, and that the maximum number recorded from the British Isles was 22. Litters of 20 or more are rare however. They are born under cover, and the female improvises a kind of 'nest' with the circular motions of her body. The young are normally born at the end of August or beginning of September, though they may appear as early as mid-July or, after an unfavourable summer, as late as October, November, or even the following spring. The usual period of pregnancy is about three months. The female displays no further interest in her offspring once the eggs are laid.

The young are encased in a transparent membrane from which they free themselves by thrusting their heads forward several times, until the membrane is punctured. They then emerge straight away. The vestigial egg-tooth is insufficiently developed to be of use in this process, and appears to be completely non-functional. It is even less developed than that of the common lizard, and does not project beyond the mouth. It is normally shed within two days of hatching, rarely on the third or fourth day (Petzold, 1971). At this stage they measure from 65 to 90 millimetres, and the tail constitutes a little under half the total length. Smith (1969) states that the members of any one brood do not vary in length by more than 10 millimetres. He reports that after a year slow worms measure between 152 and 180 millimetres, and that after another year they have reached between 210 and 230 millimetres.

Maturity Maturity is reached when the slow worm measures about 25 centimetres. The male is apparently able to reproduce in its third year, females a year or two later.

Siamese twins Reichenbach-Klinke (1963) refers to a case of Siamese twins, which possessed only a single head. In addition the upper part of their bodies had grown together.

Hibernation

In England the slow worm disappears during the second half of October, although in mild weather the young may sometimes be seen about until the end of that month. Angel (1946) states that in France it retires at the end of October or in November, often in groups of 20 or 30. Some slow worms may hibernate singly. The winter quarters are carefully selected to avoid northerly and easterly winds. *Anguis fragilis* sometimes hibernates in crevices in banks and amid the roots of bushes and hedgerows, under piles of leaves or wood, as well as heaps of stones or rubble. In regions where the winter is likely to be severe, it may hibernate deep down in the earth, up to 70 centimetres deep (Petzold, 1971). Where ready made cavities are not available, it makes burrows with the snout. The entrance to the hole is said to be blocked from the inside with moss, grass or earth. The largest specimens congregate at the bottom, while the young settle nearer the entrance.

Hibernation sometimes takes place with other species of reptiles, including snakes. It has even been found in company with the adder, and about 100 slow worms were discovered in Norway in retreat with some 40 of the latter species. Petzold reports that it has also been found with the fire salamander (*Salamandra salamandra*).

Mild, sunny spells during the middle of winter have been known to draw it out. It is one of the first reptiles to be seen in spring, and in western and southern Europe it often emerges early in March or occasionally even in February. In central and eastern Europe its appearance is usually delayed until late March or April. In the extreme north of its range, as in northern Scandinavia, it is not seen about until the beginning of June. The young generally emerge before the adults.

Ecdysis

Periodically the slow worm sheds its skin; in the young at least this happens some three or four times a year (Petzold, 1971).

General response

On being discovered, the slow worm frequently shows little reaction, remaining immobile as though nothing had happened. If unmolested it usually, after a short pause, retreats slowly into nearby undergrowth. It is easy to catch. Sometimes however I have found basking specimens of the eastern race to be more alert when approached, making off quite rapidly into the undergrowth. Though adult slow worms readily shed the tail if this is seized, the young can quite safely be picked up by this method. When first caught the slow worm struggles considerably and usually defecates. The males often protrude the penes. This species seldom bites, old males and pregnant females being most inclined to do so. Once however I was bitten by a one-year old specimen. Only on one occasion have I known the slow worm to draw blood. Usually those specimens which did bite fastened their jaws firmly onto my hand for a considerable time. One even clung on for about half an hour. When placed on the grass below, it showed no interest in escaping, but obstinately maintained its grip. Knowing this creature's dislike of water, I placed it under a tap with running cold water. This too was of no avail. I eventually removed it by gently easing its head from side to side, and by pulling the skin of my finger slowly away. Rarely have I known specimens disgorge a recent meal.

The Slow worm soon becomes tame in captivity, and does not object to being handled. It feeds readily and will soon learn to accept food offered in the hand. The adults, in my experience, live well with other species of lizard as well as with grass snakes. Certain old males may occasionally attack other slow worms. In suitable conditions it can survive for many years, and no other species of lizard appears to have surpassed its records for longevity. It has been known to attain ages of 33 and 35 years, although the famous case of a slow worm surviving for 54 years in Copenhagen appears to be open to some doubt (Petzold, 1971).

I have sometimes released specimens after a period of several months in captivity, at precisely the same spot where originally found, usually under a stone or piece of rusty metal. On being freed, they normally disappear quite quickly into the surrounding vegetation, though I have know them to return, even within half an hour, to take up their former place of residence under the metal.

Distribution

The slow worm has a very wide range covering most of Europe as well as parts of northern Africa and western Asia.

There are however no records of slow worms from Corsica, Sardinia, Sicily or the Balearic islands.

Anguis fragilis fragilis The western form *Anguis fragilis fragilis* is well represented in the British Isles, and extends to the extreme north of Scotland, though it is absent from Ireland, the Isle of Man, as well as from the Orkneys and Shetlands. It is on record from Lewis, Skye, Mull, Jura and Arran off the west coast of Scotland. Of the islands off the coast of Wales it is known from Anglesey, Bardsey, Ramsey, Skomer, Skokholm and Flat Holm (Lockley,

1970), and Steep Holm in the Bristol Channel. On the mainland it is widely distributed, but is most common in the south-west. It is found on the Isle of Wight and some of the Channel islands: Jersey, Guernsey, Alderney, Herm and Jethou.

NORTHERN AND CENTRAL EUROPE   It inhabits all of mainland France and the île d'Yeu, as well as Belgium, Luxembourg and Holland, where it is most common in the Veluwe district, and the diluvial parts of Utrecht and southern Limburg. It ranges throughout the mainland of Germany, and is represented on the islands of Rügen, Usedom and Wolin. It is widespread in both Poland and western Czechoslavakia. In Denmark it occurs throughout Jutland as well as on the islands of Fyn, Falster and Zealand. In Norway it extends as far north as 63° 30', but is common only in the south, as in the Oslo fjord region. In Sweden it reaches 65°N. It is common on the island of Öland, and has been reported from Gotland. It is a widespread species in both Switzerland and Austria, and it is also found in western Hungary. Although this form predominates in the hilly regions of the Danube in northern Hungary, some specimens there possess *colchicus* characteristics (Dely, 1972).

SOUTHERN EUROPE AND AFRICA   In southern Europe it inhabits Portugal approximately as far south as 40° lat. (Petzold, 1971); Spain—from the mountains of Galicia and the north of Leon province to the Pyrenees, as well as the Iberian and Central mountain ranges (Salvador, 1974b); Italy, including the island of Palmaria near La Spezia (Lanza, 1968); Yugoslavia (Slovenia and Croatia, including Krk and various other Adriatic islands); and a few isolated districts in Algeria. Smith (1969) also mentions it from Ain Draham in Tunisia. Recent research has shown that *Anguis fragilis fragilis* reappears in the central and western mountainous districts of Bulgaria, overlapping with *colchicus* somewhere between 500 and 600 metres. Certain populations of Romanian slow worms show the influence of this race, which actually predominates in the Bihar district.

Blue-spotted Anguis fragilis fragilis   Blue-spotted specimens of this sub-species are known from the British Isles, where they have been found from the south coast to as far north as south Aberdeenshire (Taylor, 1963). Most occur in southern England, and I have even found them at Tooting in London. They are also known from Germany and Austria, while Smith (1969) mentions it from Fontainebleau in France and I found two male specimens in the Camargue. This form has not been reported from Denmark nor, as already mentioned, Scandinavia.

Anguis fragilis colchicus   The eastern sub-species *Anguis fragilis colchicus* is found to the east of the Alpine region, and south of the Carpathians. It thus inhabits north-eastern Hungary, Romania, central and southern Yugoslavia, Bulgaria, Albania, European Turkey and most of Greece with the exception of the Peloponnese, but is present on some of the Ionian islands, and the island of Thasos. In south-western Asia it occurs in Turkey, Cyprus, and in the Caucasus as well as in northern Iran: near the Caspian sea region and possibly at Kopet Dag. The Caucasus probably forms the northern border of this particular range (Petzold, 1971).

Of great interest is the recent discovery that this race is indigenous to Finland, which has prompted the need for a closer taxonomic investigation of the slow worm in the north eastern parts of its range, particularly in Russia. Specimens from this area were formerly assumed to be referable to *Anguis fragilis fragilis*. In Finland *Anguis fragilis colchicus* has been reported as far north as Oulu and Kajaani. Specimens from the Ahvenanmaa islands presumably belong to the western sub-species.

Recent investigation has shown that most specimens occurring in eastern Czechoslovakia belong to *Anguis fragilis colchicus*, and only an estimated 6.4 per cent of all male specimens lack the characteristics of the eastern form. Petzold (1971) suggests that this may already replace the western sub-species in part of Poland, possibly to the east of the river Vistula.

More research is needed in the Balkan region, and in Italy, to gain a detailed picture of the distribution of these two sub-species. Voipio (1962) refers to a specimen from the French *département* of Côte d'Or, which had a slightly visible ear cavity.

SOVIET UNION   In the Soviet Union the slow worm is represented mostly in the European part, north of the steppe region, and it is thus absent from the Crimean peninsula. Its range includes the Baltic states, together with the islands of Saaremaa and Hiiumaa (Kauri, 1946). East of Finland it is still found to the north of lake Onega; its northern border continues eastwards at roughly 60°N. to the Ural mountains. Its most northerly point in Russia is about 63°N. (Petzold, 1971). It does not appear to occur further east than the valley of the river Tobol (Terent' ev and Cernov, 1949).

Anguis fragilis peloponnesiacus   The remaining sub-species *Anguis fragilis peloponnesiacus* **Štěpánek** is endemic to the Peloponnese region in southern Greece.

Nomenclature *in northern and central Europe*
  English   Slow worm, Blind worm
  Dutch   Hazelworm
  German   Blindschleiche
  Danish   Stålorm

Norwegian   Blindorm, Kobberslange
Swedish   Ormslå
French   Orvet
Italian   Angue fragile, Orbettino
Romanian   Năpîrcă
Hungarian   Lábatlan gyík, Törékeny gyík
Finnish   Vaskikäärme
Czech   Slepýš křehký
Slovakian   Slepúch obyčajný
Polish   Padalec zwyczajny
Serbo-Croatian   Sljepić
Russian   Веретенница Ломкая

THE
SNAKES

The Grass Snake
Natrix natrix
(formerly *Tropidonotus natrix*)

Sub-species found in northern and central Europe:
Natrix natrix natrix (**Linnaeus**) 1758
Terra typica restricta: Sweden

Natrix natrix helvetica (**Lacépède**) 1789
Terra typica: Mont Jura, Switzerland

Natrix natrix persa (**Pallas**) 1814
Terra typica: Persia
Plates 18, 19, 20, 21, 22

The grass snake has a strong and moderately slender body, which is rather thicker and longer in female specimens. The barred grass snake (*Natrix natrix helvetica*) is the most strongly built of the three sub-species, and the female of this form has a markedly broad head. The grass snake's head is oval and stands out clearly from the body. The snout is short and rounded and the moderately large eyes are laterally situated, as are the nostrils. The tail varies from about a quarter to a sixth of the total length and is broader at the base in males.

The females of the largest sub-species, *Natrix natrix helvetica*, have been known to attain a length of 1.7 metres in northern Europe, and specimens of 2 metres or even slightly longer have on rare occasions been recorded from the south of its range. Male specimens have only exceptionally been known to exceed 1 metre. Though the females of *Natrix natrix natrix* may occasionally grow to 1.5 metres, males rarely exceed 90 centimetres in length. Females average about 75 centimetres, males about 60 centimetres.

Scalation
Dorsals: 19 longitudinal mid-body rows—strongly keeled except lowest row or two on either side, which is either smooth or weakly keeled. 163–183 *ventrals*; 53–78 paired *subcaudals* (*Natrix natrix natrix*). 157–179 *ventrals*; 49–73 paired *subcaudals* (*helvetica*). 167–188 *ventrals*; 55–89 paired *subcaudals* (*persa*). *Anal* divided. *Rostral* broader than deep, visible from above. 9 large plates on top of head. 1 *preocular*; 2–4 (usually 3) *postoculars*; 1 + 2 *temporals*. 7 (rarely 6 or 8) upper *labials* (3 and 4 bordering eye).

Colouration
Dorsal region   The basic colour of the grass snake is brown, olive grey or olive

green, though not infrequently specimens of *Natrix natrix natrix*, and sometimes *Natrix natrix helvetica*, display a distinct bluish tinge. Sexual dimorphism does not occur in this species. Just behind the head, which is a little darker than the general colouration, there are two large whitish, pale or bright yellow, or orange blotches, which form a collar. On rare occasions these blotches may connect on top of the neck. In some old females this collar often fades, and may even disappear. Behind these markings is a black crescent-shaped patch. The upper labials are yellowish, orangy, cream or whitish, but the sutures between these shields are black. The young are similar to the adults, though the preoculars, and sometimes the postoculars are yellow. Some of the sutures between the head plates may sometimes be finely edged with black.

NATRIX NATRIX NATRIX   The pattern on top of the back and on the sides varies according to the sub-species. *Natrix natrix natrix* normally has from four to six more or less distinct longitudinal rows of small black spots. Within this sub-species however, considerable variation may be found, especially in the Alpine region. Specimens from the Swedish island of Gotland sometimes have vertical bars on the flanks, a feature in common with *Natrix natrix helvetica* (Gislén and Kauri, 1959).

NATRIX NATRIX HELVETICA   This sub-species has a longitudinal row of black vertical bars on each side, each measuring about 1 centimetre, while two more or less distinct alternating rows of black spots are normally present on top of the back. On many specimens a further row of black spots occurs on the lower part of each side, usually alternating in position with the vertical bars. The yellow collar is more frequently absent from this form than from the previous sub-species, and the black patches of the neck are usually large and prominent. On some specimens a pair of tiny whitish or greenish cream flecks may occur on the upper and lower foreparts of many of the scales, a feature sometimes characteristic of the previous sub-species.

NATRIX NATRIX PERSA   *Natrix natrix persa* shows a great degree of variability. Apart from its usually relatively narrow head and long tail, the normal characteristic is a pair of whitish or yellowish dorso-lateral stripes, which commence immediately behind the black neck patches. Two rows of small black spots are often present on top of the back, and a longitudinal row of black spots or, more usually, vertical bars, occurs on the sides. As in *Natrix natrix helvetica*, a further row of spots may exist on the lower part of the flanks. By comparison with the previous two sub-species, the two halves of the yellow collar are normally widely separated behind the head as are the succeeding black patches. Although the majority of specimens possess longitudinal stripes, these may be completely absent on some. As Bodenheimer (1944) has reported, both striped and unstriped grass snakes may emerge from eggs laid by the same mother. During the course of two days searching for grass snakes near Plovdiv in Bulgaria, I saw large numbers of striped specimens, but only a single unstriped individual.

Ventral region   In all three sub-species the dorsal and lateral patterns are continued on the tail. The underside of the grass snake normally consists of a chequered pattern of black or bluish black patches, superimposed upon a whitish, pale yellow or greenish cream background. The throat region is normally uniformly white or pale yellow, while near the tail the dark colouration becomes predominant, the tail itself usually being mainly, sometimes exclusively, black. The eye is black, apart from the golden or dirty yellow ring around the pupil. The tongue is uniformly black, but may sometimes have a reddish tinge. In the new born the tips of the tongue are white, remaining so for about a week.

Colour variation   Occasionally specimens of *Natrix natrix natrix* and *Natrix natrix helvetica* have been found devoid of markings on the back and flanks. An interesting variety of *Natrix natrix natrix* found in Aneboda in Sweden, had a uniformly light belly (Gislén and Kauri, 1959). I once found a specimen of *Natrix natrix helvetica* in western Hampshire whose belly was predominantly black. A parallel pair of greenish white flecks was present on each of the belly plates. These flecks diminished in size and disappeared towards the tail end. Isolated individuals have been found with the belly completely black.

Melanism and albinism   Cases of total or partial melanism are on record for all three sub-species. Until recently melanistic specimens had not been recorded from Britain. In 1975 however a female was found in north Staffordshire (Halfpenny and Bellairs, 1976). Although rare on the Swedish mainland, they are common on Gotland (Gislén and Kauri, 1959). Cases of partial or total melanism in *Natrix natrix persa* are particularly prevalent on some of the Greek islands. Melanistic forms are more usually associated with moorlands and mountainous regions. There are also records of partial albinism in *Natrix natrix natrix* and *Natrix natrix helvetica*, cases of the latter having been found in both England and France.

Grass snakes with adder-like patterns   Grass snakes with an adder-like zigzag band are sometimes found on Gotland, very rarely on the Swedish mainland. Gislén and Kauri (1959) suggest that this pattern may be associated with old age. However, in September 1974 I found several baby specimens of *Natrix natrix persa* with a blackish zigzag pattern, west of Slavonski Brod (Eastern Croatia). In the adults the pattern was either absent or very obscure. Subsequently in August 1976 I found a young individual in southern Hungary

(County Somogy) with a similar pattern. Janisch (1973) has described a male of 44 centimetres from Tiszahát (north-east Hungary) which resembled an adder in shape, colouration and pattern. The forepart of its head was shorter than normal, but the dentition was typical and the pupils of the eyes were round.

Venom glands

The grass snake is harmless to man. However, a poisonous secretion is produced by a gland in the upper jaw, and this has been shown experimentally to have an effect on guinea pigs similar to that of the aspic viper's venom (Hediger, 1937).

Habitat

As the generic name indicates (*Natrix* = water snake), the grass snake is somewhat aquatic by nature, though in fact it is the least aquatic of the three species of its genus inhabiting Europe. It favours secluded, sunny spots beside thick grass, bushy vegetation, reeds or rushes, often near stagnant or flowing water. It is thus at home in damp meadows, marshes, the banks of streams, canals and rivers, as well as in ditches, ponds and lakes. One has been observed as far as 23 kilometres out at sea, presumably carried out by the current.

Southwards, and to some extent eastwards, it becomes progressively more associated with water, especially during the summer months. Of the three races described, *Natrix natrix helvetica* in Britain is, in my experience, the least, and *Natrix natrix persa* in the Balkans the most, dependent upon water. Not infrequently, at least in the northern parts of its range, it can be found quite far away from water, occurring in hedgerows, open woodlands, clearings, along the borders of woods and cultivated fields, beside country lanes and paths, near farms, in rubbish tips, in sand and stone quarries, as well as on moorlands, sandy heaths and dry chalky hills. Dark, sheltered slopes are always avoided.

Altitude   The grass snake is most abundant in flat land, but also inhabits hilly and mountainous country. Fretey (1975) states that it occurs up to 1400 metres in the Massif central, but that it attains 2300 metres in the French Alps.

Co-habiting species   In southern England I have found this species living in the same localities as the five other species of British reptiles. In central Europe I have observed it sharing its territory with the sand lizard more frequently than with any other reptile. I have also found it in the same localities as the wall, meadow and green lizards, the dark green and Caspian whip snakes, the meadow viper, the Balkan adder and the European pond tortoise. I have witnessed it co-habiting with the viperine snake, but never with the dice snake. In Austria it occurs alongside the horned viper (Zapf, 1966; Franz, 1973), while in dry localities in France it shares its habitat with the aspic viper (Fretey, 1975).

Behaviour

The grass snake is almost completely diurnal and loves to coil up in order to bask in the sun. It is most often seen in spring while the surrounding vegetation is still low. There are occasional reports of it having been observed on warm summer nights. In April, just after emergence from hibernation, it is frequently seen in groups, and sometimes half-a-dozen or more can be found coiled up, basking together. Such groups have presumably shared the same winter quarters. After the mating season they disperse and are usually found singly.

The basking grass snake is easily alarmed and any disturbance will cause it to retreat. Often it will return to the same spot as soon as all danger appears to have passed. Sometimes however it may not return until half an hour or more later, or not even until the following day.

It does not hesitate to flee into water in times of emergency. It is a good diver as well as an excellent and graceful swimmer. When swimming or floating it keeps the head and neck raised above the surface. When alarmed it is able to submerge itself completely, hiding among weeds or mud, and it has been known to remain in such a position for up to an hour. Those that I have found swimming in Britain have presumably been hunting for food. In the warmer parts of Europe however they are frequently seen basking while floating on the surface of the water; they can bask for hours in water, changing their position intermittently.

The grass snake often retreats into the disused burrows of small mammals, though it is frequently found in concealment under piles of rubble, flat stones or rusty, discarded sheets of metal. This species is a reasonably good climber, and often climbs onto low bushes to bask. It is frequently found near human habitation, especially near farms, and it has been known to enter houses.

When discovered in retreat under stones or rubble, it has usually lost much of its alertness, and remains for a short while in a coiled-up position, before hurriedly retreating into nearby vegetation. In my experience such retreats may be favoured by many grass snakes during the course of the year, though only single specimens or a pair, not necessarily male and female, are usually found at any one time. Once however I found five coiled up together under a wooden board. On another occasion I came across a grass snake in hiding with a slow worm. The coils of the former were actually touching the latter. I have twice found a grass snake and a smooth snake whose coils were intertwined. Predictably in each instance the grass snake was the first to make off into the vegetation. I have also found it in hiding with the sand lizard.

Food

Being partially aquatic by nature, this species feeds mainly on amphibia, especially frogs, as well as small fish, though it is less adept at catching the latter than are the more aquatic dice and viperine snakes. Common toads, eagerly seized by some grass snakes, are rejected by others. Some toads may avoid being devoured by remaining immobile until the snake loses interest and goes off. When investigated closely, toads inflate their bodies with air and raise themselves high up on their limbs, in order to create a forbiddingly large impression, and this is often sufficient to deter a hungry grass snake. On the continent tree frogs (*Hyla arborea*) and green toads (*Bufo viridis*) are particularly relished (Frommhold, 1965). The fire salamander (*Salamandra salamandra*) and the warty newt (*Triturus cristatus*) are more rarely devoured. There are occasional records of lizards and even warm-blooded animals having been eaten, among them small birds, as well as such mammals as mice, voles and shrews. More unusually, there is a record of the grass snake eating honey bees (Smith, 1969).

Though inevitably hunting often takes place under water, large prey especially is brought on to the land to be consumed. All food is swallowed alive. The prey is not held in the coils. Fish are normally swallowed head first, while frogs, usually having been seized by a hind leg, are manoeuvred until they can be swallowed back first. Although the jaws of the snake can be distended to a remarkable degree, the swallowing of a large frog can be a difficult task, and sometimes it has to be released. Smith (1969) states that for an adult one or two large frogs may suffice for a few days. However as many as four or five may sometimes be devoured in a row. Boulenger (1913) states that a grass snake has been known to eat as many as 20 very small frogs in succession, and Werner refers to two specimens which ate 108 frogs between them, within a period of four months. Some frogs have been heard to emit a few anguished croaks even after having been swallowed.

The young eat baby frogs, newts and amphibia larvae. There are also reports of earthworms, slugs and even insects having been devoured by the young.

Enemies

On account of their small, rather worm-like form, very young grass snakes are devoured by a wide range of mammals and birds. The enemies of the adults include such flesh-eating mammals as hedgehogs, badgers, stoats, as well as shrews and rats. Predatory birds and poultry will seize them. The grass snake appears to be immune to the adder's venom. The two species however do not object to one another's presence.

Reproduction

Mating   The usual months for mating are April and May. This begins with a preliminary courtship in which the male follows his mate everywhere, and tries to stimulate her by rubbing his chin agitatedly on her back. During this time the male's tongue is persistently flickering in an excited manner. According to Smith (1969) young males may omit this courtship, and proceed to copulate straight away. During copulation the rear part of the bodies and tails are entwined.

Egg laying conditions The eggs are normally laid from late June until early September, the time varying according to the latitude and weather conditions, and in a very cool summer laying may be delayed until October. The kinds of conditions selected by the female for depositing her eggs are those in which heat is artificially generated, and for this reason female grass snakes are often found in the vicinity of farms at this time. Among favoured situations are manure heaps, beneath piles of compost and rotting logs, under hayricks and sawdust, amid moss, under roots and in wall cavities. Sometimes they are laid in loose soil, and even in disused mammal burrows.

Mass egg laying sites Suitable incubation conditions are said to be frequented annually by the same females, and sometimes large numbers may resort to the same place for their egg-laying. Leighton (1901) refers to an old wall at Llanelly (Carmarthenshire) in which some 40 batches of eggs had been deposited. Terent' ev and Cernov (1949) state that some 1200 eggs were found in Russia underneath a discarded door which measured 140 by 90 centimetres. As many as 1500 have been found under a single pine tree stump (Dürigen, 1897). More recently Kabisch (1967) has described further cases of mass egg-layings in Mecklenburg, including some 3500 to 4000 eggs which are apparently laid annually in the shavings cellar of a saw mill, the average number of eggs per clutch being from 30 to 32.

On 3 September 1973, near Kaszópuszta in south-western Hungary, I found a large number of eggs concealed beneath a rotting tree trunk; I counted a total of 286. It was difficult to estimate how many clutches of eggs were there, because some of the eggs had been deposited singly, while others had adhered together to form large clusters, obviously the product of several females. Two hundred and four of the eggs were empty, and the young had already hatched, as indicated by the long slits caused by the egg-tooth. One young specimen was in the process of emerging from its shell, but quickly withdrew on being discovered. A further 71 eggs appeared in perfect condition. Only seven of the eggs had shrivelled, and were probably infertile. In addition I found three eggs with dead, but almost fully developed young inside. On returning to the site the following spring, I found that most of the remaining eggs had successfully hatched.

According to Angel (1946), large clutches of the eggs of both the grass snake and the viperine snake may sometimes be found together. Having selected a suitable site, the female burrows her way in with her snout and improvises a 'nest' with the writhing movements of her body coils.

The eggs   The number of eggs depends on the size and age of the female. A young mother may produce only 8, though the usual number varies from 11 to 25. Old females may produce up to 40, rarely more. Rollinat (1934) however mentions a female which laid 53, while Mertens (1947a) refers to one which achieved a record of 73!

The eggs are pale white, and when freshly laid are moist and shiny, due to a secretion from the oviducts, this causing them to adhere together in a clutch. The first few eggs are laid in fairly rapid succession, at intervals varying from 5 to 30 minutes, but laying becomes an increasingly slow process, and the final few may not be laid until a day or two later. At this stage some of the eggs may already contain more or less developed embryos. In size the eggs vary from 21 to 37 millimetres in length by 11 to 24 millimetres in diameter, though as development proceeds and moisture is absorbed, they tend to increase somewhat in size. Some females have been known to exhibit a degree of parental instinct by guarding them for a few days. Smith (1969) refers to one which remained with her eggs for 13 days.

Hatching   Hatching normally takes place in late August or September. After a cool summer this may be delayed until October, and Rollinat (1934) found a batch of eggs on the point of hatching as late as November 14. In cold wet summers the embryos may perish. The entire brood normally hatches within 48 hours, though there are usually a few infertile eggs. The egg-tooth, though barely visible, is well developed, and as the snake makes agitated movements, the shell is punctured, often in several places. At first only the head—often just the tongue and nostrils—emerge, normally protruding for a long time, though any hint of danger will cause the young snake to retreat completely inside the shell again for several minutes. Being attached to its umbilical cord, it may remain tied to the egg for as long as 24 hours until this is finally severed. The egg-tooth is shed a few hours after hatching. The skin of the tongue is shed after a few days, though general ecdysis takes place after two to three weeks.

Growth   The babies are miniature replicas of their parents, though somewhat darker. At this stage they vary in length from 14 to 21 centimetres. They are then inconspicuous, seldom being found except under cover. At first the growth rate is quite rapid. During their first year they grow about 10 centimetres, and by the end of the following year they have added about a

further 10 centimetres to their length. After three years they measure
approximately 50 centimetres. At this stage the male is already mature, the
female reaching maturity about a year later, when she measures some 60 to 65
centimetres. After this the growth rate is much slower, amounting to an
average of about 2 or 3 centimetres per year. Records of two-headed snakes
have been reported, including one from near Truro in Devon (Davies, 1974).
Such individuals rarely survive for long however.

Autumn mating   Specimens in captivity have been known to mate during the
autumn, and even to produce eggs during the following winter. It does not
appear to have been established whether fertile eggs can result.

Hybrids   A number of experiments have been made in captivity, notably by
Hans Schweizer, in crossing various sub-species of the grass snake in order to
produce hybrids. One of the resultant male hybrids (from a male *Natrix natrix
astreptophora* and a female *Natrix natrix schweizeri*) was successfully crossed
with a female *Natrix natrix helvetica*, and with a female *Natrix tessellata*. There
is also a record of hybrids being produced from the grass snake and the viperine
snake *N. maura* (Mertens, 1950, 1956).

Hibernation
The grass snake disappears into hibernation during October. In the south of
England it may sometimes still be seen active up to the third week, while in
exceptionally mild weather it may still be found up to the end of October. The
young are normally the last to retire. They often hibernate communally; and
certainly, as already mentioned, clusters of them can sometimes be seen
basking together shortly after the spring emergence, normally in March or
April, the time varying according to the weather. The sites chosen for
hibernation include small mammal tunnels, rabbit burrows, crevices in walls,
amid tree roots, holes in thickly vegetated banks and in piles of straw and
manure (Angel, 1946). On rare occasions, it has been observed on warm days
in mid-winter.

Ecdysis
Hvass (1972) states that the grass snake sheds its skin five or six times during
the summer season. The shed skin of this species bears little trace of the
original pattern.

General response
When found basking in the sun it can rapidly uncoil and disappear into the
nearby undergrowth. It is at least as difficult to approach when basking on the
water surface, swiftly submerging to the bottom or swimming away. When

found coiled up under debris however it is quite easy to catch. On being caught it rarely bites, though old females may occasionally do so. Usually it struggles very excitedly, and resorts to its notorious habit of emitting a yellowish, unpleasant-smelling fluid from the vent, this being mixed with excreta. If cornered it hisses loudly, alternately inflates and deflates its body, and strikes repeatedly, though the mouth is usually kept closed. In addition it often emits long sustained hisses, sometimes with the tongue stretched far out, and occasionally with the tips of the tongue directed together. This species sometimes disgorges a recently devoured meal when freshly caught. On very rare occasions blood droplets may appear in the mouth (Grzimek, 1971). Only once have I observed this with a newly caught specimen.

Sometimes newly-caught specimens feign death by lying quite limp and motionless, usually on their backs. The mouth is kept wide open with the tongue protruding, the two tips of which are once again often closed together. This behaviour may even be renewed several times for a quarter of an hour or more. The exact significance of this act is not fully understood. Most if not all of its predators would just as readily seize it in this state as when fully active. The animals most likely to ignore motionless prey are other reptiles and amphibians, none of which are regular predators of the grass snake.

One long striped specimen, which I captured in southern Hungary, and held for a while by the tail, continually revolved its body around, in the manner normally associated with *Coluber viridiflavus*.

Taming With continual handling its wildness disappears, and after a few weeks it usually becomes fairly tame, though for some while it may initially struggle to escape each time it is picked up. Later it often becomes used to being handled, and will coil around one's hand to bask in the sun. Though prey is often refused initially, the grass snake when tame normally accepts food readily. A few specimens may persist in rejecting all food offered and are best released. Dead food, if reasonably fresh, may sometimes be accepted. The grass snake is able to fast for several months. Frommhold (1965) refers to an individual specimen of 83 centimetres which took only water for a period of 14 months. It was active until shortly before its death, and during this period it lost 39 per cent of its body weight.

In captivity the grass snake lives well with other species of snakes, and I have kept them quite safely with slow worms as well as with lacertids. The grass snake has been known to live for 20 years in captivity (Stemmler, 1971). One specimen that I kept for several months as a pet became very tame. I eventually released it at exactly the same spot where found. A few weeks later I recaptured it in the same vicinity, but on being picked up it behaved as wildly as any other freshly caught grass snake.

Distribution

Natrix natrix natrix is an inhabitant of Scandinavia and of central Europe, where it is the most abundant species of snake. Its range extends from Germany, where the river Rhine more or less forms its western boundary, through Poland, where it is widespread, though it becomes rare in the mountainous districts, to the Baltic States and European Russia. According to Kauri (1946), it is common in western Estonia. The approximate eastern limits of its range are the River Dnieper and Lake Ladoga.

Of the German islands it is known from Borkum and Juist. It is absent from northern Denmark and rare in western Jutland, while in eastern Jutland and on the larger islands, it is common. It does not however occur on the smaller islands.

In Norway it extends as far north as the province of Nordland, and is fairly common in the eastern lowland regions, while in Sweden the northern limit is by Edefors (66°N.). In the cultivated parts of western Sweden it is rare. Among the Baltic islands it is known from Bornholm, southern Gotland and Öland (where it is local and rare), Gottska Sandön, Saaremaa, Hiiumaa and the Ahvenanmaa islands. The north-eastern limit of its occurrence is said to be south-west Finland, though the exact status of Finnish grass snakes has yet to be established.

In the south of its range it occurs in north-eastern Switzerland: in a small area around Lake Constance, and the lower course of the river Thur. In Austria it has a wide range, occurring in the provinces of Salzburg, Upper and Lower Austria, Styria, Burgenland and Carinthia. Its presence in the eastern Tirol is unconfirmed, but in the north Tirol it inhabits the eastern part (Eiselt, 1961). Elsewhere it ranges over north-eastern Italy (Julian Alps), Czechoslovakia, Hungary, Romania, Yugoslavia (Slovenia, Croatia, Bosnia and Serbia) and northern Bulgaria.

Natrix natrix helvetica This sub-species is found throughout most of England. Its presence as a native Scottish species is open to doubt. It is sparsely distributed in the north of England, and does not surpass Cumbria or southern Northumberland. It is probably extinct in Lancashire. Lockley (1970) says that it is present in all the Welsh counties. It inhabits Anglesey and the Isle of Wight, but has not been recorded from the Isle of Man. In the Channel islands it is known only from Jersey.

It extends throughout France, occurring also on the île d'Yeu and île d'Oléron off the Atlantic coast, and on the îles d'Hyères in the Mediterranean. In Belgium it is found in the provinces of Namur, Limbourg, Liège and Luxembourg, as well as the Campine region. It has been introduced into Brabant. In Holland it is almost exclusively associated with diluvial sand areas, notably in the regions of Utrecht province, Veluwe and Drente (Bund, 1964). It is found in Luxembourg, while in Germany the river Rhine generally appears to be its eastern limit, though according to Mertens (1947b) it extends beyond this river at some points, being found for example in the Bergstrasse and the Taunus region, as well as extending for a little way along the valleys of the Lahn, Main and Neckar.

Its range covers most of the central, southern and western parts of Switzerland, hence the sub-specific name *helvetica*, as well as the Austrian province of Vorarlberg and the western part of the northern Tirol. It is not yet established which race inhabits the eastern Tirol. Finally, it is represented in northern Italy, Istria and Slovenia. According to Kramer (1970), grass snakes from Mount Jura in Switzerland are more similar to *Natrix natrix natrix* as regards pattern.

Natrix natrix persa   This sub-species, whose exact status is still a matter of dispute, is predominantly an inhabitant of south-eastern Europe and south-western Asia. The precise limits of its range are hard to define however in those peripheral areas where other sub-species are also represented and where intermediate forms occur. Striped grass snakes from the eastern part of Lower Austria are considered by Mertens (1947b) as belonging to *Natrix natrix natrix*, while those from northern Italy he regards as being *Natrix natrix helvetica*. In Lanza's view however (1968) those from north-eastern Italy (Paduan plain and southern Venetia) are referable to *persa*, as are those from parts of Istria, which Mertens still classifies as being *helvetica*, but mixed with the *persa* strain. Striped specimens from Carinthia and Styria as well as south-eastern Czechoslovakia are probably to be regarded as being *Natrix natrix natrix*. In Hungary *Natrix natrix persa* has been mentioned from the Bükk district in the north-east, in the region of the rivers Hernad and Bodrog (Vásárhelyi, 1965), as well as parts of the Alföld (Fejérváry-Lángh, 1943). I have found striped specimens in the lower Somogy region, and at a locality north of Budapest.

In Romania striped grass snakes are found mainly in the south-eastern part, especially the Dobruja region. Fuhn and Vancea (1961) however recognise only *Natrix natrix natrix* as being indigenous to Romania. Striped grass snakes from the southern Ukraine are sometimes identified as *persa*, but Mertens regards these as referable to *Natrix natrix scutata*. *Natrix natrix persa* is found over much of western and southern Yugoslavia, extending almost as far north-west as Istria (Mertens and Wermuth, 1960). Its range includes much of Croatia, Serbia, Bosnia and Hercegovina, and Macedonia. Elsewhere in Europe it is known from Bulgaria (south of the Balkan mountains), Albania, Greece, including Euboea, the Cyclades and Dodecanese, as well as European

Turkey. Finally it is found in Asia Minor, Cyprus, Transcaucasia, the southern coastal region of the Caspian Sea, northern Iran and south-western Turkmenia.

Other sub-species Eight other sub-species are at present recognized, at least by some authorities, and they extend the range of this species elsewhere in Europe as well as in north Africa and south-western Asia. *Natrix natrix astreptophora* (**Seoane**) occurs throughout the Iberian peninsula, as well as in Morocco, Algeria and Tunisia. Grass snakes appear to be absent from the Balearic islands however. *Natrix natrix lanzai* **Kramer** is a recently described central Italian form. The limits of its known range are Genoa and Rimini in the north, and Salerno, Campobasso and Termoli in the south. *Natrix natrix corsa* (**Hecht**) is found on Corsica, *Natrix natrix cetti* **Gené** on Sardinia, and *Natrix natrix sicula* (**Cuvier**) in Calabria and Sicily.

Natrix natrix schweizeri **Mueller** appears to be confined to the islands of Milos and Kimolos in the southern Aegean, while *Natrix natrix syriaca* (**Hecht**) is endemic to Syria and Israel. In the Soviet Union, east of the River Dnieper (including the Crimean peninsula), *Natrix natrix natrix* is replaced by *Natrix natrix scutata* (**Eichwald**), a form which extends into Asia as far as eastern Kazachstan, Buryat-Mongolia, Lake Baykal and eastern Siberia. In addition it is found in the Black Sea region of north-eastern Turkey.

Nomenclature *in northern and central Europe*
  English   Grass snake, Ringed snake
  Dutch   Ringslang
  German   Ringelnatter
        Barren-Ringelnatter (*Natrix natrix helvetica*)
        Gestreifte Ringelnatter (*Natrix natrix persa*)
  Danish   Snog
  Norwegian   Buorm
  Swedish   Ringorm, Allmän Snok
  French   Couleuvre à collier
  Italian   Natrice, Biscia dal collare
  Romanian   Şarpele de casă
  Hungarian   Vízi sikló
  Finnish   Tarhakäärme
  Czech   Užovka obecná
  Slovakian   Užovka obyčajná
  Polish   Zaskroniec zwyczajny
  Serbo-Croatian   Obična bjelouška (*Natrix natrix natrix*)
        Prugasta bjelouška (*Natrix natrix persa*)
  Russian   Обыкновенный Уж

The Dice Snake
Natrix tessellata
(formerly *Tropidonotus tessellatus*)

Sub-species found in northern and central Europe:
Natrix tessellata tessellata (**Laurenti**) 1768
Terra typica: Karst, north-western Yugoslavia
Plate 23

The dice snake has a long and slender body. Its head is long and narrow, and distinct from the neck; the snout is obtuse, and the rather small eyes and the nostrils are turned upwards and outwards. The tail varies from about a sixth to a quarter of the total length. As in the grass snake there is a tendency for females to develop a somewhat thick-set body, and in addition the rear part of the head frequently appears swollen. The dice snake normally reaches a maximum length of about 75 centimetres, but may exceptionally attain a length of 1 metre in the north of its range, while in the south a length of 1.5 metres has been known.

Scalation
Dorsals: 19 longitudinal mid-body rows—strongly keeled excepting lowest row or two on either side, which is smooth or weakly keeled. 160–187 *ventrals*; divided *anal*; 48–79 paired *subcaudals*. *Rostral* broader than deep, visible from above. 9 large plates on top of head. *Nasal* often partially divided; 2 or 3 *preoculars*; 3 to 6 *postoculars*; 1 *temporal*; 8 (rarely 7, 9 or 10) upper *labials* (4, 4 and 5 or rarely 3 and 4 bordering eye).

Colouration
The basic colour of the upper surface, including the top of the head, is olive green, grey green, olive grey, brown, or yellow brown, sometimes with a reddish tinge. There are four, or more usually five longitudinal rows of dark brown or black squares or blotches. These rows tend to alternate with one another in position. Sometimes however the upper pair of squares unites with one another across the top of the back to form cross-bars—a pattern not unlike that of *Vipera aspis*. On the neck there is a more or less distinct black ʌ-shaped marking. The head retains the basic colouration, though irregular dark stains may be present on top. The upper and lower labials are whitish, though the sutures are usually very dark. The pupil of the eye is round and black; the iris is golden, bronze or coppery-red.

The throat is whitish, while on the belly a black chequered pattern is superimposed upon a white, pinkish-white or, particularly in older specimens, a yellowish, reddish or orange background. In some specimens the black colouration may predominate towards the centre of the belly, and often the tail is entirely black. The pattern of this species appears markedly more vivid when it is submerged in water. Little difference is to be observed between the young and the adults in colour and pattern, though in old specimens the pattern sometimes tends to fade.

MELANISM AND ALBINISM   Melanic forms are rare. They are known from a locality at Lake Balaton in Hungary, and occurred, formerly at least, at a site near Lake Lugano in Switzerland. According to Stemmler (1971) this colony is probably extinct now due to the construction of a motorway. A few isolated albino specimens are also on record.

Venom glands
This species is completely harmless to man, although its poison glands are apparently similar to those of the grass snake (p. 130).

Habitat
The dice snake is more aquatic than the grass snake, spending most of its active life in and around water, usually on stony soil. It tends to avoid muddy localities. It is in fact the most aquatic of European snakes, and shows a preference for clear, flowing water. Although it inhabits rivers and streams, it is not restricted to flowing water, being found also in ponds and lakes. According to Trutnau (1975), this species is fond of sunning itself for hours, often in large numbers, on the branches of trees and bushes overhanging the water.

It does not object to salt water. In Bulgaria it is sometimes found on the stony banks on the Black Sea, and Boulenger (1913) states that it also inhabits the sea shore near Odessa. Occasional individuals may be encountered quite far away from water outside of the mating season, though certainly not during the hotter months of the year.

Altitude   It is found mainly in low lying areas, though it is sometimes present in hilly country. Stemmler (1971) reports that it is very rarely seen above 1000 metres in Switzerland. In Bulgaria it is never found in the high mountains (Buresch and Zonkov, 1934), but occurs from the sea littoral to 1100 metres.

Co-habiting species   Boulenger states that it sometimes co-habits with the viperine snake in areas where their ranges overlap. It is sometimes said to avoid territories inhabited by the grass snake. However, in Slovakia at least, these two species share the same habitat (Ponec, 1965). In a rocky district of northern Croatia I have found the dice snake basking beside a hedgerow where the horned viper was common. I also found a smooth snake there.

Behaviour

It is diurnal in its habits, and likes to bask in the sun at the water's edge. In its movements it is agile both in and out of water, more so than the grass snake. It is a good diver and an excellent swimmer, and is able to submerge itself for long periods at the bottom of the water, where it can spend hours lying on top of suitable rocks or stones, while occasionally rising towards the surface for air and allowing only the snout to protrude. When swimming the head is usually held above the water. It is also fond of meandering along the bottom. It appears to be quite a sociable creature, frequently living near other specimens. I have discovered it among debris and discarded strips of rusty sheet-metal, under which it was not unusual to find two or three specimens. I have also found it basking upon low bushes.

Food

Its diet consists of aquatic life, especially small fish, as well as frogs and tailed amphibians. Steward (1958) states that it readily attacks all fish, including sticklebacks. The latter are often rejected eventually, on account of the spines however. While hunting for fish this snake remains totally submerged. Small, easily manageable fish are usually eaten straight away in the water, while larger fish are first brought onto land. The young devour tiny fish, the larvae of amphibia and possibly worms also.

According to Kabisch (1966), in the Black Sea region of Bulgaria dice snakes are best observed feeding in the early morning. They sometimes lie in wait in shallow water under stones for the approach of shoals of young fish, these being attacked at high speed. Others actively swim around the boulders hunting for gobies, which appear to form the main part of their diet. These snakes apparently lie in the water for one or two hours with their bodies swollen with food intake, and are skilfully anchored under two to three stones.

Reproduction

Mating takes place on land, from March to May, and large numbers have sometimes been found together at this time. The courtship procedure is similar to that of the grass snake (p. 133). According to Zapf (1969), the males are far more common than females in Carinthia, and in warm days in March and April bundles of entangled dice snakes can be found at the water's edge, consisting of many males and a single female.

After mating both sexes return to the water, though the female later returns to the land to lay from 5 to 25 eggs under leaves, rotten wood and other decaying vegetation, amid tannery refuse or in the fissures of rocks and walls, in loose soil, and under stones. They are normally laid in July or at the beginning of August, and hatching usually occurs in September. The eggs measure from 30 to 40 millimetres by 20 to 24 millimetres. A second mating in the autumn has been observed.

HYBRIDS   Hybrids have been obtained in captivity as a result of crossing this species with a viperine snake. Another hybrid was achieved by crossing a female dice snake with a male grass snake (see p. 135).

Hibernation

From the end of September until the end of October, depending on the climate and latitude, the dice snake leaves its aquatic environment and takes up residence in dry rocky crevices or in holes in the ground. In Switzerland emergence takes place late in March, or at the beginning of April. In Germany however, emergence may be delayed until the end of April.

General response

This species is often difficult to approach when basking beside water, as it rapidly dives in at any hint of danger. When freshly caught it behaves wildly—struggling vigorously and hissing furiously. Like the grass snake it releases an unpleasant-smelling fluid from the vent, and may even similarly feign death (p. 136). It does not bite, however. It soon settles down and does quite well in captivity, becoming fairly tame. Food is normally readily accepted.

Distribution

Germany and Switzerland   In Germany it is found on the eastern side of the Rhine valley between Lahnstein and Bingen, and in the Lahn valley between Lahnstein and Nassau. Southwards it extends from Bingen along the Nahe valley towards Bad Kreuznach. It is also associated with two other tributaries of the Rhine: the Mosel valley, where it may be extinct, and the Ahr valley, from where it has recently been reported (Raehmel, 1977). Elsewhere in Germany it is known from near Pirna and Meissen in the Elbe valley in Saxony. Near Meissen it is believed to be extinct, not having been reported there for several years, its disappearance partly having been associated with the construction of a motorway. In Switzerland it is found with certainty only in Tessin and Vierwaldstättersee.

France, Italy and Austria   Fretey (1975) reports that it is found in France only very exceptionally. Its position as an indigenous species in France is, I believe, open to doubt. Its range covers most of northern Italy (Piedmont, Lombardy, Trentino-Alto-Adige, Venetia, Liguria and Emilia) and it extends southwards down the peninsula, approximately as far as Naples. Its presence in Sicily has not yet been confirmed (Lanza, 1968). In Austria it is found in lowland regions in the provinces of Vorarlberg, Lower Austria, Burgenland, southern Styria and Carinthia (Eiselt, 1961). According to Zapf (1969) in Carinthia it is confined to Wörthersee and the Drava district.

Eastern Europe and Balkans   In Czechoslovakia it is widespread, extending in Bohemia about as far northwards as Prague. According to Ponec (1965), in Slovakia it is much rarer than the grass snake. There are no authentic records of its occurrence in Poland. It has a broad, somewhat uneven range in Hungary, where it appears to be absent from the dryer, hotter parts of the plain. It is an inhabitant of Romania, Yugoslavia, Albania, Greece and many of the islands, including Crete and Corfu. Karaman (1939) states that it is absent from the islands of Yugoslavia. In Bulgaria and in both European and Asiatic Turkey it is found throughout. In Russia and the Ukraine it occurs in the steppe regions, and seldom surpasses a latitude of 53 to 54°N. It is present on the Crimean peninsula and in the Caucasus region.

Asia   It extends eastwards into central Asia (Kazachstan, the Turkmen, Uzbek, Tadzhik and Kirgiz republics) and southern Siberia, as far as the river Irtysh, the northern Altai mountains and Sinkiang province in north-western China. Finally in south-western Asia it occurs on Cyprus, in Syria, Israel, Iraq, northern Iran, Afghanistan and northern Pakistan.

Black Sea sub-species
The sub-species *Natrix tessellata heinrothi* (**Hecht**) is confined to the island of Serpilor (now Ostrov Zmeinyi) in the Black Sea.

Nomenclature *in northern and central Europe*
  English   Dice snake, Tessellated snake
  Dutch   Dambordslang, Dobbelsteenslang
  German   Würfelnatter
  French   Couleuvre tessellée
  Italian   Natrice tessellata, Biscia tessellata
  Romanian   Şarpele de apă
  Hungarian   Kockás sikló
  Czech   Užovka podplamatá
  Slovakian   Užovka fŕkaná
  Polish   Zaskroniec rybołów
  Serbo-Croatian   Kockasta bjelouška
  Russian   Водяной Уж

1 Common lizards (*Lacerta vivipara*). This species has a wider range than any other terrestrial reptile, extending from Ireland across Eurasia to the Pacific island of Sachalin.

2 Pontic lizard (*Lacerta praticola pontica*). This is a little-known species closely related to the common lizard.

3 Female (upper) and male sand lizards (*Lacerta agilis agilis*) from western Hampshire. Although a rarity in Britain, the sand lizard is common in some European countries.

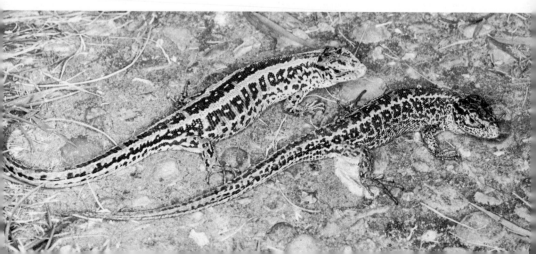

4 Female red-backed sand lizard (*Lacerta agilis agilis* var. *erythronotus*). This variety is distinguished by its absence of a pattern on top of the back.

5 **Above** Balkan form of sand lizard (*Lacerta agilis bosnica*). This race is most easily recognizable by its almost continuous white vertebral stripe.

6 **Below** Male (upper) and female green lizards (*Lacerta viridis viridis*). Although absent from Britain, this species occurs on Jersey and Guernsey, and on the continent it extends from the Atlantic coast to western Russia.

7 **Above** The eyed lizard (*Lacerta lepida lepida*) is Europe's largest species of lizard. As this illustration shows, young and adult specimens are very dissimilar in appearance.

8 **Below** Male (upper) and female wall lizards (*Podarcis muralis muralis*). This is one of Europe's most abundant reptiles. As its name indicates, it is frequently found basking upon walls.

9 **Above** Male (left) and female wall lizards (*Podarcis muralis oyensis*) from the island of Yeu. This race is endemic to the islands and coastal regions of north-western France.

10 **Below** Wall lizards with well defined dorsal markings and with black-flecked bellies (*Podarcis muralis maculiventris*) occur in parts of southern Switzerland, northern Italy, north-western Yugoslavia, and in south-western Romania.

11 Ruin lizards (*Podarcis sicula campestris*) are mainly associated with Italy. In central Europe their range is confined to the extreme south of Switzerland.

12 The meadow lizard (*Podarcis taurica taurica*) is fairly similar to the ruin lizard in appearance. In Europe it is found mainly on the Balkan peninsula, but extends as far north as Hungary.

13 The Balkan skink (*Ablepharus kitaibelii fitzingeri*) is one of Europe's smallest lizards, often being less than 10cm in length. This race inhabits Hungary and a few localities in southern Slovakia.

14 This race of Balkan skink (*Ablepharus kitaibelii stepaneki*) is very similar to the preceding form. It occurs in parts of Romania as well as in certain regions in the north of the Balkan peninsula.

15 Although essentially a Mediterranean species, the three toed skink (*Chalcides chalcides striatus*) also inhabits a few localities near the Atlantic coastal region of France.

16 Young male (lower) and pregnant female slow worms of the western race (*Anguis fragilis fragilis*). The absence of limbs makes this lizard unique in northern and central Europe.

17 The slow worm is an ovo-viviparous species. This female of the east European race (*Anguis fragilis colchicus*) is shown with her recently-born young.

18 Grass snakes (*Natrix natrix natrix*). In many areas of central Europe this is the commonest form of snake.

19 Female barred grass snake (*Natrix natrix helvetica*). This race, found in Britain and north-western Europe, is most readily distinguished by the vertical bars on its flank.

20 Striped grass snake (*Natrix natrix persa*). More usually associated with the Balkan peninsula and the Middle East, this form of grass snake also inhabits parts of the Pannonian plain.

21 Baby grass snake (*Natrix natrix persa*). Its unusual zigzag marking is similar to that of the adder. It retains however the bright yellow flecks behind the head, characteristic of typical grass snakes.

22 Communal egg-laying site of grass snake (*Natrix natrix natrix*). These clusters of eggs were found under a rotting log in south-west Hungary.

23 Dice snake (*Natrix tessellata tessellata*). This species is Europe's most aquatic snake.

24 Viperine snake (*Natrix maura*). As its name indicates, some specimens, like this one, have a dorsal zigzag pattern similar to that of certain vipers.

25 Variety of viperine snake (*Natrix maura*) with two dorso-lateral stripes.

26 Aesculapian snake (*Elaphe longissima longissima*). The fragmentary occurrence of this species in certain northern localites of its range has prompted the theory that such populations have descended from specimens imported by the Romans, who at one time introduced them into their temples.

27 Dark green whip snake (*Coluber viridiflavus viridiflavus*), one of the largest and fiercest snakes of western Europe. It sometimes exceeds one and a half metres in length.

28 Dark green whip snake (*Coluber viridiflavus viridiflavus*). The juvenile form of this species differs considerably from the adult in appearance.

29 Above Black whip snake (*Coluber viridiflavus carbonarius*). Young specimens are similar in markings to those of the previous race. The upper surface of the adults is uniformly black.

30 Below Caspian whip snake (*Coluber jugularis caspius*). This is one of the largest snakes found in Europe. Specimens from Asia Minor have been known to exceed 3m in length.

31 Below Baby Caspian whip snake (*Coluber jugularis caspius*). As with the previous species, the young of this snake differ considerably from the adults.

32 Female smooth snake (*Coronella austriaca austriaca*). This species is Britain's rarest reptile, though on the continent it is common in many regions. This specimen is from east Dorset.

33 Smooth snake (*Coronella austriaca austriaca*). Many continental specimens, like this male from Hungary, have two stripes extending from the back of the head.

34 Female (left) and male southern smooth snakes (*Coronella girondica*). Similar in appearance to the preceding species, this snake is however more slender in build, and typically has a horse-shoe shaped marking on top of the head.

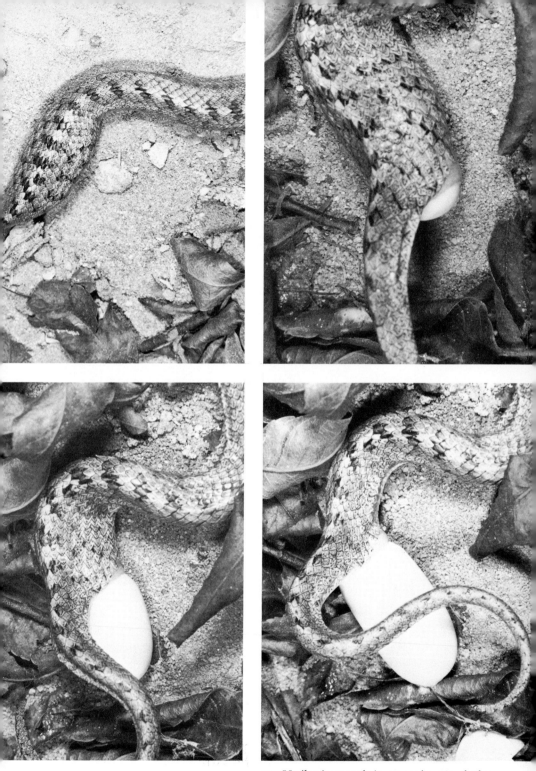

35 Until quite recently it was not known whether the southern smooth snake reproduced by laying eggs, or by giving birth to fully-developed young. Evidence for the former method is shown in the above sequence.

36 Meadow vipers (*Vipera ursinii rakosiensis*) such as these from central Hungary have, despite their adder-like appearance, acquired a reputation for being quite pacific by nature.

37 Female adder (*Vipera berus berus*) sunning itself. Adders do not attack humans except when molested.

38 Melanistic adder (*Vipera berus berus*) from north-west Hampshire. The outline of a dorsal zigzag pattern is only very faintly discernible.

39 Balkan adders (*Vipera berus bosniensis*). The upper snake (male) is a melanistic variety showing no trace of a dorsal zigzag. The lower specimen (female) is more typically marked.

40 Young aspic viper from eastern France (*Vipera aspis aspis*) sunning itself.

41 Aspic vipers. The upper form (*Vipera aspis francisciredi*) is found mainly in Italy, but extends northwards into the Swiss canton of Tessin. The lower snake (*Vipera aspis atra*) is mainly associated with the Swiss Alps.

42 The horned viper (*Vipera ammodytes ammodytes*) can readily be distinguished from the other snakes by the so-called 'horn' projecting from the end of its snout.

43 The Greek tortoise is endemic to Europe. This race (*Testudo hermanni hermanni*) mainly inhabits Italy and the Balkan peninsula. It is also found north of the river Danube in south-west Romania, from where this specimen originates.

44 Although long extinct in Britain and Scandinavia, the European pond tortoise (*Emys orbicularis*) still has a very extensive range, extending from the Atlantic coast of Europe to western Asia.

The Viperine Snake
Natrix maura (**Linnaeus**) 1758
(formerly *Tropidonotus viperinus*)
Terra typica: Algeria

Plates 24, 25, see also colour plate

The viperine snake has a moderately slender body, which eventually can become quite thick-set, especially in old females, and a shortish oval head, which stands out quite distinctly from the short neck. The snout, though round, is somewhat blunt, and the rather small eyes, like the nostrils, are turned obliquely upwards. The tail varies from a sixth to a quarter of the total length, and is enlarged at the base in male specimens. The male attains a maximum length of 83 centimetres, the female 96 centimetres (Angel, 1946).

Scalation
Dorsals: 21 (rarely 19 or 23) longitudinal mid-body rows—strongly keeled excepting smooth or weakly keeled lowest row on either side. 147–164 *ventrals*; divided *anal*; 46–72 paired *subcaudals*. *Rostral* broader than deep, visible from above. 9 large head plates. *Nasal* usually partially divided; 1 or 2 *preoculars*; 2 or 3 *postoculars*; 1 + 2 (or 3) *temporals*; 7 (rarely 8) upper *labials* (3 and 4 or 4 and 5 bordering eye).

Colouration
The basic colour of the viperine snake is quite variable, ranging from grey, greyish brown, olive, olive green, brown, reddish, reddish brown to yellowish. According to Fretey (1975), specimens with a reddish dorsal colouration are males, while those which are greenish are females. The dorsal pattern is also variable. Normally however there are either two alternating longitudinal rows of dark brown or black spots, or a similarly-coloured wavy zigzag band which usually becomes fragmented near and on the tail region. In some individuals inconspicuous whitish spots may occur on the zigzag line. On each side is a row of black roundish spots, each of which has a yellowish or whitish centre. These spots run parallel with the indentations of the dorsal zigzag. The head is usually darker than the body, but has lighter, often symmetrical patches. A dark ∧-shape, beginning on top of the head, extends to the temples. A similar dark marking is sometimes also present behind this. The upper labials are usually yellow or a dirty white, with black bars in the sutures between the shields. Sometimes these are mainly black, each one containing only a single small yellow spot. The throat is whitish, while the ventral side is quite variable,

being reddish, yellow, whitish or a dirty green, and is well but irregularly distributed with black squarish blotches. On the belly of some specimens the black colour may predominate; in others it may be completely black. Sometimes the black markings on the belly may be connected by dark vertical bars to the lateral ocellations. The pupil of the eye is black, the iris being golden or orange, and often tinged with brown.

The young are similar to the adults, but the markings are more sharply pronounced. As in the dice snake, the pattern of this species is more vivid when it is submerged in the water. The somewhat oval head and comparatively short body, together with the dorsal zigzag pattern, have led many people, including even eminent naturalists, to confuse this snake with the adder. Its identity can however be established by a glance at the eye, which has a round pupil, unlike that of the adder, whose pupil is vertical.

Variations   Specimens possessing a pair of yellowish or reddish dorsal stripes (var. *aurolineatus*) occur mainly in Sardinia, southern France, the Iberian peninsula and north Africa. In south-western France however they occur in the Gironde *département*. In such specimens the zigzag stripe is often fragmented into a row of spots.

Melanism and albinism   A few cases of melanism and albinism are on record.

Venom glands

The viperine snake is harmless to man. As in the grass snake and the dice snake, the poison glands of the upper jaw secrete a venom, which experimentally has been shown to have an effect on various animals similar to the venom of the aspic viper.

Habitat

The viperine snake is most frequently found in and around water, occurring in the vicinity of marshes and swamps, and beside ponds, lakes, streams and rivers. However, it may sometimes be encountered in fields and ditches some distance from water outside of the dry season. In mountainous regions it can occasionally be observed swimming amid torrents of cold water. It can also be found in marshy coastal districts.

Altitude   This species is at home in flat, hilly and mountainous areas, reaching up to 1200 metres in the Alps of south-western Switzerland, 1500 metres in the Pyrenees, and 2300 metres in Morocco.

Co-habiting species   In France I have found this species co-habiting with the slow worm (p. 116), the green and wall lizards, the grass snake as well as the European pond tortoise. In Spain I have seen it sharing its territory with the three toed skink and Spanish terrapin (*Mauremys caspica leprosa*). Boulenger (1913) states that in northern Italy it occurs alongside the dice snake, while in the Geneva region it co-habits with the aspic viper (Stemmler, 1971).

Behaviour
Like the previous species of snakes, the viperine snake is diurnal in its habits. Though fond of sunning itself, often communally, particularly in springtime and in the mornings, it dislikes a strong sun, and spends much of its time in retreat, under rocks, sometimes under walls, in moss, crevices in banks beside water, and of course in the water itself. Here it lies amid floating plants or under submerged branches, though it may often be seen swimming around quite casually. Sometimes it swims on the surface of the water, in which case the head is held above water level. According to Steward (1971), when surfacing from shallow water in order to breathe, it raises itself vertically, with its tail resting on the bottom, and only the nostrils and eyes protude above the surface of the water.

Food
The diet of this species is similar to that of the dice snake, fish, including eels, as well as amphibia and their larvae being preferred. The young eat small fish and the larvae of amphibia. Earthworms are devoured by both adults and young. Occasionally salamanders are taken. Sometimes several individuals may be seen in the water, lying in wait for their prey. Small fish are swallowed in the water, while larger prey is taken on land to be eaten. Captive specimens at least will readily try to seize fish out of the mouths of other snakes, and tug-of-war scenes may be frequent. There are also a few records of both mammals and birds having been consumed. The viperine snake is very voracious during the summer months.

Enemies
The chief foes of this species are predatory birds, and such mammals as hedgehogs and shrews. Poultry will also seize them if given the opportunity. They are often killed by man because of their resemblance to the adder.

Reproduction
The viperine snake mates in March or April, the courtship pattern being similar to that of the grass and dice snakes. The female lays from 4 to 20 whitish eggs in late May, June or July. These are sometimes deposited in the abandoned holes of mice, voles or moles, under tree roots, compost, moss or

rocks, but always in close proximity to water. The eggs, like those of the dice snake, are somewhat elongate, and when first laid measure from 29 to 31 millimetres by 15 to 18 millimetres.

Hatching takes place from August to October, and the young then measure about 17 or 18 centimetres. They immediately set off to seek water. Within three days of hatching the egg-tooth is shed. According to Steward (1971), in September or October baby specimens often assemble in large numbers in shallow water in order to feed. Grass snakes at this stage are far less frequently seen.

Sometimes a second, autumn, mating may occur, but according to Boulenger (1913) egg-laying takes place only during the summer. There is however a record of a captive female, which, despite the absence of a male, produced several clutches of eggs, sometimes laying twice within a single year. The eggs were of course infertile (Sievers, 1969). By the end of their first year the young reach a total length of about 22 centimetres. Females become mature at about four or five years, males a little later (Fretey, 1975).

HYBRIDS   Hybrids have been produced in captivity as a result of the mating of this species with a dice snake, and with a grass snake. Hybrids have also been produced from a mating of the striped and flecked forms of this species (Mertens, 1964).

Hibernation
In the north of its range it disappears into hibernation at the end of October or beginning of November. Frequently it hibernates communally, and sometimes its retreat is shared with other species of snake. For its refuge it chooses holes in the ground, crevices in tree trunks and rocky cavities. Railway embankments are sometimes favoured. March is the usual time for emergence although this can be delayed until April. Further south however hibernation is either very short, or perhaps non-existent. This species has in fact a remarkable degree of resistance to the cold.

Ecdysis
The viperine snake sheds its skin at least four times a year (Angel, 1946).

General Response
Unless cornered in its retreat, this is not an easy species to catch, for it is very alert in its movements, both on land and in the water, being like the dice snake an excellent diver and swimmer. It is also able to remain submerged for long periods. When freshly caught it behaves very excitedly, struggling wildly, hissing, and often releasing an unpleasant smelly fluid, similar to that released

by the grass and dice snakes. According to Boulenger (1913) some specimens may bite, although I have never experienced this.

Normally it soon tames reasonably well however, and thrives in captivity. At first it may refuse to feed, but before long food is usually seized eagerly, and even dead prey is often taken. Angel however refers to specimens which refused all food during periods of 370 and 464 days. The viperine snake lives well in captivity with other members of its own species, as well as with other snakes.

Distribution

France and Switzerland The viperine snake is an inhabitant of central and southern France, occurring as far north as southern Brittany and the *départements* of Seine-et-Marne and Aube (Angel, 1946). Fretey (1975) states that it is rare in the *départements* of Cantal and Aveyron, and very rare in Jura. An isolated population exists near Metz (Moselle). It also occurs on the Atlantic île d'Yeu, and on the îles d'Hyères off the Mediterranean coast. According to Rollinat (1934) it is more common than the grass snake in watery regions of France. In south-western Switzerland it is found in the Rhône district, and in the cantons of Geneva, Vaud and Valais.

Southern Europe In northern Italy it is confined to Piedmont, Lombardy and Liguria. It also occurs in Sardinia, the Isola S. Antioco, as well as throughout Spain, the Balearic islands, and Portugal, where it is very common. It appears however to be absent from Corsica, and its presence in Sicily requires confirmation.

North-west Africa Outside of Europe the viperine snake seems to be restricted to north-western Africa. Its range there extends from Morocco, where it is found throughout, across northern Algeria and Tunisia to western Libya. Apparently it penetrates for some way into the north of the Sahara.

Turkey Two specimens, reportedly brought from near Maraṣ in southern Turkey, were preserved in a Berlin Museum (Bodenheimer, 1944).

No sub-species are at present recognized.

Nomenclature *in northern and central Europe*
Dutch Adderringslang
German Vipernatter
French Couleuvre vipérine
Italian Natrice viperina, Biscia viperina

The Aesculapian Snake
Elaphe longissima
(formerly *Coluber longissimus*)
Sub-species found in northern and central Europe:
Elaphe longissima longissima (**Laurenti**) 1768
Terra typica restricta: Vienna, Austria
Plate 26

This snake has a long, moderately slender but strongly-built body, and a small, narrow but longish head, which is not very distinctly set off from the neck in the adult, though it is more clearly defined in the young. The snout is rather blunt. The long, slender and tapering tail constitutes from about a fifth to a quarter of the total length. The Aesculapian snake grows to a length varying from 1.4 to 2 metres, 1.8 metres being the maximum length reached in the north of its range.

Origin of name
The Aesculapian snake derives its name from Aesculapius, the god of medicine in Ancient Greek mythology. He is portrayed carrying a long stick around which a snake is entwined. The Romans, who at one time regarded these snakes as sacred, introduced them into their temples, and the present-day, rather patchy occurrence of this species in the north of its range, in Germany and Switzerland—often in the vicinity of former Roman Spas, has led to the theory that these populations have originated from such introductions. Other authorities however regard these scattered localities as mere remnants of what was originally a much wider range. The presence of this species in Poland, and until recently in Denmark, can obviously not be attributed to the Romans, whose empire did not extend to these regions.

Scalation
Dorsals: 23 (rarely 21) smooth and shiny, longitudinal rows at mid-body, slightly keeled on top of posterior part. 212–248 *ventrals* with distinctly angled edges; divided *anal*; 60–91 paired *subcaudals*. *Rostral* broader than deep, visible from above. 9 large plates on top of head. 1 *preocular*; 2 *postoculars*; 2 long, narrow *temporals*; 8 or 9 upper *labials* (4 and 5 or 5 and 6 bordering eye).

Colouration
Adult colouration   There does not appear to be any difference between the two sexes with regard to size and colouration. The basic colour of the upper surface varies from yellow-grey to dark olive-brown, though exceptional specimens

may be straw-coloured or black. The fore-part of the body is always lighter than the rear part. Many of the scales are stippled with small white flecks, sparse on some individuals, numerous on others. These occur on the upper corners of the dorsal and lateral scales. Sometimes they are so densely distributed as to form a network. Above, the head is similar to the basic colouration, but the upper labials are usually pale yellow, and a pair of yellow patches behind the temples forms a collar reminiscent of that of a grass snake, though much less distinct. These patches do not connect with one another. There is usually a fairly distinct dark bar just behind the eyes, tilted slightly downwards, and a dark fleck situated just below the eye. The tongue is a pinkish-brown colour. The pupil of the eye is round, and the iris is normally brown or dark grey. The underside, including the throat, is devoid of markings, being a uniform pale yellow, whitish or even greenish.

Juvenile colouration　　The young are often darker than the adults and have from four to seven longitudinal rows of dark brown spots on the back and flanks, which may tend to form cross-bars towards the head. The yellow blotches forming the collar are far brighter than those of the adult, and there is a black ring shape just behind these. A dark brown transverse bar crosses the head just in front of the eyes, and there is, as in adults, a vertical fleck just below each eye. The belly is yellowish-olive or greyish, often speckled with black on the fore-part, and becoming grey in the rear part.

Colour variations　　Melanic forms, which are black both above and on the belly, are rare. Less rare are albinos, a number of such specimens having been recorded from France, Austria and Serbia. In the Zemplén range of northern Hungary a grey form var. *subgrisea* occurs.

Venom glands
Phisalix (1922) states that this species is devoid of poison glands, unlike some other colubrids.

Habitat
The Aesculapian snake is an inhabitant of shrubby and lightly wooded, especially deciduous areas, sunny glades, forest borders, clearings and meadow land. It is often found in stony districts, and may be encountered basking on or hiding in old and ruined walls, sometimes on garden walls. It occasionally suns itself by the roadside. In hilly regions it inhabits only slopes that are well protected from the wind, and in the north of its range lives mainly on south facing slopes. Although it may sometimes occur in arid regions it avoids damp and marshy localities. On rare occasions it may penetrate into dark and densely-wooded areas, and is apparently the only European snake to

do so. It is equally at home on flat and hilly country. In the south of its range it prefers a stony soil (Frommhold, 1965).

Altitude   It ascends to 1250 metres in Switzerland, 1500 metres in Provence, and 2000 metres in Bulgaria.

Co-habiting species   Near Passau in Bavaria it shares its habitat with the green lizard. Zapf (1969) has even witnessed the two species basking together during an entire summer in Carinthia. In the Balkans I have found it in the same localities as the Caspian whip snake. But the extent of its territory does not appear to be large when compared with that of the whip snakes. I have also observed it co-habiting with the slow worm.

Behaviour
As stated, it is a sun lover, and is often found basking upon rocks and walls, as well as on and in bushes and in sunny clearings amid thick vegetation. While basking it frequently holds its head up in a horizontal position. However it dislikes excessive heat, and during the warmer part of the day retires into the shade, often under stones, or sometimes even haystacks. On one occasion I discovered one hiding in the lining of a discarded anorak! It has been observed to crawl about at night. In many of its localities in Carinthia, Zapf (1969) observed it living in pairs throughout the year.

It is fairly slow in its movements, but is an excellent and, when necessary, agile climber, and not infrequently it ascends trees, where it likes to bask with its body draped loosely around a thin branch. It has powerful muscles, and Gadow (1901) has remarked on its ability to scale vertical walls by skilfully taking advantage of any unevenness in the surface. It is a good diver and swimmer, and in hot weather sometimes enters water, particularly when about to slough its skin. On such occasions it has been seen to remain immersed for a long period. This species has some power of constriction. It is also able to raise the head and upper third of its body vertically.

Food
The adults eat small rodents principally, and are responsible for devouring large numbers of mice and voles. They are thus of considerable economic value to agriculture, a fact which, alas, is not always appreciated. Zapf (1969) believes that the young eat mainly mice, the adults devouring principally rats. Moles and shrews may sometimes be devoured, and on occasions even birds and their eggs, frogs and, more rarely, fire salamanders (*Salamandra salamandra*) (Frommhold, 1965). The young are often stated to eat lizards also. Prey is held in the snake's coils, and may sometimes be killed by constriction.

Enemies

Hedgehogs, weasels, badgers, predatory birds and poultry are listed among the foes of the Aesculapian snake.

Reproduction

Mating Mating takes place from the middle of May until the middle of June. Before mating the male wildly and excitedly pursues his partner, and they then perform a curious dance in which they face one another with the anterior parts of the body raised vertically in an S-shape. During this time the hind parts are entwined. The resultant pattern thus resembles a lyre. This dance may last up to an hour or even longer. During copulation the hind parts remain entwined and the male often holds the female firmly in his jaws by the neck.

Egg laying At the end of June or in July the female normally lays 5 to 20 dull white eggs. These are elongated in shape, and measure from 35 to 45 millimetres by 19 to 24 millimetres. They are usually deposited in compost heaps, rotting vegetation, dried moss, manure, in tree hollows, cavities in walls, rubble, and other warmth-providing conditions. Thus at this time of year they are sometimes found in stables.

Hatching The young usually hatch in September, and are much less slender proportionally than the adults, being rather similar in appearance to young grass snakes. They measure from 14 to 25 centimetres, the tail comprising about a fifth of the total length. As soon as they have hatched they are ready to bite any unwelcome intruder. According to Angel (1946) they measure about 35 centimetres by the time they are one-year old. Maturity is reached in their fourth or fifth year (Zapf, 1969).

Hibernation

This species, although disliking great heat, is also sensitive to the cold. Even in the southern parts of its range it has often disappeared into its winter retreat by the end of September. It emerges comparatively late in spring, and even on the French Riviera may not appear until May. In south-eastern Slovakia the adults disappear already during the middle of August, the young still being found up to about the end of September. Emergence there takes place in the middle of May. In Hungary also it emerges about this time.

Sites chosen for hibernation quarters include crevices amid rocks, tree hollows, cavities in the soil and even piles of manure. Only rarely does it leave its hibernation quarters to warm itself or drink, according to Fretey (1975).

General response

It is not usually a very difficult snake to catch, since like the smooth snake it often remains stationary when found, and can therefore easily be picked up. When caught however it struggles wildly and strikes rapidly, trying to bite. If it succeeds, it does not normally fasten its jaws on its adversary for long. The teeth are small, and though they can cause bleeding, are unable to do any serious damage. When held by the tail it is sometimes able to climb up by coiling around its own body—a habit characteristic of *Coronella*.

For a while in captivity it can become quickly alarmed, but normally it tames quite soon, and does well provided it has plenty of space in which to roam, sunlight, a cool retreat and facilities for climbing. Food is usually readily accepted, though certain individuals may stubbornly refuse everything that is offered. It has been reported to have fasted for fourteen months before dying. Normally it can be persuaded to accept even dead food. The adults may often seize food more readily than the young. They seem reluctant however to take food from the hand, though they often appear to enjoy being handled. In captivity they usually get on well with other species of snakes, though some may prove rather quarrelsome towards members of their own species.

Distribution

Elaphe longissima longissima has a fairly wide range in Europe, being found over much of the central and southern parts of the continent.

France   In France it has a widespread but rather broken range, being quite common in the western region between the Loire and Dordogne, in the central region, the Dauphiné and the south. The northern limit of its range extends from the south of Brittany through the *départements* of Orne, Seine-et-Marne, Côte-d'Or and Haute-Saône (Angel, 1946).

Germany   In Germany it has now become very rare. According to a report by Bechtle it has not been found within recent years in its former localities at southern Odenwald, near Lörrach in the Wiese valley (Baden) and at Hirschhorn on the Neckar. In Bad Schlangenbad (Taunus) it has become rare, though it was at one time very common. It still occurs near Passau on the Danube in south-eastern Bavaria, and here efforts are being made to help ensure its survival (Bechtle, 1970). The population which still occurs at Schlitz in upper Hessen has descended from 40 specimens which were collected at Schlangenbad during 1853 and 1854 and subsequently released at Schlitz. The only danger to their survival at present appears to be cars, since these snakes apparently have a habit of basking on the road (Jaeschke, 1971). It has not been found in Denmark (South Zealand) since 1863, though it was apparently quite common near Copenhagen at the end of the eighteenth century (Boulenger, 1913).

Switzerland and Austria   In Switzerland it inhabits the cantons of Vaud (the Rhône valley and the Lavaux region), Valais and lower Tessin. It also occurs in the region of Geneva. In addition it has been reported from near Dornach (Soleure) (Dottrens, 1963). In Austria it is found in the province of Lower Austria, with the exception of the eastern plains. According to Eiselt (1961), it also occurs in the provinces of Styria, Burgenland and Carinthia as well as in northern Salzburg and the eastern part of Upper Austria. Its presence in the north of the province of Tirol requires confirmation.

Eastern Europe   Štěpánek (1949) states that in Czechoslovakia the Aesculapian snake has been found several times in western and south-western Bohemia, but is more commonly met with in Moravia and Slovakia. It is apparently quite abundant in suitably warm areas of southern Slovakia (Ponec, 1965). It still occurs in south-eastern Poland, though it may well be extinct now near Cracow (Berger, Jaskowska and Młynarski, 1969). In Hungary it is mainly an inhabitant of forested, hilly and mountainous regions. In western Hungary it is widespread though rather localized. It is found around Budapest and in the Danube region to the north of this. Further east it is known from the Körös valley. It inhabits Romania, Bukovina, Moldavia and the Ukraine, though it does not reach as far east as the river Dnieper.

Southern Europe   In Spain it is very rare, but has been reported from the Basque district and the regions of Gerona and Barcelona. Recently a dead specimen was found near the Picos de Europa in the Cantabrian mountains (Salvador, 1974a). In Italy it inhabits the northern and central regions, where it extends along the high Apennines as far south as the province of Lazio and the Lago di Matese. There have apparently been no reports of its occurrence in Corsica, though it is present on Sardinia. It ranges more or less over the entire Balkan peninsula. In Yugoslavia it is represented almost everywhere, though according to Radovanović (1941), it is nowhere very abundant. Among the Yugoslav islands it is found on Mljet, Brač, Šolta, Rab and Hvar.

Asia Minor   Mertens (1952) states that it is limited to the northern-most part of Asia Minor, where it is very rare. It occurs in the western Caucasus, but is absent from Armenia. Finally it is known from northern Iran.

OTHER RACES   In Iran another race, *Elaphe longissima persica* **Werner**, also occurs. The southern part of Italy and Sicily are inhabited by the striped form *Elaphe longissima romana* (**Suchow**). The form living on the island of Amorgos in the Cyclades is now considered by some authorities to be a form of *Elaphe quatuorlineata*; others regard it as a separate species, *Elaphe rechingeri* **Werner**.

Nomenclature *in northern and central Europe*

Dutch Aesculaapslang
German Äskulapnatter
Danish Aeskulapsnog
French Couleuvre d' Esculape
Italian Colubro di Esculapio
Romanian Şarpele lui Esculap
Hungarian Erdei sikló
Czech Užovka stromová, Užovka Aeskulapova západní
Slovakian Had hôrny
Polish Wąż Eskulapa
Serbo-Croatian Eskulapova zmija
Russian Эскулапова Змея

The Dark Green Whip Snake and the Black Whip Snake
Coluber viridiflavus

Sub-species found in western Europe:
Coluber viridiflavus viridiflavus **Lacépède** 1789
(formerly *Zamenis gemonensis* var. *viridiflavus*)
Terra typica: Southern France

Coluber viridiflavus carbonarius **Bonaparte** 1833
(formerly *Zamenis gemonensis* var. *carbonarius*)
Terra typica restricta: Sicily
Plates 27, 28, 29, see also colour plates

This species, represented by these two principal races, has a very long and slender body, and a very long, finely tapering tail, which varies from about three-tenths to a quarter of the total length. The head is clearly distinct from the neck, and the snout is rounded. There is a slight concavity on either side of the head, situated just in front of the eyes. This species reaches a maximum length of about 1.9 metres. Fretey (1975) states that males are larger than females, and also have larger heads.

Scalation
Dorsals: 19 (sometimes 17 or 21) smooth, polished, longitudinal mid-body

rows. *Ventrals*: 160–208 (males), 208–230 (females); divided *anal*; paired *subcaudals*: 102–131 (males), 85–113 (females). *Rostral* broader than deep, visible from above. 9 large plates on top of head, including long, bell-shaped *frontal* and 2 wide *supraoculars*, protruding slightly outwards. 1 *preocular*; 1 anterior *subocular*; 2 or 3 *postoculars*; 2 (rarely 1) +2 or 2 + 3 *temporals*; 8 upper *labials* (4 and 5 bordering eye).

Colouration

Coluber viridiflavus viridiflavus   In appearance the adult dark green whip snake with its long whip-like form and striking colouration is a beautiful creature. There appears to be no sexual variation regarding colouration. Its ground colour is dark green or black, and it is covered with bright yellow, greenish-yellow, or sometimes, particularly in younger adults, light olive green markings. These are in the form of blotches or transverse bars on the anterior part of the body, while on the posterior part and tail each scale has a narrow longitudinal streak, thus more or less continuous parallel lines are formed. The top of the head is mottled with various shades of dark brown or black and a white or yellow dash is present on each supraocular scale, and sometimes behind each of the parietals. The preocular and postocular shields are also blotched with yellow as are the upper labials, which have black bars in and around the sutures. The fairly large reddish eye has a round black pupil. The throat is white, the belly yellow, pale grey or greenish white, either uniform or with occasional dark flecks, particularly towards the edges of the belly plates.

JUVENILE COLOURATION   The young are uniformly grey green, olive green or olive brown above, and the head markings are particularly vivid at this stage. A narrow whitish crossbar, almost connecting the postocular shields, is interrupted on the frontal plate. Behind the parietal plates there is usually a V or W shape marking, the latter sometimes being broken up on top of the head. In some cases this marking is further extended and an adjacent pair of loops may be formed.

Coluber viridiflavus carbonarius   The young of the black whip snake appear to be almost identical to those of the other sub-species until they reach the age of about three. Then the upper surface darkens, and eventually becomes a highly polished deep uniform black or blue-black, while the yellow markings on top of the head usually disappear. This colouration is particularly vivid after sloughing has occurred. The yellow or pale cream markings may be retained to some extent on the side of the head, notably on the preocular and postocular shields, and on the upper labials. Underneath, the colour is dark ash grey or dirty whitish yellow, and is lightest towards the centre of the belly. Very tiny sporadic dark flecks may be present, particularly at the bottom of each belly plate. The lower surface of the tail is often a steely or iron grey. The throat and chin are yellow or whitish. The black whip snake has sometimes been confused with the Aesculapian snake.

Venom glands

This species is harmless to man, but possesses a parotid gland which secretes venom. According to Phisalix (1922) the poison glands of this species are relatively small, and venom is apparently not produced throughout the year. None the less a guinea-pig became paralysed after receiving an injection, and died within an hour.

Habitat

Both races of this species have a varied range of habitat, though they are rarely found near water, and generally avoid all damp areas. They occur in flat, hilly and mountainous country, ascending to an altitude of 1800 metres, but in the Massif central, *Coluber viridiflavus viridiflavus* does not appear to surpass 900 metres (Fretey, 1975). Both these forms occur in bushy or shrubby areas, especially on stony or rocky ground, as well as near vineyards, in sunny glades, beside paths, and on the borders of woods. They are sometimes to be found living near human habitations.

Western race   In south-western France I have quite frequently found the western race on the flat and sandy heathlands and in pine forests around the vicinity of Bordeaux, while further north-west, near Marennes, I have found it on dry land surrounded by oyster beds. In Italy I have discovered it beside a path, on either side of which were large expanses of intensively cultivated land; evidence of its roaming disposition.

In various localities I have observed this form sharing its terrain with the wall lizard, the ruin lizard, the green lizard, the aspic viper and the grass snake.

The eastern race   Typical situations where I have found the eastern race have been beside country roads, on piles of rubble, amid olive groves, on garden walls, by stony walls surrounding agricultural plots, in grassy meadows and on a railway embankment. I have found it occurring in the same vicinity as the green lizard and the horned viper.

Behaviour

This species is diurnal by nature, spending much of its time sunning itself on top of rocks, piles of stones, old walls, rubble or in clearings beside thick vegetation. I have noticed how some specimens of both races show a fondness for basking with the body almost vertically outstretched on a very steeply inclined wall or sandy or rocky slope. Sometimes however I have found it in hiding coiled up under discarded pieces of metal or piles of rocks. Usually this snake is difficult to approach, being very alert and extremely agile. Its German name *Pfeilnatter*, meaning arrow snake, is very appropriate, for when alarmed it shoots off at an incredible speed, particularly on a downward slope.

It is a very skilful climber, and is able to scale almost vertical rough slopes. When climbing it is able to raise, unsupported, about half of its total body length in a horizontal position. I once found a specimen basking outstretched on a very steep cliff face that was about 6 metres high. Its tail would have been just within my reach, but as I approached it quickly climbed to the top of the cliff. On arriving at this point of safety it proceeded to crawl rapidly along the edge of the cliff, and suddenly fell down on to the ground near where I was standing. It appeared however to be none the worse for its fall, and when I picked it up, it writhed with all the furious energy so characteristic of this species.

In the earlier part of the morning, before the sun has become strong, this snake is normally less alert and is most easily approached. At other times however it races off into the undergrowth at the slightest disturbance. It often returns to the same place some while later, since a favourite spot is frequently visited daily, often over a period of several months or even years.

Food

Coluber viridiflavus viridiflavus when adult eats lacertids and their eggs, snakes, frogs and young birds, sometimes climbing into bushes in order to find them in their nests. Small rodents such as voles and mice, as well as slow worms are said to be particularly favoured. Even poisonous snakes have been known to be devoured, and instances of cannibalism are on record. Amphibia are devoured when other food has become scarce. Grasshoppers and large moths are sometimes eaten. On one occasion near Pisa I observed a ruin lizard darting out of a hedgerow onto the path, just ahead of me. It was closely followed by a large *viridiflavus* which was too preoccupied to be bothered by my presence. The young eat mainly grasshoppers and lizards. The diet of *Coluber viridiflavus carbonarius* includes such frogs as *Rana dalmatina* and *Rana latastei*. Schreiber states that in the Karst district of north-eastern Yugoslavia orthoptera are devoured predominantly. Struggling prey is sometimes killed by constriction before being swallowed.

Reproduction

Mating usually takes place in April and May. This is preceeded by rivalry among the males, and violent struggles take place. During courtship the male often holds the neck of the female firmly in his jaws, and the tails are entwined.

The whitish eggs are normally laid at the end of June or beginning of July, more unusually as late as September, and number from 5 to 15. They are round and elongate in shape, measuring from 28 to 40 millimetres by 14 to 22 millimetres, and they are sometimes joined in pairs. They are disposed by the female in crevices in the soil or among rocks, in well sheltered, sunny places. The incubation period varies from 6 to 8 weeks, and the very long and slender young measure about 25 centimetres on emergence. The approximate lengths attained after the first, second and third years are, according to Angel (1946), 31, 47 and 78 centimetres respectively.

Hibernation
This species appears to be active from March or April until September or October, when it disappears. Apparently it may sometimes interrupt its hibernation in order to bask and drink (Fretey, 1975).

Ecdysis
Angel states that healthy specimens shed their skins some four or five times during the summer.

General response
Not only is it one of the fastest of European colubrids, it is also one of the fiercest. When freshly caught it struggles violently and furiously lashes its tail to and fro like a whip, hence its name. It readily bites, fastening its jaws around one's hand, making persistent slow chewing movements. The bite, although unpleasant, is not of course dangerous, nor even very painful, though one may find the hand covered with blood. The bite can normally be avoided if one holds the snake at arm's length by the tail. Though it will writhe wildly and try to leap towards one with open jaws, it cannot do much harm. Often when held in this position it begins to spin its entire body round and round in a circle, making it necessary for one to adjust one's hold in order to re-establish a firm grip. Occasional specimens, however, are so long that even when held at arm's length they are able to leap far enough to seize one's hand or part of one's clothing in their jaws. Some newly-caught specimens may emit an unpleasant smelling fluid from the vent—similar to that of the grass snake though not as powerful. I have observed this habit in both racial forms.

Some whip snakes retain their savage disposition for months in captivity, but in my experience, most of them become tolerably tame and can be handled freely. When they tire of this however and wish to venture off, but are prevented from doing so, they not infrequently resort to biting. On account of their roaming disposition, these whip snakes are not really suitable for keeping in captivity. Much roaming space is required as well as a warm and dry atmosphere; without these they quickly succumb to illness. Food is normally accepted readily. Sometimes I have known individuals of this species behave aggressively with others of their kind.

Distribution

Dark green whip snake   The dark green whip snake is found in France, where it is normally encountered to the south of a line extending approximately from Nantes to Strasbourg (Angel, 1946). It is found above all in the *départements* of the south-west, bordering the Atlantic. It is rare in much of the north of its range, as in such *départements* as Maine-et-Loire, Vienne, Indre, Yonne, and Haute-Saône, while in central France, according to Rollinat (1934), it is no longer to be found in such *départements* as Cher, Nièvre, Corrèze and Puy-de-Dôme. It is on record from the *départements* of Aisne and Moselle (near Thionville), the latter locality being situated near Luxembourg, from where it has also been reported, according to Mertens and Wermuth (1960).

A number of specimens have been found in Belgium, notably in the province of Brabant—presumably having escaped from captivity. In Spain it is found only in the Pyrenees, and in the Montseny and Basque regions. In Switzerland it inhabits mainly the southern Alpine district and is known from near Geneva, Aigle (Vaud), and the *cantons* of Valais, Tessin and Graubünden. In Italy it occurs in the north-western and central parts, including Monte Argentario, as well as on Capraia, Elba, Pianosa, Giglio, Corsica, Sardinia and some minor islands. This species, in its two forms, is the most commonly encountered snake in Italy.

Black whip snake   The black whip snake extends over most of the north-eastern region of Italy, about as far north as Bressanone (Brixen) in the Alps, and at least as far south as Ravenna. Although absent from central Italy, it curiously reappears in the south, as well as on Sicily and Malta. In addition it is found on Ischia and Capri, while off the Adriatic coast it inhabits some of the Tremiti islands. It is also represented on Palagruža. In Switzerland it is confined to Bregaglia and a locality near Poschiavo, from where Kramer has reported it (at an altitude of 1400 metres), in the *canton* of Graubünden.

Elsewhere it is known from Yugoslavia, where it inhabits Istria and its islands, south-western Slovenia, the Balkan coast of Croatia at least as far south as Senj, and the island of Krk. There are old reports mentioning it from the Tokaj district of north-eastern Hungary. However Vásárhelyi (1965) does not refer to this species as being indigenous to Hungary. It does not occur within the present frontiers of Austria. According to Müller (1974), hybrids from these two sub-species occur in the region of the Abruzzi National Park at the Lago di Barrea.

Montecristo race   Specimens from the island of Montecristo have recently been classified as *Coluber viridiflavus kratzeri* **Kramer.**

Nomenclature *in northern and central Europe*
Coluber viridiflavus viridiflavus
  English   Dark green whip snake, European whip snake
  Dutch   Gevlekte toornslang
  German   Gelbgrüne Pfeilnatter, Gelbgrüne Zornnatter
  French   Couleuvre verte et jaune
  Italian   Colubro comune, Colubro verde e giallo, Biacco
  Polish   Połoz żółtozielony

Coluber viridiflavus carbonarius
  English   Black whip snake
  Dutch   Zwarte toornslang
  German   Schwarze Pfeilnatter, Karbonarschlange
  Italian   Colubro carbonaro

The Caspian Whip Snake
Coluber jugularis

Sub-species found in central Europe:
Coluber jugularis caspius **Gmelin** 1789
(formerly *Zamenis gemonensis* var. *caspius*)
Terra typica restricta: Steppes of the lower Ural river, Russia
Plates 30, 31

This species is closely related to *Coluber viridiflavus*, and in fact these two snakes were at one time classified together as different forms of the same species. It is however more strongly built than its ally. It has a thick and very long muscular body, and the head stands out fairly distinctly from the neck. The tip of the snout is rounded. The very long tail constitutes from about a quarter to a third of the total length. It is almost the longest species of snake to be found in Europe, growing to a length of 150 to 200 centimetres. Old specimens exceeding this length are rare nowadays in the north of its range. Some specimens found in Asia Minor have been known to exceed 3 metres.

Scalation

Dorsals: 19 (rarely 17 or 21) smooth, shiny longitudinal rows at mid-body. 160–211 *ventrals*; divided *anal*; 87–131 paired *subcaudals*. *Rostral* broader than deep, visible from above. 9 large plates on top of head, including long, bell-shaped *frontal* and 2 wide *supraoculars*. 1 (rarely 2) *preoculars*; small anterior *subocular*; 2 or 3 *postoculars*; 2 + 2 *temporals*; 8 upper *labials* (4 and 5 bordering eye).

Colouration

Adult colouration Above, the colour varies from light yellow brown to nut-brown. It may be pale olive, grey brown or reddish brown, and often a greenish tinge can be observed. Across the middle of each individual scale is a yellowish or pale brown longitudinal streak. Thus there are some 19 more or less continuous, pale longitudinal lines extending along the body. The head is mainly brownish red, rust, dark greenish brown, or ginger, and tinged with sporadic darker shades. The upper labials are yellowish with brown sutures. The belly is light red, orange, yellow or even whitish, and is unmarked, but the colour may become more intense towards the sides. The throat region may be similar to the belly or it may become a creamy white. The large eye is maize yellow, and the round pupil is black. Usually the tongue is black, though the tip can be dark pink. Some specimens, notably those from some of the Greek islands, are almost entirely black.

Juvenile colouration The young are greyish brown with dark brown spots along the back and on the sides. Towards the neck cross-bars often occur on top of the back. In the posterior part of the body and on the tail the markings fade considerably. The dark brown head has symmetrical yellowish flecks or streaks on top, and the lip shields are light yellow with dark sutures. Its underside is yellow and this may be speckled with orange spots at the sides. The juvenile characteristics may persist until a length of about 1 metre is attained.

Habitat

Its habitat, like that of *Coluber viridiflavus*, is very varied. In Hungary it is associated with bushy country in low limestone mountain regions. According to Vásárhelyi (1965) it is rarely found in vineyards there. On the Balkan peninsula it occurs chiefly on warm, dry and rocky hill and mountain slopes. In Russia it inhabits hot, dry and flat countryside, often on sandy soil. Here it may be found in areas with sparse vegetation, including steppelands and semi-desert regions. Damp localities are normally avoided. However I once came across a shed skin entangled in a grassy bank that sloped down to a stagnant stream. This stream divided large expanses of cultivated land, terrain that seemed most ill-suited to this species. I have frequently come across this snake near ruined buildings, piles of stony rubble overgrown with shrubbery, and beside country paths and roads.

Altitude   In Bulgaria it reaches an altitude of 1000 metres (Beškov and Beron, 1964). It does not appear to ascend higher than from 1400 to 1500 metres.

Co-habiting species   Other species that I have known to share its territory are the Pontic, wall, and green lizards, the three lined lizard (*Lacerta trilineata*), the Balkan skink, Aesculapian snake, Dahl's whip snake (*Coluber najadum dahlii*), the horned viper, as well as the Greek tortoise and the spur-thighed tortoise (*Testudo graeca*).

Behaviour

The Caspian whip snake is diurnal by nature, and spends much of the day basking in the sun, usually in the neighbourhood of thick bushes or piles of rocks into which it may retreat when disturbed. Having selected a suitably sunny spot, it will, in my experience, often bask there on successive days.

It is a very alert species, its eyes being quick to detect movements around it, and it is thus difficult to approach. It is an excellent climber. I have found a very young specimen sunning itself inside a cavity in a high, shady and almost vertical bank, devoid of vegetation. Normally I have found it basking on rocks and piles of brushwood. I have also discovered it in hiding underneath discarded wooden planks. It is extremely agile in its movements. When cornered it may savagely leap forward with great force, and can spring up to as high as a man's chest. In fact when springing up it has been said to alarm donkeys and horses sufficiently for them to panic and throw their riders.

During the second week of April 1964 in Macedonia I found one which shared its retreat with a specimen of *Coluber najadum dahlii*. I always found these two snakes basking near one another, and as I approached they would both shoot away. They appeared to co-habit quite harmoniously. Unfortunately I was never able to get close enough to identify their sexes. After having been disturbed, the Caspian whip snake often returns to the same spot to resume its basking, sometimes almost straight away, and sometimes, I have noticed, several hours later.

Food

Its diet consists of such mammals as mice and rats, birds up to the size of a blackbird, lizards and snakes. Some prefer mice to reptiles. Prey is seized and held in the jaws rather than in the coils. In my experience mice are often already dead before the swallowing process is under way. According to Vásárhelyi (1965) it can swallow up to six or eight mice in succession. It is thus of considerable use as a pest controller. Some snakes are eaten although grass snakes are usually rejected, and I have kept the two species living quite happily together. Dead food is normally accepted in captivity.

Enemies
Few details are known regarding its enemies. Predatory birds such as hawks are known to devour this species. Doubtless man ranks as its most significant foe, by reducing much of its natural habitat.

Reproduction
Mating takes place in May, and at the end of June or beginning of July the female lays from 5 to 15 eggs. Vásárhelyi (1965) states that they are deposited in moss, under leaves or in soil-covered rocky crevices. They measure some 50 millimetres in length. The incubation period is presumably similar to that of *Coluber viridiflavus*. In southern Yugoslavia I have found recently born specimens about in late August.

Hibernation
In the Russian Caucasus it emerges from its winter quarters in late March or early April. In 1964 I found several specimens about in southern Yugoslavia on 10 April, two days after a snow storm. In Hungary it is normally first seen in May.

General response
The speed with which it retreats and conceals itself makes it one of the most difficult of all European snakes to catch. It is very nervous, and flees into the undergrowth at the slightest disturbance. When caught it writhes wildly with great strength and energy. It tries to bite, and if successful, is inclined to cling on for some while, clasping its adversary firmly in its jaws. The teeth are able to draw blood, though they can do no real damage to man.

I have found it to be more adaptable to life in captivity than *Coluber viridiflavus*, and compared with other members of its genus it becomes relatively docile, though in my experience some individuals become markedly more tame than others. It is not however suited to captive life as it needs a great deal of living space in which to pursue its roaming activities. If kept, its living quarters should be made very secure, since this species has a muscular strength far greater than most European snakes.

When tame it does not usually mind being carefully handled. Due to its nervous disposition however it may quickly become alarmed when approached, even after some weeks in captivity, and it may still attempt to bite at first. I have found that prey is readily accepted, though I have not so far succeeded in persuading one to accept food from the hand. Some specimens may even dislike being watched while eating. One that I kept consistently ignored its prey in my presence, though this was invariably quickly devoured as soon as I was out of sight.

Distribution

Eastern central Europe   In contrast to *Coluber viridiflavus* this species has an east European range. In Hungary it is found mainly in isolated colonies in the hilly regions to the west of Budapest, where it is becoming rare. The demand for this species among pet dealers is thought to have contributed to its decline. In southern Hungary it has been found in the Mecsek and Villányi hills. Although there have been isolated reports from Bohemia, Moravia and Slovakia, its presence in Czechoslovakia has not yet been verified. Its occurrence in Poland is doubtful (Berger, Jaskowska and Młynarski, 1969), though in the past there have been unconfirmed reports from Olkusz and Maczek. In Romania it inhabits the southern Banat as well as the regions of Bucharest, Galaţi and the Dobruja.

South east Europe   In Yugoslavia it occurs especially in the eastern half, where according to Radovanović (1941) it is one of the commonest species of snakes. In eastern Slavonia it is known from Morović and Kupinovo, and it has been reported from the Fruška Gora. In Bosnia it extends as far west as Derventa, Banja Luka and the Ivan mountains near Sarajevo, while elsewhere it is found in Hercegovina, Montenegro, the island of Lastovo and more or less throughout Serbia and Macedonia. It occurs in Albania, while in Bulgaria it is encountered nearly everywhere in low-lying districts (Buresch and Zonkov, 1934). Its range also includes Greece, with Corfu and many of the Aegean islands, and European Turkey. According to Wettstein (1953) it is found only in the eastern parts of the Greek mainland, and is quite rare there.

Asia and Russia   In south-western Asia it extends from northern Asia Minor eastwards to the Caspian Sea. In Russia it is found principally in the southern steppe region, where, according to Schreiber (1912) it is the commonest snake. Here it ranges from Bessarabia to the lower reaches of the Ural river. In the Ukrainian and Russian steppelands it reaches about as far north as 48 to 49°, though its exact range is unknown. On the Crimean peninsula it occurs in the steppe districts, while in the Caucasus region it is found only in the coastal districts of the Black Sea (Terent' ev and Cernov, 1949).

Other races Two other races are known. *Coluber jugularis schmidti* **Nikolsky** occurs in eastern Turkey, Georgia, Armenia and southern Daghestan. It is absent from the Black Sea coastal region. *Coluber jugularis jugularis* **Linnaeus** occurs in southern Turkey, on Rhodes, Cyprus, Syria, Lebanon, Israel and Jordan. The exact ranges of the three races in Asiatic Turkey awaits fuller investigation.

Coluber jugularis asianus **Boettger**, associated with Iraq and Iran, is no longer regarded as an independent sub-species, but merely a form of *Coluber jugularis jugularis*, which has retained its juvenile pattern into adulthood (Wettstein, 1953).

If a recent reclassification of these snakes is accepted as valid, all three races will have to be regarded as independent species, the European form becoming simply *Coluber caspius*.

Nomenclature *in northern and central Europe*
English Caspian whip snake, Balkan whip snake
German Balkannatter, Pfeilnatter
Romanian Șarpele rău
Czech Užovka východní kaspická
Slovakian Užovka východná
Hungarian Haragos sikló
Russian Желтобрюхий Полоз

The Smooth Snake
Coronella austriaca
(formerly *Coronella laevis*)
Sub-species found in northern and central Europe:
Coronella austriaca austriaca **Laurenti** 1768
Terra typica: Vienna, Austria
Plates 32, 33

The smooth snake has a slender, moderately long body. The head does not stand out markedly from the body, but is distinctly larger in male specimens. The snout is fairly prominent, and somewhat depressed. The tail in the female is considerably shorter than in the male, being about a sixth of the total length, as compared with up to a quarter in males. The average length of both sexes is about 50 centimetres, though individual specimens have been known to attain a length of 75 centimetres. Two individuals measuring 83 centimetres have been recorded in Sweden (Andrén and Nilson, 1976), while a specimen from Russia measured 92 centimetres. The longest smooth snake from Britain mentioned by Smith (1969) measured 623 millimetres, but on 28 May 1966 I found a female specimen in western Hampshire with a length of 71 centimetres, and a small fragment was missing from the end of her tail. The longest continental specimen I have found was a male from Hungary which measured 80 centimetres.

Scalation
Dorsals: 19 (rarely 17 or 21) smooth, highly polished longitudinal rows at mid-body. *Ventrals*: 150–164 (males), 162–200 (females); divided (rarely single) *anal*. Paired *subcaudals*: 54–70 (males), 40–56 (females). Occasional *ventrals* can be paired, or *subcaudals* can be undivided. *Rostral* at least as deep as broad, making triangular indentation between *internasals* (rarely separating them). 9 large plates on top of head. *Nasal* often divided; 1 (rarely 2) *preoculars*; 2 *postoculars* (I have found an English male and a Hungarian male with only single *postoculars*); 2 (rarely 1) + 2 or 2 + 3 *temporals*; 7 (rarely 8) upper *labials* (3 and 4 or 4 and 5 bordering eye).

Colouration
General characteristics   The smooth snake has sometimes been mistaken for the adder, possibly because of the dark, somewhat heart-shaped marking on top of the head, the rear part of which bears a slight resemblance to the ∧-shaped marking at the back of the adder's head. It is from this marking that the generic name *Coronella* (meaning coronet) derives. The dorsal pattern however differs considerably from that of the adder. This consists of a row of small, rather indistinct dark spots, arranged in pairs on top of the back and extending longitudinally to the end of the tail. A careful examination shows this to be quite unlike the prominent unbroken zigzag stripe characteristic of the adder. In some specimens each pair of spots may be united towards the neck region, forming a series of cross-bars across the back. A fairly thick dark streak extends along the side of the head from the nostril until a short way beyond the neck. This streak is interrupted by the eye, and in some specimens in the neck region also.

Along each side of the body there is a very indistinct longitudinal row of dark spots. Easily overlooked are four parallel, rather shadowy, longitudinal bands, one occurring on either side of the back and one on each flank. It is upon these bands that the dorsal and lateral series of spots are situated. The apical pits on each of the body scales are punctuated by tiny dark dots.

The upper lip shields are whitish, greyish-white or light brown, and are sometimes speckled with darker tints. The tongue is dark red or reddish brown. The eye is yellowish, light orange or copper, with a round, black pupil.

In some individuals the dark marking on top of the head is further extended for a short way behind the neck by two short, parallel stripes. I have never found this characteristic in English specimens however, though it is present in most of the Iberian as well as the east European specimens I have seen. On rare occasions these stripes may join up with the first dorsal cross-bar to form a horseshoe shape, reminiscent of that of the southern smooth snake.

Sexual dimorphism   Examination of a large number of English specimens from western Hampshire led me to the opinion that there is a distinct difference in the colouration of the sexes (Street, 1967). On the upper parts the males are brown, reddish brown, silvery- or light grey, with dark brown or dark grey markings, while females are a darker grey with dark brown, black or deep bluish-black markings.

The underside of the male is a complex mélange of orange, greyish-purple and brown, and finely powdered white or pinkish flecks are present on either side of each belly plate. These flecks also occur, though less distinctly, on the underside of the tail. I have found Hungarian males with an almost uniformly orange belly. The throat region is normally orange or mustard, and is likewise flanked on either side by white flecks.

By contrast the female's belly is a vivid, uniform, shiny black, but with similar whitish flecks on either side of each belly plate. Towards the throat and on the chin, this whiteness predominates, though black flecks may also be present. Orange tints are sometimes found on the throat of some females.

Juvenile colouration   When born the sexes are identical in colour, being dark grey with very distinctive velvety black markings. The underside is a dark pinkish red. The distinctive sexual variation begins to emerge in the second year of life.

Effects of ecdysis   It is sometimes difficult to identify the sex of a smooth snake by its colouration alone prior to ecdysis. Both sexes are particularly beautiful after ecdysis, and often have a steely-blue sheen. When seen in sunlight the scales are highly iridescent in appearance.

Variations   A few smooth snakes have been found, mainly in Alpine districts, where the dorsal marking consisted of extended cross-bars which formed a ladder-like pattern. Some have been found with a dorsal row of large, dark

flecks, being similar to *Coronella girondica* in appearance. In exceptional cases
the spots of the body and sides may be further extended to form longitudinal
stripes. Specimens devoid of any markings are very rare, as are cases of
melanism and albinism.

Venom glands

This species is harmless to man, but none the less possesses a tiny venom gland
in the roof of the upper jaw. Experiments with the venom show it to have a
strong neurotoxic effect, similar to that of the cobras, and capable of causing
respiratory paralysis in various cold- and warm-blooded animals.

Habitat

The smooth snake is predominantly a native of central and southern Europe,
where it is a frequent inhabitant of dry, rocky and mountainous conditions.

Northern Europe   In southern England, as in Holland, much of northern
Germany and northern Poland, it becomes more localised and favours a sandy
soil. Here it is found in lightly wooded countryside, and more especially on
heathland. In the English localities familiar to me it favours dry south-facing
slopes, covered with thick heather, where scattered pine trees may also be
growing. In such areas I have often observed marshy heathland close by.
According to Dalton (1950), its range in Dorset is not confined to heathland,
there being two records of its occurrence from southern Purbeck.

   Much of its habitat in the coastal regions of western Sweden and the adjacent
parts of Norway is heathland, though the soil appears to be mainly rocky there.

Central and southern Europe   In the central and southern parts of Europe
however it is at home in a wide variety of conditions, inhabiting bushy slopes,
stony wastes, stone and sand quarries, rocky walls, dry woods, forest clearings
and borders, grasslands and moorlands. It has been found in meadows, beside
country paths, roadsides, and even in cultivated fields, as well as in the
neighbourhood of vineyards. In a locality of south-western Hungary I found it
quite frequently on a railway embankment. This species often avoids plains,
especially marshy lowlands, preferring dry or slightly damp conditions, but
frequently within easy reach of water. In Russia it is fairly rare in the flatter
steppe regions.

Altitude   It ascends to 1200 metres in Germany, 2000 metres in Switzerland
(Stemmler, 1971), and 2200 metres in Bulgaria (Beškov and Beron, 1964), and
it has occasionally been found on bare mountain sides.

Co-habiting species   In much of France, Switzerland and Italy it shares its habitat with the aspic viper, and is frequently mistaken for, and killed as such. In southern England its territory is sometimes shared by the five other species of British reptile. Its limited range there is similar to that of the sand lizard, while interestingly enough, in north-eastern Germany and Poland its occurrence was at least formerly associated with the green lizard, though the latter species now appears to be almost extinct in that part of the world. In Croatia I have found it in the same territory as the dice snake and the horned viper, while in Hungary I have observed it living near the grass snake, Balkan adder and the European pond tortoise.

Behaviour

Although diurnal, it is not a very conspicuous snake, as it basks in the sun relatively infrequently. Occasionally I have come across an isolated specimen sunning itself on a warm morning in early spring, while late in the afternoon during the summer months I have sometimes discovered pregnant females basking, and on 3 August 1960 I observed two lying side by side. In such cases sunny banks and clearings among shrubbery are favoured.

Far more often however I have found it hidden in some warm and shady retreat, such as amid a pile of rocks, under a flat stone or piece of rusty sheet-metal, and other suitable debris discarded by man. I have less often found it under pieces of wood. In suitable conditions it will remain hidden for hours, often in a somewhat elliptical-shaped coil. I once found one tightly coiled up inside the wet and soggy discarded inner tube from a car wheel. In areas where such rubbish is not available it rests under rough vegetation. On the Hungarian railway embankment referred to above, it was not unusual to find it basking in the morning sunshine under sparse vegetation, not coiled up, but lying with its body loosely extended.

I have frequently known it to return daily to a favourite hiding place, but also to desert one haunt in favour of another, usually in the same vicinity, though it is quite likely to return to the original haunt after several weeks or months or even after a year or more. Meanwhile during the period of absence, the original site may become the temporary residence of another smooth snake or possibly a succession of different individuals. It may also become inhabited by a grass snake or a slow worm. Some particularly good sites I have known have, in reasonable weather conditions, almost invariably yielded a smooth snake.

It is difficult to explain why a snake should leave one good haunt for a period, and then return sometimes after a month or more. I have rediscovered a marked specimen in hiding some five minutes' walking distance from where it was originally found. Perhaps such individuals go off in search of food and when their hunger is satisfied, settle down at the nearest suitable retreat. Yet the fact that a successor may arrive so soon afterwards suggests that food supplies cannot be scarce. There is also the possibility of territorial rivalry, and that the original snake may have been driven off by a more dominant rival. This possibility suggests a more or less complex hierarchical system.

Smooth snakes are not in my experience gregarious, for I have seldom seen them basking side by side, and never more than two together, mostly some distance apart. However on two occasions I have found a smooth snake and a grass snake lying still together, entangled peacefully in each other's coils. It is a reasonably good climber, though it does not ascend bushes in order to bask.

The smooth snake may be found on any bright and sunny day, provided it is not too hot. I have also met it in dull and cloudy weather, when it has been sufficiently warm. I have noticed too how the warm, very close weather preceding a thunderstorm frequently attracts it out. During a spell of very hot weather it may disappear completely. In the areas I know in Hampshire, adult females seem to be much rarer (or more discreet) than adult males.

Unlike most snakes, the smooth snake when discovered in its retreat frequently shows no sign of alarm, and if unmolested, may remain coiled up in the same position for a while, as though unaware of one's presence. I once waited for just over twenty minutes before a newly-discovered specimen casually crawled away: yet its slight reflex movements whenever I moved indicated that it was perfectly conscious of my being there. Normally however if discovered and left undisturbed, it will casually make its way into the nearby undergrowth, usually returning within several hours, though possibly not until the next day. Sometimes it may not return at all.

On many occasions I have picked up a completely wild specimen and handled it for a few minutes, before releasing it. Although such specimens on being released invariably glide hastily into the surrounding heather, I have on more than one occasion found the same snake the next day in retreat at exactly the same spot. One summer I found one particularly bold male coiled up under a piece of rusty metal. I picked it up and examined it for a few minutes. When I placed it once again on the ground, as expected, it rapidly disappeared into the undergrowth. Then I restored the metal to its original position. Prompted by impulse I lifted the metal again, less than thirty seconds later, and to my amazement I found the same snake coiled up peacefully underneath. I prodded it gently, and again it vanished into the heather. On lifting the metal yet again after only a few seconds, I discovered it one more, contentedly coiled up.

Smith (1969) refers to two specimens which settled in a garden in Hindhead, Surrey, and lived beside a small pond, into which they dived on being disturbed. They apparently hid themselves in the mud at the bottom of the pond. Smith himself did not witness any similar performances, nor have I. Dr.

Miklós Janisch however tells me that in a sandy district of central Hungary, during a period of hot weather, he has seen the smooth snake dive into a nearby pool on being disturbed. In England I have found them on occasions coiled up at the edge of a small pool of water. These particular specimens invariably retreated into the heather behind them when alarmed.

Food

Lizards form the favourite and predominant item of the smooth snake's diet. As already mentioned, in England and also in many other parts of northern Europe, it shares its habitat with the sand lizard, and small specimens of the latter together with common lizards of all sizes form the chief items of its diet. For many smooth snakes an adult sand lizard, though readily attacked, finally proves too much to cope with, and is eventually released, though often minus its tail. Smith (1969) states that no preference is shown for any of the three British species of lizard in captivity.

Although the slow worm is certainly devoured by some smooth snakes, I have never succeeded in persuading captive Hampshire specimens to eat them. Occasionally I observed some heroic efforts to devour them, but the majority of those I kept displayed absolutely no interest in the lizard, and I have even kept the two species living quite harmoniously together. But one specimen which I caught in the Sauerland in Germany however disgorged a large female slow worm, and in captivity accepted slow worms without hesitation. Among the reptiles, the smooth snake is regarded by Petzold (1971) as being the most significant enemy of the slow worm.

I should add that common lizards were readily available for my Hampshire specimens, and were seized without hesitation. They appeared to thrive on one, or sometimes two in succession, every week. In much of Europe wall lizards, small green lizards and doubtless all other lacertids of suitable size are taken. Rollinat (1934) states that voles are accepted, and shrews and field mice are also known to be eaten. Dr. Robert Stebbings informs me that many of those which he observed in eastern Dorset fed on nestling mammals. Young birds too are reported as having been devoured on rare occasions.

Some instances of cannibalism have been reported, and one continental specimen is on record as having eaten an Aesculapian snake as long as itself (Boulenger, 1913). On one occasion I carried a newly-caught smooth snake and a young adder together in the same container. As I happened to glance down I observed the smooth snake holding the adder in its jaws. Naturally enough this provoked the latter into striking at the smooth snake, whereupon it was immediately released. The performance had to be repeated however, before the smooth snake lost all interest in its companion. It did not seem to suffer from any after-effects, and thus appears, like the grass snake, to be immune to the adder's venom. In western Sweden the adder apparently does form part of its diet (Andrén and Nilson, 1976). At one time I kept a pair of newly hatched grass snakes together with a number of adult smooth snakes. The latter showed interest only in lizards, completely ignoring the young snakes.

Young smooth snakes eat young lizards, but are also said to eat earthworms, insects and spiders. Those that I have kept in captivity showed interest only in lizards however. I have seen young specimens attempt unsuccessfully, but with much perserverance, to eat a large adult common lizard.

Method of predation   The smooth snake advances stealthily toward its prey and when sufficiently close, pauses, then suddenly strikes forward with considerable speed. If the prey should escape, the snake makes nervous, agitated movements of the head, flickers its tongue probingly around and then follows in pursuit. Compared with most European snakes this species has considerable power of constriction. Any struggling prey is held firmly in its coils, the purpose being principally to restrain the victim's movements rather than to kill it, though this sometimes occurs. Prey is normally swallowed alive. The size of the mouth is comparatively small, and although the swallowing of a moderately large common lizard may be accomplished within ten or fifteen minutes, larger prey may, according to Smith, take up to five hours.

When firmly secured in the body coils, the prey is carefully manipulated so that it can be swallowed head first. The jaws normally seize the victim somewhere about mid-way along its body. A lacertid usually reacts by fastening its jaws for as long as possible onto the snake's neck region. Then, accompanied by much writhing of the coils, in an effort to restrain the lizard's struggles, the snake slowly works its jaws along the side of the victim towards its head, until the lizard has to release its grip, and eventually the head becomes conveniently situated inside the snake's mouth. The process of swallowing can then commence.

I once saw a smooth snake successfully eat a common lizard starting with the tail end. So securely was the lizard held in the snake's coils that it was unable to struggle and use its favourite device of voluntarily shedding its tail.

Evidence of the poor sight of this species is shown by one occasion when a captive specimen sprang towards a nearby common lizard, missed, and clasped its jaws around its own tail. After releasing its hold it struck once more, and again seized its own tail, this time even more vehemently. The lizard meanwhile had escaped.

According to Gadow (1901), food is hunted mainly in the late afternoon and evening.

Reproduction
Male rivalry and mating   Most continental writers state that mating occurs at

the end of April or beginning of May. In Sweden it is reported to mate in May. I have not yet been able to observe the spring-time mating in the wild. Sometimes however an autumn mating takes place, and this I have observed with captive English specimens. Prior to mating, rival males challenge one another with the head and fore-part of their body erect, then they seize their opponent in their jaws. A tussle then ensues, in which the two rivals become an entangled mass of coils. Eventually a victor emerges who is then able to commence courtship with his mate. During copulation the male frequently holds the female in his jaws, and the lower part of his body is entwined firmly around hers.

On 2 August 1957, I found a young adult female, that was not pregnant. I took her home and placed her in my terrarium, which contained several other smooth snakes. Sixteen days later I captured a large adult male at exactly the same spot, which I also placed in the terrarium. A few days later, the male followed the female everywhere she went. Whenever she coiled up to bask, he would settle beside her and likewise coil up. He invariably snapped viciously at the other males on sight, although these had shown no apparent interest in the female. On the morning of 25 August, at 10.15 a.m. I found the two mating. The male held the female in his jaws, and the lower parts of their bodies were entwined. I picked them up, to which they showed no objection. They remained almost static until 1 p.m. when they separated. For the rest of the day the male continued to follow the female, and would coil up to bask beside her. On the following morning at 9.15 a.m. I found them mating again, and they did not separate until 2.50 p.m., after which the male lost all interest in his mate.

Rollinat (1934) reports that some of his captive smooth snakes mated while still inside their hibernation quarters—on 17 and 18 March, and later on 28 March (1930). According to Andrén and Nilson (1976), this species reproduces every two or three years in the north of its range.

Birth of young The smooth snake is an ovo-viviparous species, and the young, varying in number from 2 to 15, are born in late August, September or, after a cool season, even October. The number of young depends on the size and age of the mother. Out of 50 litters the number of young recorded by Rollinat varied from 4 to 12, with the exception of a single litter of 13.

When born they are encased in a transparent membrane from which they free themselves after a few violent struggles. Some do not hatch straight away, however, the process being delayed for an hour or two. On one occasion I observed one impatient individual force its head out of its membrane while actually in the process of emerging from its mother. Six other specimens from this brood had all hatched within five hours, and a further specimen was still-born. At this stage the young measure between 12 and 20 centimetres. The poorly developed egg-tooth is shed within approximately 48 hours. A few cases of dicephalus (two-headed) smooth snakes have been reported (Boulenger, 1913). I have never known the female in captivity to take any interest in her newly-born young.

The skin is said to be shed for the first time some 10 or 12 days after birth. Of four specimens born in captivity on 21 September 1956, one shed its skin on 8 October, two on 12 October, and the other on 14 October. The young, according to Rollinat (1934), are born with a reserve supply of fat which assists them throughout the hibernation period, even helping them to grow a little.

Maturity   The male becomes mature at the age of three, the female a year later (Fretey, 1975).

Hibernation
Most central European observers report that the smooth snake hibernates from October to April. Angel (1946) states that in France it retires in September or October, reappearing at the end of March or beginning of April. In England I have found that by the beginning of October it is less frequently to be seen. A few courageous individuals may occasionally be found during the second or even third weeks of that month. In 1960 I found a young specimen as late as 17 October, while on 16 October, 1965, I came across two full-grown males. Two days later I saw them both again. On 19 October, I found a youngish adult male and a very young specimen, while on 21 October I discovered only the former. The following day was sunny but somewhat cooler, and despite thorough searching I found no more smooth snakes that year. In my experience it does not emerge generally until the middle of April, though I have encountered individual snakes before then, the earliest dates being 20 March, 1966 (surprisingly a young adult female) and 30 March, 1957 (an adult male).

Knight (1965), states that this species retreats into disused rodent holes, or buries itself in the sand beneath the roots of gorse or heather, or retires into clefts in sandy banks. This species appears to hibernate in groups, even in large numbers.

Ecdysis
The smooth snake, like other species of snakes, casts its skin several times a year. Rollinat (1934) mentions a male specimen of his which shed its skin four times between 15 May and 27 August. There is little trace of the head and dorsal markings on the cast skin.

General response
Because of its slow movements and its frequent habit of remaining coiled up

when found, it is normally a very easy snake to catch. However, it may be observed to move unexpectedly swiftly if followed through the undergrowth or seen in pursuit of its prey. Occasionally I have known a freshly caught smooth snake in England strike rapidly and fiercely, giving a surprisingly unpleasant bite. More usually however it struggles to and fro for a short while, and then appears to calm down. But shortly after it casually fastens its jaws around any convenient finger, administering quite a prolonged bite, which though hardly painful, may well draw blood. The teeth are small, and can do no harm.

Several observers have remarked that newly-caught specimens may sometimes release a smelly fluid from the vent, similar to that emitted by some other snakes, though much less pungent than that released by the grass snake. In my experience the odour seems to be stronger with female smooth snakes, who appear to be more prone to this habit. When angered or alarmed the smooth snake usually flattens and broadens its head, thereby presenting a more menacing appearance. Unlike many snakes it does not hiss wildly when caught, though I have sometimes heard a curiously isolated single hiss.

The smooth snake has a remarkably prehensile tail, and when suspended by it is able to entwine its way up around its own body, thereby reaching the hand that holds it. It has little difficulty in crawling along a horizontal wire.

Referring to Italian specimens, Bruno (1966) remarks on the resemblance of its fiery temperament to that of *Coluber viridiflavus*. Certainly I have known this species in Hungary to behave far more aggressively than English smooth snakes, striking repeatedly and hissing at the slightest provocation, and taking much longer to lose their wildness. The German specimens I have captured behaved more like English ones.

Taming   After capture and with careful handling, the smooth snake usually loses much of its wildness quite rapidly, even within an hour. Only very rarely have I known it to refuse all food in captivity, and one specimen accepted a common lizard within five minutes of being captured. It is usually quite responsive, becoming very tame, and it may soon learn to accept food offered to it from the hand. In fact it seems to enjoy being handled, winding its way contentedly around one's fingers, until it has found a comfortable position in which to bask in the sun. In hotter weather however I have known this species to become rather irritable, even snapping when an attempt is made to pick it up. One frosty morning in January 1956 I discovered a captive male specimen, which for some reason had become active, and had left its hibernation quarters. It was now exposed to the cold air. I picked it up at once to return it to a warmer place, whereupon it started to hiss repeatedly with a ferocity more typical of newly-caught grass snakes.

Some smooth snakes, although tame, may behave pugnaciously towards other captive smooth snakes, attacking them without any apparent provocation. It should be emphasized however that they are now protected in Britain, and it is illegal to keep them in captivity without a special licence. They are also protected in Sweden, Germany, Switzerland and Hungary. This species has been known to survive for eight years in captivity.

I have quite frequently rediscovered specimens formerly kept in captivity, after having released them at exactly the same spot where originally found. So far, after an initial, brief struggle, all recaptured smooth snakes quickly became docile, showing complete familiarity with being handled. One released snake I failed to find for a whole year, and then not again for a period of almost two years. At both times of recapture it made no attempt to bite, but casually and quite contentedly coiled itself around my fingers.

Revisiting the same spot I was able to observe this particular individual over a period of seven years, and am of the opinion that the smooth snake is content to spend its entire life within a comparatively small locality, except when presented with drastic ecological changes.

Distribution

England In England this species was first discovered as recently as June 1853, a specimen having been captured on Parley Heath, Dorset, by Mr. Frederick Bond. However, it was not recorded as a British species until 1859. In 1868 it was reportedly found in scores in the region where Bournemouth now stands, and large numbers were killed. Since then its numbers in that region, and in all other areas of England, have steadily diminished. Even since the Second World War, it has been severely reduced or exterminated in areas where it was formerly common, due mainly to the urbanisation and afforestation of its habitat. Heath fires too have made a significant contribution to its decline. Its extinction in this country would appear inevitable were it not for the fact that a few areas have been set aside as nature reserves. Its range in England is restricted to a few southern counties, and being almost exclusively confined to heathland is thus found in eastern Dorset; in and around the New Forest district of Hampshire and the adjacent south-eastern corner of Wiltshire; on the Hampshire–Surrey border between Farnham and Haslemere; and in north-western Sussex. It appears to be extinct now in Berkshire. There is a recent record of its occurrence in the south-west of the Isle of Wight (Taylor, 1963).

Northern Europe On the European continent however it is widely distributed. In Norway it is quite common in some localities, but its range is rather broken. It extends along the coastal region from Oslo to Stavanger, and inhabits the sunny valleys of the south-west as well as the eastern lowlands. Its northern limit is approximately 60° Lat. It has been recorded from about 170 localities in the southern part of Sweden, where it generally extends about as far north as Stockholm. In 1958 an isolated specimen was reported from Hudiksvall (Hälsingland) and there is a record from the early part of the century from Ångermanland (62° 35′) (Gislén and Kauri, 1959). It has apparently not been reported from western Scania, but occurs on the islands of Gotland and Öland. According to Dürigen (1897) it inhabits the islands of Mörkö and Tjörn in the Gothenburg region. Although absent from the Finnish mainland, it has been reported from the Ahvenanmaa islands. It does not appear to have been recorded from the Estonian islands of Saaremaa and Hiiumaa.

France and Benelux In France it inhabits most of the northern and central regions, and is common in many localities, but Fretey (1975) states that it is rare in certain western *départements* (Loire-Atlantique, Vendée and Gironde). It is also rare in the south, except in the *départements* of Hautes-Alpes and Basses-Alpes, and in the *départements* bordering the Mediterranean, where it is found mainly at higher altitudes, being generally replaced by the southern smooth snake elsewhere. In Belgium it is found in the Campine region, and in the provinces of Liège, Namur and Luxembourg. It is also an inhabitant of Luxembourg itself, and of parts of Holland, particularly the Veluwe region. According to Bund (1964) its range in Holland is similar to that of the grass snake.

Central Europe It is found almost everywhere in southern Germany, and is widely distributed in the hilly parts of central and northern Germany. According to Rühmekorf (1970) it is widespread on the heaths, sand dunes and dry moors of the north-west German Plain. In Brandenburg and Mecklenburg it becomes very localized, and it is absent from the Mecklenburg lake region. However, it is on record from the Baltic islands of Fehmarn, Rügen and Usedom. In Denmark it has been found in northern Jutland and southern Sealand, but according to Gislén and Kauri (1959) it has not been observed there since 1914. It occurs throughout Switzerland and Austria, whence its specific name derives.

Eastern Europe In Poland it is widespread, but is principally associated with the southern regions, though it becomes rare in mountainous districts. East of Poland it extends to a little north of the Duna river in Latvia, but it is absent from Estonia (Kauri, 1946). From European Russia it extends through the Ural mountains, where its northern limit is 58°, southwards to a small area in western Kazachstan, about as far east as the river Irgiz.

It is found in most of Czechoslovakia, according to Štěpánek (1949). In

Hungary it is mainly an inhabitant of hilly and forested regions of the west and north. It is seldom encountered on the Great Plain. In Romania it is a fairly widespread species.

Southern Europe   Elsewhere in Europe it occurs in the northern half of the Iberian peninsula, mainly at higher altitudes. According to Salvador (1974b) it extends from the Pyrenees, through the Basque and Cantabrian regions to Galicia, recurring in the Iberian and Central mountain ranges. In Italy it is widespread, being particularly common in parts of the Alps, but in Sicily it is very rare.

In the Pannonian region of Yugoslavia it is found near Deliblato, but is mostly absent from the flatter parts, being associated with such hilly regions as Vršac, and the Fruška Gora region in Syrmia. In the remainder of Yugoslavia, it occurs almost throughout, with the exception of a narrow belt along the Adriatic. Karaman (1939) mentions it from the island of Brač. Its range also includes Albania, Macedonia, Bulgaria—where it is quite widespread, European Turkey and northern Greece. Wettstein (1953) states that it is rare in the southern part of the Balkan peninsula, but confirms its presence on the Peloponnese (at Am Lawka) and on the island of Samothráki.

Outside Europe   Outside of Europe it is found in Asia Minor, north-western Iran and the Caucasus region, where it inhabits Georgia, Armenia and Azerbaydzhan.

Other sub-species   The sub-specific status of *Coronella austriaca fitzingeri* (**Bonaparte**) from southern Italy and Sicily, is now under dispute (Bruno, 1966).

Nomenclature *in northern and central Europe*
  Dutch   Gladde slang
  German   Glattnatter, Schlingnatter
  Danish   Glatsnog
  Norwegian   Slett-snok
  Swedish   Slät Snok, Hasselsnok
  French   Couleuvre lisse
  Italian   Colubro austriaco, Colubro liscio
  Romanian   Şarpe de alun
  Hungarian   Rézsikló
  Czech   Užovka hladká
  Slovakian   Zmijovec hladký
  Polish   Gniewosz plamisty
  Serbo-Croatian   Smukulja
  Russian   Медянка

The Southern Smooth Snake
Coronella girondica (**Daudin**) 1803

Terra typica: Bordeaux, France
Plates 34, 35a, b, c & d

This snake is a close relative of the smooth snake and is very similar in appearance. Its body is distinctly more slender, however; the head a little longer, and the snout less prominent, being more obtuse. The tail constitutes about a fifth of the total length in males, and a sixth in females. Fully grown adults normally reach a maximum length of about 60 centimetres, though some females have been known to attain 80 centimetres. Bruno (1966) refers to an exceptional female which measured 95 centimetres.

Scalation
Dorsals: 21 (rarely 19 or 23) smooth, shiny longitudinal rows at mid-body. *Ventrals*: 170–200; divided *anal*; paired *subcaudals*: 59–72 (males), 43–64 (females). *Rostral* broader than deep, just visible from above. 9 large plates on top of head. 1 (rarely 2) *preoculars*; 2 or 3 *postoculars*; 2 (or 3—especially in females) + 3 *temporals*; 8 upper *labials* (4 and 5 bordering eye).

Colouration
Adult colouration   According to Bruno (1966) there is no difference in the colouration of male and female specimens, a conclusion which agrees with my own observations.

The southern smooth snake is sometimes mistaken for a viper and consequently killed as such. I once even saw two specimens preserved in a bottle in a natural history museum in southern France; the bottle was labelled 'Vipère Péliade'.

Dorsal region   Above, the colour is brown, light greyish-brown, light grey, yellowish or reddish, often with a pinkish or salmon-coloured tinge, particularly on the sides towards the belly region. On top of the back is a longitudinal row of black or dark brown spots. In the fore-part of the body these spots are larger and usually form an irregular sequence of transverse and oblique cross-bars. In some specimens the spots may divide into pairs on the rear of the back and on the tail. Like the smooth snake this species has indistinct, dark longitudinal bands, two along the back and one on each side.

Similarly there are tiny dark dots situated on the dorsal scales just before the *apical* pits.

At the back of the head are two parallel dark streaks which are normally united by a cross-bar on top of the neck, thus forming a horseshoe-shaped marking. The upper part of this pattern sometimes dissolves imperceptibly into the dark shadowy markings on top of the head which are irregular in shape. In some specimens however I have found this pattern incomplete, two detached parallel streaks only being present, as in some smooth snakes. Beneath the eye there is usually, though not invariably, a dark spot, and a dark streak extends from behind the eye, sloping downwards along the side of the head and terminating a little beyond the side of the neck. A similar but somewhat arched dark streak extends over the *prefrontal* shields, and connects the eyes. The latter are somewhat projecting and have round, black pupils. The iris is yellow or lemon with black and red marblings. The lower part of the iris may in some cases be a darker shade than the upper part. The throat and chin are whitish, but tiny dark flecks are usually present on the fore-part of the latter. In some cases the chin is mainly blackish however. This species is particularly striking in appearance after having sloughed its skin. Even brown specimens display a beautiful silvery sheen on their backs when exposed to sunlight.

Ventral region It is perhaps by its underside that it is most readily distinguished from the previous species. It is usually yellow or orange, and on each ventral plate there are mostly one or two squarish blotches, either black or bluish-black. The belly thus bears some resemblance to the checkered pattern of the *Natrix* species. In some specimens however the dark blotches are arranged in pairs and may even interconnect so that two parallel, longitudinal stripes extend along the entire belly.

Juvenile colouration The young are similar to the adults, although the basic colour of the belly is coral red. The dark blotches are already present however.

Venom glands
Despite being a harmless snake this species also possesses a poison gland in the upper jaw. Bruno states that its venom is much less toxic than that of the smooth snake.

Habitat
The habitat is variable, but this snake seems to be restricted to very warm and dry regions, being absent from damper localities sometimes inhabited by the smooth snake. It occurs on sandy soil, being found for example on the

heathlands of south-western France, but it is particularly at home in stony, rocky and mountainous regions. It is a common inhabitant of the dry Mediterranean *garrigues* and *maquis*. It occurs on grassy or bushy slopes, at the edges of paths, fields and woods, as well as in vineyards, stone quarries, rubbish dumps and in ruined walls. Such quarters are frequently favoured by scorpions and large Mediterranean centipedes, and I once found one of the latter in refuge with this snake under the same stone. I have sometimes come across it right beside cultivated areas, and in the coastal region of eastern Spain I have observed it inhabiting rocky enclaves amid orange groves.

Altitude   According to Lanza (1968) it extends from sea-level up to 1500 metres in the Basses-Alpes. In Morocco it occurs in the Rif and Atlas mountains between 700 and 3200 metres (Saint-Girons, 1956). Much of its range in Spain is above an altitude of 700 metres. Like the smooth snake it sometimes inhabits completely barren mountain sides, at least in the south of its range.

Co-habiting species   In the south of France I have found it living in the same localities as the Montpellier snake (*Malpolon monspessulanus*), the ladder snake (*Elaphe scalaris*), as well as with wall, green and eyed lizards, and the Spanish sand racer (*Psammodromus hispanicus*). In one locality I know in northern Spain, it shares its habitat with the midwife toad (*Alytes obstetricans*), this being quite abundant. In some parts of its range it co-habits with the smooth snake (Boulenger, 1913; Bruno, 1966).

Behaviour
Though particularly sensitive to the cold, the southern smooth snake appears to dislike bright light and is therefore rarely to be seen basking in the sun. In fact it is seldom found about at all during the day. However it has often been seen to roam freely at twilight and has also been observed crawling about in moonlight. It leads a rather sedentary life, spending much of its time coiled up in hiding under stones, amid walls and in piles of rocks and wood. It has also been found under hedges and in deserted mole holes. On 7 October 1961, in southern France, however, I found a very young specimen basking in the midday sun at the edge of a small cavity some 7 centimetres deep in a sandy bank. The side of the bank was almost vertical, and the hole itself was about 1 metre from the ground, seemingly well out of reach for such a small snake, there being no nearby vegetation to assist it in climbing.

In its movements it is normally rather slow. Although I have often known it to remain coiled up when discovered in its retreat, I have sometimes seen it exhibit a surprising alertness by making off quite quickly into the undergrowth. It is a good swimmer, and Bruno (1966) reports having found it hidden in vegetation that had got caught up in streams of water. In my experience the young of this species are more frequently encountered than are those of the smooth snake.

Food
Its diet consists principally of lizards, the species preferred varying according to the locality. Lacertids of the genera *Psammodromus*, *Podarcis* and *Lacerta* are devoured as well as the two geckos *Tarentola mauritanica* and *Hemidactylus turcicus*, which so often share its range in coastal regions. Boulenger (1913) refers to one specimen which had devoured a fully grown skink *Chalcides chalcides*. Lizards are normally sought at dusk or during the night, when they have settled in their retreat and are not too difficult to catch. Prey when seized is held in the coils, in the manner associated with *Coronella austriaca* (page 174).

One individual which I captured in eastern Spain readily consumed the sand racers (*Psammodromus hispanicus*) which I had found in the same locality, but totally ignored the wall and common lizards which I offered it. When my supply of sand racers became exhausted it still refused the other lizards and maintained a fast for about a month. But from then onwards both wall and common lizards were seized without hesitation, no preference being shown. Angel (1946) states that this species has cannibalistic tendencies, although I once kept an adult with two very young specimens in the same cage for several months, who appeared to live quite happily together, all of them feeding on lizards.

Reproduction
Mating is generally stated to take place in May, and large numbers have apparently been seen congregating together at that time. In the past there has been a conflict of opinion as to whether this species is oviparous or ovo-viviparous and detailed data have been lacking (Street, 1973). Lataste (1876) relates how he found a freshly-killed female lying on the road between Cestas and Bordeaux on 26 June 1873. It was full of eggs, none of which appeared to contain embryos however. Boulenger (1913) concludes that as it would have been at least two months before the young would have been born, this evidence was insufficient to settle the matter either way. More recently Angel (1946) remarked that this question had still not been solved.

On the morning of 14 May 1972, I was searching for reptiles in a quarry on the outskirts of Burgos in northern Spain. I was not optimistic about finding anything, as it was cold, the sky was heavily clouded, and there were frequent outbreaks of drizzle. It had also been raining during the previous night, and the ground had become thoroughly wet. I turned over a few rocks and noticed that even the soil beneath them was very damp. Then to my surprise I found two southern smooth snakes, each in hiding under a rock, these being situated only a few metres apart. Both snakes were uncharacteristically cold and clammy, one even having a slug attached to its back. After identifying the snakes as male and female respectively, I decided to bring both specimens back to England, as I could not be certain that mating had already taken place. The female, which was slightly larger than the male, measured 49 centimetres. Despite constant observation I did not subsequently witness any mating and believe that this had taken place prior to the date of capture, and therefore not necessarily between the two snakes in my possession. A month later the female showed signs of being pregnant. Then at 11.15 on the morning of 23 July I discovered an egg amid the female's coils, and between this time and 15.04 on the following day six more appeared. These were laid at long intervals, the shortest of which was a duration of about two hours—between the laying of the third and fourth egg. The period between the first visible sign of an egg and the completion of the act of laying varied from 1 minute 15 seconds to 3 minutes. The shells were tough and leathery, opaque, and uniformly ivory in colour, with barely visible longitudinal striations. Their measurements were:

Length in millimetres		Diameter in millimetres
20	×	14
23	×	13.5
23	×	14
23	×	15
23.5	×	14
24	×	14
25	×	13

They did not adhere together when laid, presumably because the sticky secretion had dried up during the long intervals between laying. The female displayed no interest in her eggs, once laid. I placed the eggs on moist sawdust and covered them with damp moss, attending to them daily to ensure that the moss remained damp. I kept them at a fairly constant temperature of about 22°C. and for three and a half weeks they appeared to do well, even increasing in size. Soon after however they started to shrivel and did not respond to increased humidity. It became obvious that they had perished.

Statements claiming this species to be ovo-viviparous may have been made on the assumption that a species so closely related to *Coronella austriaca* would reproduce in a similar manner. It is however possible that it may be an ovo-viviparous species in some parts of its range.

Female southern smooth snakes are said to reach maturity at the end of their fourth year. I have no data concerning the males.

Hibernation

Few details are known about the winter quarters of this species. According to Schreiber (1912) it has been found in gardens, and it has also been discovered amid piles of manure and refuse heaps. Fretey (1975) states that it disappears early in autumn and emerges late in spring. The earliest and latest dates I have found it are: 14 April 1965 (north-eastern Spain) and 7 October 1961 (southern France).

Ecdysis

The southern smooth snake sloughs its skin quite frequently. The head and dorsal markings are retained as a brown imprint on the cast skins and stand out more clearly than those of the smooth snake.

General response

The statement that it is less inclined to bite than the smooth snake is certainly true of many specimens. However I have found this species to be rather nervous by disposition, and some that I have caught have bitten without hesitation and have continued to do so whenever picked up, even after several weeks in captivity. Most frequently in my experience it has been extremely docile, betraying no hint of aggressive behaviour. I have also known it to discharge its excrement when caught and even, like the smooth snake, to release a smelly fluid from the vent. Some that I picked up have disgorged a recently swallowed lacertid or gecko. So far I have only known lizards to be vomited. Such habits often persisted for weeks in captivity, despite the ironic fact that food was usually readily accepted. One individual even consumed a lizard it had disgorged over an hour earlier. I have known this species to eat on the very day of capture, and one freshly-caught specimen, on being placed inside a bag which contained a wall lizard, started to devour this almost immediately. As with the smooth snake I have sometimes heard this species emit an isolated single hiss when first picked up.

Although exposure to a bright and hot sun is generally avoided, my captive specimens showed a fondness for lying with their body partly in the sun and partly in the shade. In such circumstances they remained for hours, periodically readjusting their position very slightly. This species normally becomes very tame, but some individuals do not, in my opinion, always tame to quite the same extent as the smooth snake, tending to writhe about somewhat awkwardly and restlessly when held, rather than peacefully coiling up around one's fingers. On the whole however it does well in captivity, but being a more southerly species than its close ally, is more sensitive to the cold and thus requires a warmer atmosphere. In suitable conditions it has been known to survive as a captive for more than fifteen years.

Distribution

France   As its scientific name indicates this snake occurs in the Gironde *département* in south-western France, although its range appears to be quite fragmented there. Lataste stated (1876) that he had never found a single living specimen in that area. The northern limit of this species' range in France extends from the *département* of Charente-Maritime south of the Charente river to the Dauphiné district. According to Fretey (1975) it is rare in the Landes and sporadic in the Gironde and neighbouring *départements*. Cantuel (1949) does not mention it from the Massif central. It is fairly common in the Mediterranean *départements* however. It has been reported from the south of the île d'Oléron, and has been found on some small islands off the coast of Provence: Ratonneau, Pomègue, Riou and Porquerolles. It does not appear to be on record from the *département* of Charente.

Italy   In Italy it is found in Liguria, particularly in coastal regions, as well as in the southern part of the province of Trentino where it just passes 46°N. and attains the most northerly point of its entire range. (This area is usually referred to as the south Tirol.) Elsewhere in northern Italy it is known from only a few sporadic localities in Piedmont, Lombardy and near Verona. In peninsular Italy it has been reported mainly from the western regions and appears to become progressively rarer further east and south. It also occurs in a few localities in Sicily, where it is the rarest species of snake. Its presence on Sardinia requires confirmation. A detailed account of its Italian range is provided by Bruno (1966).

Iberian Peninsula   It is found in most parts of Spain, being absent only from the north-western provinces of La Coruña, Lugo, Asturias, Santander, and the Basque region (Salvador, 1974b); and in Portugal where it is common throughout (Lopes Vieira, 1897).

North west Africa   Finally it inhabits north-west Africa (Morocco, Algeria and Tunisia), north of the Sahara.

SUB-SPECIES   The form known as *Coronella girondica amaliae* (**Boettger**) from north Africa should probably not be regarded as a valid sub-species (Saint-Girons, 1956).

Nomenclature *in northern and central Europe*

   English   Southern smooth snake, Bordeaux snake
   German   Gironde-Natter, Girondische Glattnatter
   French   Couleuvre Bordelaise
   Italian   Colubro del Riccioli

The Meadow Viper
Vipera ursinii
Sub-species found in central Europe:
Vipera ursinii rakosiensis **Méhely** 1894
(formerly *Vipera ursinii ursinii*)
Terra typica: Rákos plain, Hungary
Plate 36

This species was first reported by Count Orsini at Gran Sasso in the Abruzzi mountains of Italy. Subsequently in 1835, it was first described by the Italian herpetologist Bonaparte. Years later some specimens were collected on the Rákos plain near Budapest, and these were sent to Werner in Vienna where they were described as being a form of *Vipera berus*. Later however Boulenger correctly identified them as belonging to *Vipera ursinii*.

The meadow viper has a short and moderately slender body. Its somewhat oval shaped head, which is a little narrower in male specimens, does not stand out distinctly from the neck, and is shorter than that of the adder. The snout is obtusely pointed, and the very small eyes have vertical pupils. Each of the eyes is normally smaller than the *nasal* shield. The tail is very short, consisting of about an eighth or ninth of the total length in males, and as little as an eleventh or a twelfth in females. The meadow viper normally attains a maximum length of 40 to 45 centimetres; specimens reaching or exceeding 55 centimetres being rare. Dr. Miklós Janisch of Budapest has informed me of one individual which measured 63 centimetres. The female is normally longer than the male.

Scalation
Dorsals: 19 (rarely 20 or 21) longitudinal rows at mid-body—strongly keeled on top of back, less so on sides; lowest row on each side is smooth. *Ventrals*: 120–136 (males), 125–142 (females); single *anal*; paired *subcaudals*: 30–37 (males), 20–28 (females). *Rostral* as deep or deeper than broad, visible from above. 1 (rarely 2) shields immediately behind *rostral*. Normally 5 large plates on top of head: long *frontal*; 2 *parietals* (rarely replaced by small shields); 2 long, narrow *supraoculars* (each normally separated from *frontal* by 1–3 small shields). Single *nasal* (I have found a central Hungarian specimen with a divided *nasal*); 6–10 (usually 8 or 9) small scales bordering eye below *supraocular*; smooth *temporals*; 6–9 (usually 7 or 8) upper *labials* (3 or 3 and 4 separated from eye by a single row of small scales).

Colouration

Sexual dimorphism   As in the adder there is a difference in colouration between the two sexes, though this is far less conspicuous. And in view of the close resemblance to the adder the points which distinguish the two species should be closely observed. The ground colour of the male is straw-yellow, yellowish brown, grey, greenish grey or olive green, while that of the female is darker, usually more brown. Many meadow vipers have a distinct greenish tinge. The ground colour on top of the back is markedly lighter than that on the sides. Along the top of the back is a continuous wavy band, usually black in males, and brown or reddish in females. This has a deep black narrow border on either side. The wavy band is not so sharply zigzag as in the adder. Along each side is a row of large spots, though a smaller longitudinal row of spots may also exist between the side spots and the wavy band.

At the back of the head is a ∧, X or even H-shaped marking, and a thick dark stripe extends from behind the eye as far as the side of the neck. Symmetrical dark patches are present on top of the head. The lip shields are either uniformly white or yellowish, or are speckled or bordered with brown or black. The chin and throat are pale white or yellowish white, occasionally spotted with black. The underside is yellow grey, grey white, slate-grey or black. This may be either uniform in colour, or spotted with whitish flecks—or if the belly is light, with dark dots. The ventral spots sometimes form quite regular longitudinal rows. The tip of the tail is similar to the belly in colour. In some specimens the dorsal wavy band is partially or completely broken up into a series of elliptical or rhomboidal patches.

Melanism   According to Méhely (1911), melanic forms are frequently found in the Balkan sub-species, *Vipera ursinii macrops*.

Habitat

This particular race of meadow viper is an inhabitant of wide, open plains and low, bushless hills. It avoids high altitudes completely. Kramer (1961) states that it occurs between 120 and 240 metres. In Romania however it has normally been found at an altitude of 300 metres. It inhabits flat, grassy meadows, especially dried-up marshy grasslands, on dry hillocks surrounded by water-logged countryside, and in ditches that have been drained. The Balkan form (*macrops*) on the other hand is not found below 1000 metres, except on the island of Krk, and in the Dinaric Alps ascends to 2100 metres (Werner, 1897). The Italian and French forms are also montane, the latter occurring between 1400 and 2700 metres (Fretey, 1975). Though principally a lowland form, *Vipera ursinii renardi* in southern Russia ascends almost to 3000 metres (Terent' ev and Cernov, 1949).

Co-habiting species   The areas known to me where *rakosiensis* occurs are also inhabited by the sand lizard, the slow worm and the grass snake. According to Boulenger (1913) this species never appears to be present in localities inhabited by the adder. This may be true regarding this lowland form. Apparently, however, in southern France, where this species is represented by *Vipera ursinii wettsteini*, the two species co-habit on Mont Ventoux (Vaucluse) (Angel, 1946). The Italian form *Vipera ursinii ursinii* similarly shares its territory with the aspic viper.

Behaviour

In its habits it is mainly diurnal, though it avoids the midday sun and is seldom seen about in hot weather. It may sometimes be found on dull, cloudy days, and has been observed to crawl about by night. For its retreat it chooses the deserted burrows of small mammals such as field mice and ground-squirrels. It is fond of basking, and likes to coil up on exposed patches of sand, or on top of mole-hills, provided there is sufficient cover nearby. I have noticed that, like the adder, it sometimes likes to flatten its back towards the sun, in order to expose itself to the maximum amount of warmth. It is quite an alert species, and is somewhat quicker in its movements than most other European vipers. When pursued it flees into nearby sandy holes or clumps of thick grass.

Food

According to Boulenger (1913) the meadow viper in Laxenburg feeds chiefly on sand lizards and small rodents. Its diet also includes crickets, grasshoppers, beetles and other insects, as well as shrews. These are normally hunted during the day. It has been stated that this species is less likely to use its poison apparatus with lizards, than with warm-blooded prey such as mice.

However on one occasion in central Hungary I observed the tail of a sand lizard slightly protruding out of a sandy hole in the ground. By carefully enlarging the entrance to the hole, I was able to slip my hand far enough inside to be able to grab the lizard by the rear part of the body. I pulled it right out and to my amazement found that its head and neck were engulfed inside the jaws of a meadow viper. The latter was easily caught since it refused to release the lizard until I had placed them both inside a cloth bag. The lizard later showed very obvious signs of having been poisoned. Within an hour the viper regained interest in the lizard, which was devoured with little resistance. Normally prey is swallowed as soon as it has been seized, the viper not waiting for the venom to take effect. The fangs are unlikely to be used on insects. According to Vásárhelyi (1965) in captivity it is not unusual for this species to devour its own young, if insufficient food is provided. Feeding largely on rodents and insects, it is of considerable benefit to agriculture. Méhely (1911) reports that specimens of the Balkan sub-species ignored all the mice and lizards offered. This form appears to feed exclusively on grasshoppers. One specimen was discovered with a large lump inside its stomach, which on investigation proved to be a mass of over a hundred grasshoppers. An examination of the excrement of French specimens also revealed orthoptera debris (Dreux and Saint-Girons, 1951).

Enemies
This snake is known to be preyed upon by such mammals as hedgehogs, weasels and martens. Other important enemies are birds, including great bustards and pheasants, and these are known particularly to take the young.

Reproduction
Mating in Hungary normally takes place in early April, if the weather is mild (Vásárhelyi, 1965). Austrian specimens also mate in April, according to Guglia and Festetics (1969). As with the adder, a ritual combat 'dance' may occur between rival males. The generic name *Vipera* is said to derive from the way in which almost all members of this genus bring forth fully-developed young. The meadow viper is in fact ovo-viviparous, and the young are normally born in July or early August. Young females produce from 2 to 10 offspring, while older females may produce as many as 18. Boulenger (1913) refers to an exceptional female from Lower Austria which was reported to have given birth to 22. The newly-born measure from 12 to 15 centimetres, and may reach a length of 20 centimetres before going into hibernation.

Hibernation
In Hungary at least the meadow viper emerges early from hibernation, sometimes while the snow is still thawing. In early April it is often to be found about in considerable numbers. It is reported to disappear in late October or early November. The montane forms however have a longer period of hibernation, those in France, for example, disappearing from the end of September to April or May (Fretey, 1975).

General response and effects of venom
By nature it appears somewhat excitable when first caught. It hisses and may repeatedly strike at its captor, yet it normally never bites unless seriously hurt. Méhely (1911) reported that some school children were seen innocently playing with wild specimens in the district of Angyalföld (now a built-up suburb of Budapest). I myself have handled it freely, and I have seen a Hungarian authority on this species casually put his hand into a dark bag and bring out a handful of writhing specimens. It is however advisable to wear

gloves as a precaution. Although it tames quickly in captivity and readily accepts food, it is said not to be a hardy captive, and it is difficult to bring it successfully through the winter months. Before long it loses much of its characteristic swiftness.

Owing to the pacific nature of this species, instances of snake bite are rare. There is however some conflict of opinion as to how serious its bite really is. Compared with other vipers, it uses its fangs, which are quite short, relatively seldom, being largely an insect eater. The venom therefore accumulates, and according to Mertens (1964) this species is at least potentially dangerous to man. This is confirmed by Dr. Miklós Janisch, who informed me of a case in Hungary of a six-year old child who died as a result of being bitten. Vásárhelyi (1965) remarks that its bite is serious if a vein is punctured. The venom is to a large extent neurotoxic in action. Despite its former abundance in Laxenburg, no accident appears to have been recorded there.

OTHER RACES With regard to *Vipera ursinii renardi*, Terent' ev and Cernov (1949) report that no fatal accidents have been recorded with certainty, despite its vast range in European and Asiatic Russia. According to Méhely (1911), an accident involving the Balkan form *macrops* resulted in no after-effects.

A contrast in temperament was displayed by the French specimens observed by Dreux and Saint-Girons (1951). They possessed an irritable disposition, and even in captivity hissed and struck, with the fangs erect. Fretey (1975) remarks that this snake may sometimes feign death.

Distribution

Austria This species was formerly very common in the Viennese basin, and was particularly abundant in the grounds of the Imperial castle at Laxenburg. At one time the intendant of the castle paid a premium for all vipers caught there, and in the course of one month (July 1892), many hundreds were killed. During the course of that year over a thousand specimens were brought to the intendant. Méhely (1911) still refers to it as being enormously abundant in that area. Since those times however its numbers have dramatically declined, partly because of agricultural development, and also on account of over-collection. According to Guglia and Festetics (1969), in Burgenland it has been caught in hundreds during the past. Today it is very rare in Austria, where it is now a protected species. It is confined to the provinces of Lower Austria and Burgenland, occurring to the south of the Danube, and east of the Vienna woods. In the former area, the limits of its range are Laxenburg, Fischamend and Bruck an der Leitha. In Burgenland it occurs between Weiden and Podersdorf in the region of Neusiedler Lake (Eiselt, 1961), but here it is now practically extinct.

Hungary It also occurs sporadically to the south of this lake within Hungary. Elsewhere in Hungary it is known from Lébény-puszta, the Hanság district (where it has become rare), and from a number of scattered localities situated in the lowland region between the rivers Danube and Tisza, the latter area being the principal centre of distribution for this particular race. Its Hungarian name *Parlagi vipera* means 'common viper'. However the opening up of virgin steppelands, and the development of heavy agricultural activity in recent years have steadily contributed to a decline in its numbers, and in some areas it is becoming extinct. Furthermore much of its territory is at present being used for military manoeuvres. I know of one locality where plunderers from western Europe have collected on a large scale, removing up to fifty in one visit! There is thus a danger that before long it may become rare in that country, though fortunately it has recently become protected there. It does not appear to the east of the river Tisza in Hungary.

Eastern limits of range It reappears isolatedly near Cluj in Romania but according to Fuhn (1969) this colony may now be extinct however. A single female specimen preserved in the Hungarian National Museum was collected in Slavonia. The exact locality does not appear to be known. More recently, however, Radovanović (1964) also mentions it from Slavonia. Finally, two specimens have been recorded from Kolarovgrad, a lowland region of northern Bulgaria.

Other races Five other races are sometimes recognized, although this classification is disputed by some authorities. In western Europe the range is curiously fragmented. *Vipera ursinii wettsteini* **Knoeppfler & Sochurek** is found at suitable altitudes in the *départements* of Vaucluse and Basses-Alpes in south-eastern France. Fretey (1975) also refers to two localities in the Alpes-Maritimes. It is now quite a rarity, and is a protected species. *Vipera ursinii ursinii* (**Bonaparte**) is an inhabitant of certain mountainous regions of Marche, Umbria and the Abruzzi in central Italy. *Vipera ursinii macrops* **Méhely** occurs in Yugoslavia—on the island of Krk near Istria, in Bosnia, Hercegovina, Dalmatia (near Vrlika, according to Karaman), Montenegro and Macedonia, as well as in northern Albania and western Bulgaria (near Sofia). Kramer (1961) regards these three forms as belonging to the same sub-species.

Vipera ursinii renardi (**Christoph**), sometimes regarded as a distinct species, is found in the Romanian Dobruja, from where it extends eastwards across the steppelands and forest-steppe regions of Bessarabia, the Ukraine as well as of European and central Asian Russia. It is also found on the steppes and foothills of the Crimean peninsula, though it is absent from the mountainous region. South of the Caucasus it extends into Georgia, Armenia, north-eastern Turkey and north-western Iran. In Asia it ranges over Kazachstan and the Uzbek and Kirghiz steppelands to western Dzungaria (north-western China) and the Mongolian Altai range. In Moldavia near Iași and Tomești, according to Fuhn (1969), there are populations of meadow vipers that are intermediate between *Vipera ursinii rakosiensis* and *Vipera ursinii renardi*. The final sub-species *Vipera ursinii anatolica* **Eiselt & Baran** has recently been described from Antalya province in south-west Turkey.

Nomenclature *in northern and central Europe*
  English   Meadow viper, Orsini's viper
  German   Wiesenotter, Spitzkopfotter
  French   Vipère d'Orsini
  Italian   Vipera dell' Orsini
  Romanian   Viperă de Fîneață
  Czech   Zmije stepní, Zmije rákošská
  Slovakian   Zmija menšia
  Hungarian   Parlagi vipera, Rákosi vipera
  Russian   Степная Гадюка

The Adder
Vipera berus
(formerly *Pelias berus*)

Sub-species found in northern and central Europe:
Vipera berus berus (**Linnaeus**) 1758
Terra typica restricta: Uppsala, Sweden

Vipera berus bosniensis **Boettger** 1889
Terra typica: Trebinje, Yugoslavia

Plates 37, 38, 39, see also colour plate

The adder has a comparatively short and thick-set body. The male however is both a little shorter and slimmer than the female. The moderately large head is fairly distinct from the neck. The sides of the head are flat and almost vertical. The eye is fairly large, but is often smaller in the female. It is about as large or a little smaller than the *nasal* shield. The short tail, which is approximately a sixth or seventh of the total length in males, and an eighth or ninth in females, terminates with a horny point. In *Vipera berus berus* a length of 60 centimetres is seldom exceeded by either sex. The female however has exceptionally been known to attain a length of 89 centimetres (Mertens, 1947a). The average fully grown adult measures about 55 centimetres. *Vipera berus bosniensis* generally attains a greater length, specimens longer than 70 centimetres often being met with.

Scalation

Vipera berus berus   Dorsals: 21 (rarely 19 or 23) longitudinal rows at mid-body—strongly keeled excepting smooth or weakly keeled lowest row on either side. *Ventrals*: 132–150 (males), 132–158 (females); single *anal*; paired *subcaudals*: 32–46 (males), 24–38 (females). *Rostral* hardly or not visible from above. 2 (rarely 1) little shields just behind *rostral*. Normally 5 large plates on top of head: *frontal* squarish or longer than broad; 2 *parietals*; (a tiny scale sometimes present between *frontal* and *parietals*); 2 long, narrow *supraoculars*—each usually separated from *frontal* by 1–4 small scales. Large *nasal* (containing nostril); 6–13 (usually 8–10) small scales bordering eye below *supraocular*; *temporals* smooth (rarely weakly keeled); 6–10 (usually 8 or 9) upper *labials*: 4 and 5 (rarely 3 and 4) separated from eye by single row of small scales; double row occasionally found in specimens throughout Alpine region (Sochurek, 1953). I have found 2 such specimens in N.E. Hampshire.

Vipera berus bosniensis   140–155 *ventrals*; 26–37 paired *subcaudals*. Plates on top of head, especially *parietals*, sometimes reduced, even fragmented; usually a double row of scales separating upper *labials* from eye; sometimes only single or partially doubled row; only 17 out 31 Hungarian specimens examined by Marián (1956) had a double row. Scalation otherwise as above.

Colouration

The characteristic pattern of the adder with its ʌ or X-shaped marking at the back of the head, and its dark, sharply zigzag dorsal pattern, which extends along the entire length of the body and tail, is well known. None the less a considerable degree of variation exists from one specimen to another.

Vipera berus berus   The sexes of the typical form *Vipera berus berus* are however usually distinguishable by colouration alone. The ground colour of the male is whitish, silvery-white, pale grey, yellowish and, in rare cases, even pale greenish. The markings are a vivid uniform black. During the mating season the contrast between the dark markings and the light background is particularly striking. Grey males with brown markings are also occasionally found. In the female the ground colour is yellowish, whitish brown, brown, reddish brown or coppery, with dark brown or dark red markings.

In both sexes there is a dark streak extending from behind the eye to a little way along the side of the neck, and this continues as a longitudinal row of roundish or oval spots along the flanks. These spots are usually parallel with the concavities of the dorsal zigzag. In both sexes the sides are darker than the top of the back. In many individuals, the ∧ or X marking on the neck dissolves into the dark colouration on top of the head. The upper labials are yellowish or whitish, with brown or black sutures. The chin and throat are white or yellowish, often tinged with black, brown, orange or reddish. In males, the scales in this region are often prominently spotted or edged with black. The belly is brownish with black spots, especially in females, or greyish, light blue, navy blue or black. It is speckled at the edges with white, ivory, pinkish white or yellow spots. The tip of the tail is usually bright yellow, dirty yellow, or pale orange below, often being a darker shade in males. The iris of the eye is normally coppery red, or reddish brown. The black pupil is vertical. The tongue is black, sometimes with a distinct reddish tinge.

JUVENILE COLOURATION   In pattern the young are similar to the adults. Their general colouration however is reddish or reddish brown, with dark reddish markings, and they are thus not unlike certain adult females.

Colour variations   In some adders the zigzag pattern is very indistinct or even absent, and may in rare instances be replaced by a continuous straight dorsal stripe. In other rare cases the zigzag pattern is partially or entirely fragmented into a longitudinal row of oval spots.

The most well-known variety is the 'black adder', sometimes referred to as var. *prester*. This is a melanic form, the black colouration being either partial or almost total. Some specimens, particularly in Britain, are a deep blue-black. In this form the ∧-marking behind the head and the zigzag pattern are often obscure or completely absent. Even in melanic specimens, a few whitish dots may however be present on the lip shields, and the underside of the tail may be tipped with yellow. The young are sometimes born black, but more usually acquire their melanic characteristics during the third or fourth year of life (Frommhold, 1969). Of rarer occurrence are specimens which are uniformly reddish brown (var. *chersea*). This variety is apparently confined to females. In addition there are a few cases of albinism on record, including one from south-eastern Devon (Hopkins, 1957).

Vipera berus bosniensis   Apart from differences in scalation, *Vipera berus bosniensis* is distinguished by its broad, slightly raised snout, and its zigzag band which tends to break up into cross-bars especially at the rear part of the body. In some specimens the zigzag is intact, while in the variety known as *pseudaspis*, associated with Slavonia, the dorsal pattern consists entirely of cross-bars. According to Sochurek (1953) the head is also stronger than in the typical form. Referring to Hungarian specimens, Fritzsche and Obst (1966), however, draw attention to the great variability of the head form, ranging from stumpy to long and narrow. There appears to be no difference in colouration between the two sexes. The ground colour is brown or brownish grey, there being less variability than in the principal sub-species. In addition its tail is relatively longer.

MELANISM Melanic or partially melanic forms are quite common in some areas. The melanic specimens I have seen in south-west Hungary were almost totally black, apart from having some white spots on the lip shields and on the throat region, and possessing a dirty yellow or orange blotch below the tip of the tail. Even the partially melanic specimens I saw had black flanks, and the top of the back was grey with a black zigzag pattern.

Habitat

The adder is at home in a wide variety of habitats. It is found on moors, sandy heaths, meadows, chalky downs, rocky hillsides, rough commons, on the borders of woods and copses, in sunny glades, forest clearings, bushy slopes and beside hedgerows. It can be found on the borders of fields, on verges beside country roads, in stone quarries, rubbish dumps and on coastal dunes. It does not avoid marshy, low lying areas provided there are sufficient dry banks. It also inhabits the banks of ponds, lakes and streams. According to Appleby (1971) it is, at least in Britain, seldom found in regions with a clay soil.

In much of southern Europe, as for example in southern France and northern Italy, it is found either on low marshy land, or at high altitudes. It ascends to about 3000 metres in the Swiss Alps. It avoids the open steppeland regions of Hungary and Russia—the areas favoured by the lowland forms of *Vipera ursinii*. In the latter country it is however present in the forest steppe zone.

Vipera berus bosniensis The Balkan sub-species *bosniensis* living in south-west Hungary prefers wooded country on sandy soil, often near marshy land, and ranges from 130 to 160 metres in altitude. This region, by Hungarian standards, is relatively damp and cool.

Black adders The black adder is chiefly an inhabitant of moorland and mountainous country, being common in the Alps. It has apparently been found up to 2000 metres.

Co-habiting species Its adaptation to a wide range of habitats enables it to coexist with many other reptiles which share its geographical range, and in Britain, for example, it can often be found in areas inhabited by the other five

indigenous species. In south-west Hungary I have found the Balkan adder
living in the same vicinity as the sand and green lizards, the slow worm, the
grass snake and the European pond tortoise.

Behaviour

The adder appears to be mainly diurnal in its habits, particularly in the north of
its range. Further south however it is reported to be active in the evening, and
also at night. There are occasional reports of its having been seen about at night
in Britain, especially during the summer months, and bonfires left burning at
night are reputed to attract it out. During the day it likes to spend much of its
time basking, though it avoids a strong sun. In springtime in England, it
emerges at about 10 a.m. but disappears before late afternoon. In Hungary I
have found the Balkan adder basking at 8.40 a.m. (C.E.T.) on 29 April (1975).

In summer the adder is most frequently encountered in the earlier part of the
morning and in the late afternoon, usually spending the middle part of the day
in retreat. At this time of the year, it may even lay out before sunrise. On very
hot days it may already disappear as early as 9 a.m. In the cooler parts of the day
the adder flattens its back towards the sun, in order to warm the maximum
surface area of its body. Favourite basking spots include sunny clearings in
dense vegetation, such as thick grass, brambles, bracken, heather or gorse, as
well as on top of large stones, logs and tree stumps. Windy conditions are
avoided, and it does not usually emerge until the air temperature reaches about
10°C. It may sometimes be seen coiled up in dull weather, and even during
rainy spells. For its retreat it frequently chooses the deserted burrows of
rodents.

The adder is not a climber, though it sometimes ascends low bushes and
banks in order to sun itself. In my experience it is less often found coiled up
amid man's discarded rubble than are the grass snake or smooth snake. I have
occasionally found it under piles of rocks, pieces of rusty metal and planks of
wood. It has also been found under piles of hay, as well as in the sheaves at
harvest time. Its movements are normally rather slow, except in times of
emergency. The adder will sometimes enter water of its own free will, being a
good swimmer. It swims on the surface of the water, and does not normally
appear to submerge, though it is on record as doing so in times of emergency.

Migration in Vipera berus berus   Recent research has cast some light on the
adder's migratory habits, revealing that in one colony two distinct areas were
inhabited during the course of the year. Mating often takes place in the same
well-sheltered dry banks where hibernation has occurred, following a period of
a few weeks spent basking. After mating both sexes disperse to water meadows
up to a distance of 2 kilometres or more away, where the summer months are

spent—an area where an abundant food supply must be available. In late summer the females return to the hibernation area, and it is here that the young are born. At the end of the active season, males and immature specimens also return to this area (Prestt, 1971).

Migration in Vipera berus bosniensis   A similar pattern of migration is reported by Fritzsche and Obst (1966) regarding *Vipera berus bosniensis* at Somogyszob in Hungary. This area consists largely of oak forests. According to local forest workers, these snakes inhabit the dry, higher slopes, and the borders of woods in spring-time, where hibernation is believed to have occurred. In summer they migrate to more low-lying areas, and in a dry season, they penetrate deep into the alder woods, while in wetter years they make for the drier poplar plantations that exist within the alder region.

Sense of direction   The adder has a well developed sense of direction, and specimens taken some distance from their home territory are eventually able to find their way back. Frommhold (1969) refers to several such experiments. In one case an adder returned from a distance of 80 metres in three days. Another found its way back twice within three days over a distance of 60 metres.

Basking   During the spring months male specimens are most frequently observed, while the majority of adders seen in late summer are females. As warm, sunny weather is vital to the development of the young, much time is spent in basking, and females often return each day to a suitable spot. Sometimes the entire day is spent basking.

Warning behaviour   When disturbed, the adder will sometimes reveal its presence by loud and often sustained hissing to warn off any potential aggressor. In my experience pregnant females are particularly prone to this habit. It is not, however, an aggressive snake, but is rather timid, and attempts to bite only when cornered or alarmed. Many accidents are caused through people or animals inadvertently treading on one. Normally any hint of danger will send it off into the undergrowth, where it will remain until all seems quiet. Then it will discreetly return to resume its basking, often in the same spot. If threatened, the fore-part of the body is drawn into an S-shape, in preparation for striking.

Food

The chief items of the adder's diet are small mammals such as mice (*Apodemus*), voles (*Arvicola*, *Clethrionomys* and *Microtus*) and shrews (*Sorex*, *Neomys* and *Crocidura*), as well as lizards, especially common lizards. Frommhold (1969) states that the adders on Lüneburg Heath usually feed on shrews. Slow worms are occasionally eaten, and there are records of weasels and moles having been taken. Captive specimens have been known to accept young hamsters. Some amphibia are devoured, among them frogs, notably the common frog (*Rana temporaria*), and newts. Salamanders have also been found in its stomach, though toads do not appear to form part of the diet. Birds, particularly nestlings, are sometimes eaten and even bird's eggs. Mr. Eric Hosking informs me that he once found an adder pilfering a woodlark's nest. Not only nests on the ground are plundered however—the adder will climb into shrubbery and bushes to seek them. In general their dietary preferences tend to vary according to the locality.

Prey is normally killed by venom. The adder approaches its victims slowly and stealthily, and when sufficiently close, the fore-part of its body forms an S-shape, and it then strikes extremely rapidly as soon as the prey makes a move. Often the prey is able to escape before succumbing to the effect of the venom. None the less the adder, either immediately or after a minute or two, sets off in search of its meal, carefully tracking down its scent with the aid of both tongue and nose. By the time the hunt is over, often several minutes later, the victim is either dead or unable to offer much resistance. A hungry adder, having tracked a female mammal to its nest may also devour an entire litter. Both lizards and small mammals are normally swallowed head first. Smith (1969) states that frogs and newts are often eaten alive. After hibernation the adults feed little until after the mating season. According to Prestt's observations (1971) in Dorset, adult males and non-breeding females feed for a period of three months—from June to August, while the breeding females, which had accumulated fat the previous year, eat little until after the birth of their young, and then feed to the beginning of hibernation.

The young feed on nestling mammals, small lizards—mainly common lizards, and small frogs. Their diet is often stated to include worms, spiders, and insects.

The adder drinks comparatively frequently.

Enemies

Predators of the adder include such mammals as hedgehogs, polecats, wild boars and pigs. Foxes and badgers may occasionally devour them. Certain predatory birds such as eagles and buzzards sometimes feed on them, as do owls, ravens, crows, jackdaws, magpies, jays, starlings, blackbirds, and, more rarely, storks, herons and cranes. They have also been found inside the stomachs of pike and eels (Smith, 1969), and Frommhold (1969) refers to a case of an edible frog (*Rana esculenta*) regurgitating a young specimen. Its most significant enemy is man.

Adder bite

In some parts of Europe it is sometimes difficult to establish whether accidents have been caused by this species or the aspic viper. Most cases involve a limb, the adder having been picked up by hand, or trodden upon. Children, elderly people, and persons in ill health are most seriously effected. However, recovery from bites may be quite rapid or take more than a year. Apart from man the most frequent victims of adder bite are dogs, cattle, sheep, goats and horses.

The fangs of this species measure about 4 millimetres in length. After repeated use the fangs do not always automatically return to the horizontal position straight away. This is eventually achieved with the aid of a yawn-like action. During the summer months each of the fangs functions for a period of about six weeks, and is then shed. New fangs are constantly growing and after fang loss it is replaced by the first of the reserve fangs situated just behind.

A common lizard, according to Smith (1969), dies in 30 seconds of being bitten. However on one occasion in captivity I observed a very young adder strike at a young adult sand lizard. This subsequently grew very lethargic and stiff, and died after about four hours, but was not devoured. The grass snake and smooth snake appear to be immune to the adder's venom. The hedgehog is often stated to be immune to its poison, but this has been shown experimentally to be erroneous. In normal circumstances the striking adder has little chance to penetrate the thicket of spines, the hedgehog's only protection.

Reproduction

In Britain, as in central Europe, the adder mates in April or May. Marián (1963) states that in northern Hungary mating occurs in the first and second weeks of May, while in Transdanubia it already takes place during the last week of April. The male, having shed its skin, sets out in search of a mate, being guided by a scent trail specially emitted by the female. Occasionally it may be necessary for it to travel hundreds of metres a day before it finds its partner. Sometimes the female does not readily respond to the male's advances, and she races off at high speed, with the male in close pursuit. Then they flow together side by side, almost streamlined, through the vegetation, until her reluctance wains. For a day or two he is content to bask beside her, often with his head on top of her.

Courtship behaviour During courtship the male constantly pursues the female, and continually flickers his tongue agitatedly along her back. The tail lashes excitedly to and fro. At no time does the male hold the female in his jaws.

If a rival male approaches it is immediately chased away, and then the two males frequently race in parallel motion for some while, in the same manner as the courting pair.

'DANCE OF THE ADDERS' Their rivalry reaches its climax in the spectacular 'dance of the adders'. In this act they confront each other with the head and the fore-part of their bodies held vertically upwards, and they make swaying movements with their bodies, and persistently try to push one another onto the ground, until one of them becomes exhausted and crawls off, to find some other female. Appleby (1971) interestingly records that he has never known the intruder to come off best in such contests, the victor having been so aroused by his frustrated courtship that he is determined not to lose his chance to mate. There is no record of any biting taking place during such performances. It seems likely that such combats will be less frequent however in areas with a relatively small proportion of males.

Prestt (1971), in his studies of the adder in southern Dorset, observed that the females there bred usually in alternate years, and notes that a biennial cycle has been reported from Sweden, Finland and Switzerland. Unlike the males, the Dorset females did not shed their skin until after mating.

Birth of young The fully developed young, numbering from 3 to 20, are born from August to late September or even October; in rare cases as early as July. In 1975 I found a female in north Hampshire on 12 July, which had already given birth. In Denmark adders are usually born during the first half of August (Smith, 1969). Following an unusually cold summer the young may overwinter, and are born the following spring. In the extreme north of its range the summer period is inadequate for the complete development of the embryos, and the gestation period accordingly requires two years.

The young are encased in a transparent sac from which they free themselves by continual writhing, and also by side to side movements of the head. The final puncture of the membrane is achieved by applying sustained pressure with the snout. In some cases the young may free themselves from the membrane while still inside their mother. The poorly-developed egg-tooth is shed a few weeks after birth. The young vary in size from 14 to 23 centimetres, usually about 17 centimetres. Already at this stage they are equipped with poisonous fangs, which they readily use whenever required. Shortly after birth, often on the first or second day, the skin is shed for the first time. The young are born with a reserve supply of yolk in their body.

Relationship between mother and offspring The female does not appear to take much interest in her offspring, and there is no evidence in support of the belief that she swallows her young in times of danger. None the less the young have been observed to remain beside the mother for several days after birth.

Late matings   Smith (1969) refers to a mating in Suffolk which took place as late as 19 June, and also to a male combat witnessed in Surrey in early October. Sometimes an autumn mating takes place. Whether such matings can result in the birth of young awaits confirmation.

Dicephaly   There are a few records of dicephalus young being born.

Growth   For the first five years of its life, the adder grows about 10 centimetres annually, thereafter growth proceeds at a much slower rate. Maturity appears to be reached by the male in the third or fourth year of life. According to Prestt's observations the female's first eggs grow rapidly during the third summer, that is, when the snake is about two years old. The first young are born during the following summer. The adder is believed to live for at least fifteen years, and some authorities believe it may surpass 25 years (Frommhold, 1969).

Hybrids   According to Boulenger (1913), in certain areas of France and Italy where the range of this species overlaps with that of the aspic viper, intermediate specimens are found which are probably hybrids. Apparent hybrids between this species and the horned viper are on record from Carinthia and Slovenia. In captivity a mating between a male *Vipera berus berus* from Spandau in Germany and a female *Vipera berus bosniensis* from Slavonia resulted in offspring (Mertens, 1950). A similar successful mating of these two sub-species with the sexes reversed is also on record (Frommhold, 1969). This author also witnessed male rivalry between a representative of each of these forms.

Abnormal behaviour   A remarkable observation was noted by Appleby (1971) in early June 1968, involving a captive male adder which, ignoring the female adders present, became interested in a female slow worm, and started to court her, eventually mounting her back as though she were a female adder. The slow worm showed no apparent alarm at this behaviour. After two unsuccessful attempts to mate with a female adder, the male returned to the slow worm to continue his courtship with her.

Hibernation

In western Europe the adder usually goes into hibernation in mid-October, though in favourable weather conditions it may still be encountered up to the end of that month. In Finland it disappears about 20 September on average (Viitanen, 1967). In eastern Europe it may similarly commence hibernation towards the end of September. For its winter quarters it chooses ready-made tunnels and crevices in thickly vegetated banks, and other elevated, sheltered and well-drained situations. The deserted burrows of mammals and cavities under roots and tree stumps are often chosen. According to Leighton (1901), it is frequently found under the roots of gorse.

Some adders hibernate singly, others in groups, which may number up to a score or more, exceptionally as many as 300 or, as reported by Viitanen, even 800 (at a Finnish locality at 63°N.). Their winter quarters may be anything up to 2 metres in depth. As recorded in Smith (1969) Volsøe, working in Denmark, noted that those that retreated under the roots of heather some 25 centimetres deep, usually hibernated singly, while those that disappeared into slopes and banks at depths of between 50 and 125 centimetres often assembled in groups which numbered up to 24. Not infrequently it may share its retreat with other snakes, and even with slow worms, common lizards and common toads (*Bufo bufo*). According to Viitanen, adders do not always return to the retreats used during the previous winter.

The adder has been seen about during the winter on sufficiently mild days. Even a thick layer of snow may not discourage it if it is sunny enough, though it will bask only in places where the snow has melted. It has no hesitation in crossing the snow in order to reach a suitable sun-trap. Volsøe discovered that in Denmark the decisive temperature was 8°C. When the temperature fell below that point it disappeared into hibernation, while it re-emerged in spring as soon as the temperature rose above this level. Prestt (1971) in southern Dorset records males spending about 150 days in hibernation and females 180.

It is one of the first reptiles to appear in spring, sometimes being found out towards the end of February. Most however awaken in March or April. Males are always the first to emerge, and they may appear from two to five weeks before the females and young. In an exceptionally cold spring emergence may be delayed until May. Shortly after hibernation the adder may often be seen in groups, and clusters, even of a dozen or more, may be found coiled up together. In the extreme north of its range (northern Scandinavia) owing to the short summer period, hibernation lasts for some eight or nine months (Smith, 1969). In his survey of Finnish adders, Viitanen estimated that some 15 per cent of the adults, and from 30 to 40 per cent of the young die during the hibernation period.

Ecdysis
According to Frommhold (1969), it sheds its skin frequently, about every four to six weeks. The first ecdysis normally takes place in April, the last usually in August.

General response
Once captured it does not persist in making frantic struggles, although it remains constantly on the alert, and sudden movements easily incite it to

strike. When cornered it often coils up tightly, keeping its eyes firmly fixed on the intruder, and always turning its head in accordance with the latter's movements. When striking it releases itself like a spring, thrusting about the front third of its body forward with extreme rapidity for a distance of some 15 to 20 or exceptionally 30 centimetres. The mouth is open, and the fangs are lowered ready to penetrate the flesh of the aggressor. At first any object placed before it will provoke it to strike, but it normally soon tires of striking at inanimate objects. Dr. Robert Stebbings however has informed me of a particularly aggressive adult specimen, which, within five minutes, struck 121 times at a cork, which was hanging from a piece of string.

It can normally be held safely in the hand by the tail, at arm's length, though it will writhe wildly, hiss, and strike with open mouth into the air. I have frequently picked them up by this method, and have never yet been bitten. It is however advisable to use thick gloves or tongs, as there have however been rare occasions when they have been known to climb up their own body, thereby reaching the hand of their captor. They are usually far less accomplished in this respect than are smooth snakes for example. Fritzsche and Obst (1966) remark that the Balkan sub-species is less temperamental than the principal form, and that it almost never hisses.

Once in captivity the adder settles down to a certain extent, losing some of its wildness. Food however is often ignored unless fairly natural conditions are provided. Those born in captivity however usually respond more readily to food. Those that do feed may even accept dead prey. Some may allow themselves to be carefully picked up without attempting to bite, provided abrupt movements are avoided.

The adder generally lives quite harmoniously with others of its kind, as well as with other species of snakes. It has been known to survive for up to five years in captivity.

Distribution

The adder is the world's most northerly distributed snake. It also has a wider geographical range than any other species of terrestrial snake, extending from the Atlantic coast of Portugal and Spain, across Europe and Asia, to the Pacific coast of Russia and the island of Sachalin. Northwards in Scandinavia and Finland it extends over the Arctic Circle, being the only species of snake to do so. In all, four sub-species are at present recognized, by far the most widespread of which is the typical form, *Vipera berus berus*.

Vipera berus berus

BRITAIN AND SCANDINAVIA   In Britain this is the commonest snake, occurring almost throughout the mainland. It is represented in all the Welsh counties (Lockley, 1970). It is absent from Ireland and the Isle of Man, but present on Anglesey and the Isle of Wight. In Scotland it extends to the extreme north, and its range includes the islands of Skye, Mull, Jura, Islay and Arran. It is well represented in Norway, and its northern limit in Sweden is Jukkasjärvi (approximately 68°N.). In western Russia it is generally found up to about 65°N., sloping down to 60° in the Ural region. It also occurs isolatedly in the south of the Kola peninsula.

FRANCE AND BENELUX   In France it is mainly found to the north of the river Loire, the *départements* of Yonne, Côte-d'Or and Jura forming its south-eastern limit. It is also found in the Massif central, Mont Ventoux (Vaucluse) and the Alpine region (Angel, 1946). It appears to be absent from Alsace and most of Lorraine. In Belgium it inhabits the Campine district of Anvers, Limburg, Flanders, Namur and the Ardennes region. Apparently only one specimen appears to have been found in Luxembourg. This was recorded from Remich in about 1850 (Ferrant, 1922). In Holland it occurs in many localities of the diluvial region (Bund, 1964).

GERMANY AND DENMARK   The adder ranges over much of Western Germany, but is absent from the Rhine-Main district, Hessen, the Odenwald region, Lower Franconia (except for the Rhön area), northern Baden and Württemberg. It is widely distributed in Eastern Germany, though it is lacking from a few areas in the south-east. In this country it is protected by law (Frommhold, 1969). Of the Baltic Sea islands it is known from Fehmarn, Darss, Zingst, Rügen and Usedom. It is common in parts of Denmark, particularly in western Jutland, and also occurs locally on all the larger islands, but is absent from most of the smaller ones. In the Baltic Sea it is found on the islands of Bornholm, Öland, Gotland, Gotska Sandön, Saaremaa, Hiiumaa and Ahvenanmaa.

POLAND, ESTONIA AND CZECHOSLOVAKIA   It is well represented in Poland where its range includes the mountains and foothills of the southern regions. It inhabits the three Baltic states, and Kauri (1946) reports that it is common on the mainland of Estonia. In Czechoslovakia it is found throughout (Štěpánek, 1949).

SWITZERLAND AND ITALY   In Switzerland where it is a protected species it occurs in the north, though it has become extinct in many places. It also lives, like *Vipera aspis*, in the mountains of the south, but it is absent from the Jura district. In Italy it is known only from the northern regions, occurring in parts of Piedmont, Lombardy, Trentino-Alto-Adige, Venetia and in neighbouring parts of Emilia as far as Ferrara. The river Isonzo forms the limit of its range in this region, while further east it is replaced by *Vipera berus bosniensis*. There are no records of adders living on Corsica, Sardinia, Sicily or the Balearic islands.

AUSTRIA AND HUNGARY   From Austria Eiselt (1961) mentions it from the provinces of Vorarlberg, the north and eastern Tirol, Salzburg, Upper Austria, Lower Austria (with the exception of the Vienna woods and the Viennese basin), Styria (with the exception of the Graz basin) and Carinthia. It is not widely represented in Hungary, being known principally from a few smallish and isolated areas. These lie in the north-eastern corner of the country: in the vicinity of Tokaj, in the Zemplén mountain region, and in the Tisza district near the border with the Soviet Union. It is not known from the Great Plain. *Vipera berus berus* is widespread in Romania, though it is absent from the south and the Dobruja (Fuhn and Vancea, 1961).

YUGOSLAVIA AND BULGARIA   It also occurs in parts of Yugoslavia: in Syrmia in the region of Fruška Gora, as well as in the Danube region (Radovanović, 1964), and at higher altitudes in Slovenia, Croatia, Bosnia, Hercegovina, Serbia and in Macedonia where it appears to be quite isolated. In Bulgaria it occurs in the north, including the Balkan mountains.

EASTERN LIMIT OF RANGE   *Vipera berus berus* is well represented in the temperate parts of European and Asiatic Russia where it extends across northern Kazachstan and southern Siberia. In the Amur district and north-eastern China, however, *Vipera berus sachalinensis* **Čerevsky** occurs. This is the form which is also found on the island of Sachalin.

Vipera berus bosniensis   Of great interest is the recent discovery that specimens found in the district of Somogyszob in south-west Hungary are referable to the Balkan sub-species *Vipera berus bosniensis* (Fritzsche and Obst, 1966). The adders from this and adjoining areas in County Somogy have more or less strong melanistic tendencies, a feature which appears to have caused this form's true identity to be overlooked in the past. Such adders are also known from Ormándpuszta in neighbouring County Zala. At present these areas appear to be the most northerly point of this sub-species' range. It apparently does not occur in Austria or Romania. Much of Yugoslavia—Slovenia, extending north-westwards to Snežnik and Pivka (Schwarz, 1936), Croatia (including the Sava district and Slavonia), Bosnia, Hercegovina and Serbia (Kopaonik), as well as northern Albania and the Pirin and southern Rila range in Bulgaria (Beškov and Beron, 1964) is the home of this sub-species. (It is worth adding however that some authorities regard *bosniensis* as a form entirely confined to the Bosnian mountains, maintaining that those from northern Yugoslavia and south-west Hungary should be regarded as a separate race.)

This species is absent from Istria and Dalmatia. There is an isolated report of its occurrence by Sabanca (near Izmit) in Asia Minor (Bodenheimer, 1944).

Iberian sub-species   The remaining sub-species is *Vipera berus seoani* **Lataste**, which occurs isolatedly in northern Portugal and in north-western Spain (Asturias and Galicia).

Nomenclature *in northern and central Europe*

English   Adder, Viper, Common viper, Northern viper
Dutch   Adder
German   Kreuzotter
Danish   Hugorm
Norwegian   Huggorm
Swedish   Vanlig Huggorm
French   Péliade
Italian   Marasso palustre
Romanian   Viperă
Hungarian   Keresztes viperă
Finnish   Kyykäärme
Czech   Zmije obecná
Slovakian   Zmija obyčajná
Polish   Żmija zygzakowata
Serbo-Croatian   Bosanski šargan (*Vipera berus bosniensis*)
Russian   Обыкновенная Гадюка

The Aspic Viper
Vipera aspis

Sub-species found in western Europe:

Vipera aspis aspis (**Linnaeus**) 1758
Terra typica restricta: Poitou, France

Vipera aspis atra **Meisner** 1820
Terra typica: Kandersteg, Switzerland

Vipera aspis francisciredi (**Laurenti**) 1768
Terra Typica: Italy
Plates 40, 41, see also colour plate

Like that of the adder, the body of this species is rather thick-set. It has a broad triangular-shaped head, well distinguished from the neck, and the tip of the snout is slightly upturned. The head of *Vipera aspis francisciredi* becomes markedly swollen behind the eyes. In addition the upper lips are distinctly visible from above in the adults of this form—not however in the other two sub-species. The tail is very short, varying from about a seventh to a ninth of the total length in females, and from a sixth to an eighth in males. In this species it is the males which attain the greater length, though they are somewhat slimmer than the females. The former have been known to reach 85 centimetres, but are rare over 75 centimetres.

Scalation

Dorsals: 21 or 23 (rarely 19 or 25) longitudinal rows at mid-body—strongly keeled excepting lowest row on each side which is more or less distinctly keeled, rarely smooth. 134–170 *ventrals* (*V. aspis aspis* has less than, and *V. aspis atra* more than 150 on average); single *anal*; paired *subcaudals*: 32–49 (males), 30–43 (females); terminal tail shield sometimes quite blunt (compared with the adder's). *Rostral* broader than deep. 2 large *supraoculars*, otherwise normally only numerous small, irregular plates on top of head—smooth or weakly keeled. Small *frontal* or even *parietals* occasionally present. (Of 9 offspring born to a female *francisciredi* which had no trace of *frontal* or *parietal* shields, all possessed a *frontal* and 7 also had distinct parietals.) Large single (sometimes divided) *nasal* containing nostril; 8–13 (usually 10–12) small scales bordering eye below *supraocular*; smooth or weakly keeled *temporals*; 9–13 (usually 9–11) upper *labials*: 4 and 5 (rarely 4–6 or 5 and 6) separated from eye by 2 (rarely 3) rows of small scales; sometimes a single scale between *labial* 4 and eye.

Colouration

The colour of this snake is even more variable than that of the adder, and sexual variation, so marked in the latter species, is considerably less apparent.

Dorsal region The ground colour varies from light grey or grey-brown to reddish brown or brick-red. Some specimens may be coppery red, orange or straw-yellow. Though females are often darker than the males, red, brown or copper coloured individuals can be of either sex. Some specimens exhibit a noticeable greenish tinge.

The dorsal pattern consists of a row of dark brown or black narrow cross-bars or squarish blotches extending along the entire length of the body and tail. Some of the cross-bars may be irregular in shape, or even broken into two halves, one of which may be situated diagonally above the other. Occasionally the dorsal bars are connected by a thin, dark longitudinal line, but only rarely is a zigzag pattern, like that of the adder formed. The cross-bars of *Vipera aspis atra* are considerably thicker than those of the other sub-species, and when they are linked, the resultant zigzag line can be reminiscent of that of the horned viper. Some *francisciredi* specimens can resemble the barred grass snake in pattern. A row of vertical cross-bars is usually present on the sides.

These normally alternate in position with the dorsal markings. Sometimes the cross-bars of *atra* may extend from the back well on to the flanks.

Head   Some aspic vipers are devoid of markings on top of the head, but usually, towards the neck region, there are two fairly thick, dark, oblique streaks forming a ʌ-shape, behind which is often a dark triangular patch. This patch is sometimes connected to the first dorsal cross-bar. Along the side of the head is a thick blackish stripe, extending from behind the eye to a little beyond the neck. The upper lip shields are whitish, cream, yellowish or pinkish, often with thin dark bars in the sutures. The eyes are small and are usually golden or coppery red, with a vertical black pupil.

Ventral region   The belly is very variable. It can be whitish, dirty yellow, light or dark grey, steely-blue or blackish, and is often, though not invariably, stippled with whitish or reddish dots. Sometimes it is pale reddish with brown dots. The belly plates may also have a white or cream-coloured fleck on each side. When present in *Vipera aspis aspis* these are small. Those of *Vipera aspis francisciredi* are almost as large as the black flecks along the flanks. The throat is often lighter than the rest of the underside, being yellowish-white or pale reddish, either uniform or spotted with black. In some males it is entirely black. On the underside the tip of the tail is bright yellow, orange or reddish, or at least is brightly spotted.

Juvenile colouration   In colour the young are similar to the adults, though less vividly marked, and some specimens have a white belly speckled with greyish dots.

Melanism   Cases of melanism are rare in *Vipera aspis aspis*, and such specimens are apparently always female. Melanic forms of *Vipera aspis atra* are of common occurrence in some Alpine regions. Those that I have found have been uniformly black both above and below, and bore no trace of the usual markings.

Habitat
The aspic viper is an inhabitant of warm and dry areas which are well exposed to the sun. Though it may sometimes be found in plains, at least in France and Italy, it is particularly associated with hilly and low mountainous districts, especially in limestone regions. Here it may be found on sunny slopes, in glades, on scrublands, in mountain meadows, forest clearings, at the borders of woods, in rubbish dumps and stone quarries. I have found one basking on a roadside verge, totally surrounded by intensive agriculture. It is also found in chalky and sandstone areas.

Altitude   The aspic viper reaches an altitude of about 3000 metres in the Alps.

Co-habiting species   Stemmler (1971) remarks that its habitat in Switzerland is similar to that of the wall lizard, while in the Geneva region it co-habits with the viperine snake. In the Swiss Alps I have found *atra* living in the same areas as the common lizard and the smooth snake, while in Italy I have observed *francisciredi* in areas also inhabited by the wall and ruin lizards, the Moorish gecko (*Tarentola mauritanica*) and the black and dark green whip snakes.

Behaviour
Like the adder, the aspic viper is fond of basking in the sun. It is sensitive to the cold as well as to intense heat, and is most often found in the earlier part of the morning or late in the afternoon. It is unable to flatten its back while basking, unlike the adder. It appears to be predominantly diurnal, but often becomes active at night during the summer months, particularly in warm, close weather. The sultry atmosphere that sometimes precedes a thunderstorm often tempts it out of its hiding place. It likes to bask upon tree stumps, or beside, or on top of, rocks, but it sometimes retires under thick vegetation, under hay or piles of cut grass—a habit which has occasionally led to accidents involving unsuspecting farm workers. The aspic viper is sometimes found living in pairs, even after springtime. When an individual has been found, a close scrutiny of the surrounding area may result in its partner being discovered. The range of its territory is quite small, and the same specimens can often be seen in the same vicinity on subsequent occasions.

In its movements it is quite sluggish, except when in pursuit of its prey or in times of danger; in my experience however it is often more alert than the horned viper. Though it will not go out of its way to attack man, it will bite if trodden upon. When threatened it inflates the body and hisses loudly.

Food
Its diet consists principally of lizards, voles and mice (e.g. *Arvicola*, *Microtus*, *Apodemys*, *Micromys*, and *Mus*) as well as shrews and moles. Lanceau and Lanceau (1974) state that the young eat mainly wall lizards. Nestling birds have been known to be taken, but amphibia and fish do not appear to form part of the diet. The very young are said to eat insects and worms. Prey is killed by the effect of the venom, seldom being swallowed alive.

Enemies
Its enemies, apart from man, are known to include hedgehogs, cats, dogs, pigs, poultry and birds of prey.

Reproduction

Mating takes place from mid-March to May, and is preceded by rivalry among the males. Breeding is an annual event given ideal conditions, but in western France there is a biennial cycle. An autumn mating may occasionally take place at least in lowland regions, in which case the young are born the following spring. Prior to copulation the male persistently follows his selected mate, and is able to detect the female's trail because of a secretion emitted by her anal glands. During the act of copulation, which according to Fretey (1975) lasts for one or two hours and is repeated five or six times, the two sexes are entwined in each other's coils. No biting takes place, however. Fretey states that they appear monogamous during the mating period. Pregnant females spend much time basking. I once found a rather cold and clammy specimen on 29 August (1975) coiled up in the shade at 8.45 a.m. (C.E.T.). The sun did not reach this basking site until some 45 minutes later.

The young are born fully-developed in August or September. The membrane in which they emerge is very thin, and is broken by head pressure. They number from 4 to 18, the usual maximum being ten. They then measure, according to various reports, anything from 14 to 24 centimetres. The skin is shed shortly after birth. Of nine specimens born in captivity on 8 September 1975, four shed their skins during the same day.

At first growth is rapid, and the length increases by some 7 or 8 centimetres annually. After maturity the growth rate is reduced to about 2 centimetres per year. Maturity is reached in the third year for males, and fourth for females.

A few cases of dicephaly are on record.

HYBRIDS Mertens (1964) refers to a male *Vipera aspis zinnikeri* from Andorra which mated with a female *Vipera ammodytes ammodytes*, who later produced offspring.

Hibernation

This species disappears at the end of October or in the first half of November. It sometimes retires singly, but quite often communally in underground cavities, in crevices at the bottom of tree trunks and in old walls. In France at least, the males retire earlier than the females. If the temperature is suitably warm, it may emerge as early as February, otherwise it does not appear until the end of March or April. According to Fretey (1975), it can sometimes be found sunning itself on warm stones during mild weather in December and January, frequently in mid-February.

General response

Though not an aggressive snake by nature, it becomes excitable when seized, and does not hesitate to try to bite. It never really tames well in captivity, and food is often refused. For these reasons it is not really suited to captive life.

Aspic viper bite The bites from this species can be more severe than those of the adder, and are very painful. According to Stemmler (1971) an estimated 4 per cent of all untreated accidents involving man prove fatal. He states that the population living in the Passwang district in Switzerland has the strongest venom found in this species. The aspic viper is responsible for about 90 per cent of snake bite accidents in Italy (Lombardi and Bianco, 1974). Statistics provided by the Herpetological Institute of Verona for the period from 1960–70 show that in the province of Tuscany there were 526 cases of viper bite, and 7 cases which were fatal.

The venom of the sub-species *zinnikeri* is more neurotoxic than that of other aspic vipers. The two fang marks, which result from a bite of this species, are situated about 7 millimetres apart.

Distribution
Vipera aspis aspis The aspic viper is confined to Europe. *Vipera aspis aspis* is found throughout most of France, but is rare in, or totally absent from, the *départements* bordering the English Channel, and Fretey (1975) regards its occurrence in Normandy as improbable. In eastern France it extends about as far north as the *département* of Meurthe-et-Moselle. Its range along the Atlantic coast includes the islands of Ré and Oléron, but it does not occur along the coastal region to the south of the Gironde estuary. Like the adder, whose range it shares in no fewer than seventeen French *départements* according to Fretey, it is absent to the east of the River Moselle. It is also absent from most of the Mediterranean region, though present near Montpellier and in the Alpes-Maritimes, while in Gascony, Andorra and in a nearby Spanish locality it is replaced by another sub-species, *Vipera aspis zinnikeri* **Kramer**.

Vipera aspis aspis however recurs in a number of localities in the Pyrenees, especially in Spain, and it is also known to the south-west of Bilbao. In Germany it is associated with one area only: between Waldshut and Thiengen in the southern part of the Black Forest, near the Swiss border. Since the Second World War however, it is believed to have become extinct there. In western Switzerland it inhabits the region of Basle, western Aargau and the Jura district, where it is common. Finally it occurs in north-west Italy.

Vipera aspis atra This race is mainly a Swiss form and is found in the region of Fribourg, the Bernese Oberland and the Alpine regions of Valais, Tessin (north of Monte Ceneri) and Graubünden, as well as in Piedmont in Italy. It apparently recurs around Lagonegro in the south-west of the peninsula (Kramer, 1970).

Vipera aspis francisciredi This sub-species also occurs in Tessin, to the south of Monte Ceneri, and this is the sub-species which inhabits most of Italy, being the commonest and most widely distributed poisonous snake there. It is however absent to the west of Lake Maggiore as well as from Basilicata and Calabria. In Trentino-Alto-Adige it ranges about as far northwards as Merano, but it is not known to occur within the present borders of Austria. In northern Italy it extends as far east as Gorizia. In Yugoslavia it is a rare inhabitant of the Julian Alps (Pozzi, 1966). Isolated specimens have been recorded from Ripanj near Belgrade, Jahorin in Bosnia and from other Yugoslav localities, but some of these reports may derive from a confusion of this species with *Vipera berus bosniensis*.

Other sub-species　The range of the aspic viper is further extended by *Vipera aspis hugyi* **Schinz**, found in Apulia, Calabria and Sicily; and *Vipera aspis montecristi* **Mertens** which is confined to the Italian island of Montecristo. A specimen reported from Harmanli in southern Bulgaria by Buresch and Zonkov (1934) is regarded by Mertens (1950) as being a *Vipera ammodytes meridionalis* with an under-developed snout horn.

The exact status of aspic vipers from Vesuvius and the French *départements* of Gard and Vaucluse has yet to be determined (Kramer, 1970).

Nomenclature *in northern and central Europe*
　　English　Aspic viper, Asp
　　Dutch　Aspis-adder, Aspis-otter
　　German　Aspisviper (*V. aspis aspis*)
　　　　　　Alpenviper (*V. aspis atra*)
　　　　　　Rediviper (*V. aspis francisciredi*)
　　French　Vipère aspic, Vipère commune
　　Italian　Vipera comune
　　Czech　Zmije jurská

The Horned Viper
Vipera ammodytes

Sub-species found in central Europe:
Vipera ammodytes ammodytes (**Linnaeus**) 1758
Terra typica restricta: Zadar in Dalmatia

Plate 42

This species is readily distinguished from all the snakes previously described by the horn on the end of its snout. This so-called horn, which grows to about 5 millimetres, is in fact soft and flexible and is covered with small scales. Unlike the vertically upright horn characteristic of the southern races of this species, the horn of this form projects diagonally forward. The body is moderately long and rather heavily built, and the broad, triangular-shaped head stands out markedly from the neck. The pointed tail is very short, varying from about a sixth to a ninth of the total length in males, and from about a ninth to an eleventh in females. This is one of the largest of European vipers.

As in the case of the aspic viper, the males of this species reach a greater maximum length than the females. The male has been known to reach 95 centimetres, though a length even of 85 centimetres is rarely observed. This northern race grows longer than the other forms of this species. The south Balkan race *meridionalis* rarely attains a length of 60 centimetres.

Scalation

Dorsals: 21 or 23 (rarely 25) longitudinal rows at mid-body—strongly keeled excepting smooth or weakly keeled lowest row on either side. *Ventrals*: 133–161 (males), 135–164 (females); single *anal*; paired *subcaudals*: 27–46 (males), 24–38 (females). *Rostral* usually broader than deep. 9–17 scales on horn, arranged between *rostral* and apex in 3 (rarely 2 or 4) transverse rows. 2 large *supraoculars* (tilting slightly upwards from front to rear), otherwise normally only numerous small, irregular, smooth or weakly keeled plates on top of head. Indistinct *frontal* or even *parietals* sometimes present. Large (rarely divided) *nasal* containing nostril. 10–13 small scales bordering eye below slightly protuding *supraocular*; *temporals* smooth or weakly keeled; 8–12 (usually 9 or 10) upper *labials* (4 and 5 separated from eye by 2 rows of small scales).

Colouration

Dorsal region

MALE COLOURATION   The ground colour of the males is light grey, greyish white or sometimes yellowish. On top of the back, extending down the entire body length is a thick black zigzag, sometimes bordered on each side by a very narrow dark edge. Along each side is a longitudinal row of rather indistinct spots. These in some cases may join up to form a shadowy wavy band extending along the lower part of the sides. The top of the head and also the horn have irregular dark brown stains. At the back of the head there is often a black blotch, /\ or Λ-shaped marking, which frequently adjoins the dorsal zigzag pattern. A thick black stripe extends from behind the eye to the angle of the mouth and a little way along the neck.

FEMALE COLOURATION   The females are similar in pattern but the colours are less strikingly contrasted. The ground colour is brownish, copper, dirty cream or brick-red, and the markings are normally brown or reddish brown. The zigzag stripe is usually finely edged with dark brown or black. The marking at the back of the head is more frequently absent in females.

Ventral region   In both sexes the tip of the tail, some 2 or 3 centimetres, is sulphur yellow, orangy red, or coral red below. The belly is variable. It can be greyish, yellowish brown or even pinkish, with black, grey brown or dark grey spots, or it can be black or dark bluish-grey and stippled with tiny white flecks. The belly plates may be edged with white on either side. In colour the chin is somewhat lighter than the belly. The tongue is usually black. As in the other vipers the pupil of the fairly large eye is vertical. The iris of the eye is golden or coppery.

Juvenile colouration   Young specimens resemble their parents both in pattern and colour.

Colour variations   Occasionally horned vipers may be found in which the zigzag pattern is fragmented, leaving only a longitudinal series of rhomboidal patches. Melanic forms are rare.

Habitat
Despite its name *ammodytes* (from the Greek ἀμμο-δύτης meaning a sand-burrower), it is not essentially an inhabitant of sandy soil. It favours dry stony hills with low and sparse vegetation, and thus is very much at home in the dry, scrubby and arid parts of the Balkan region. Densely wooded areas are avoided, but it may be found in forest clearings, beside forest paths and roads, and on the borders of woods. I have also found it on railway embankments. It occurs in meadows and beside agricultural land, particularly where there is an abundance of stone walling. Favouring sunny slopes, it is seldom found in flat country in the northern part of its range. Occasionally it lives near human habitation. It is at home amid piles of rubble, especially around vineyards. In the southern Alps and in the Karst area it appears to be restricted to limestone regions. Normally it avoids damp localities, though it may seek moister situations prior to shedding the skin, and occasionally it has been found on the banks of streams.

Altitude   In Austria it ascends to 900 metres, rarely up to 1300 metres (Eiselt, 1961). This race seems to prefer heights above 200 metres, and in the south of its range it may ascend to 2000 metres.

Co-habiting species Other reptiles I have found living close to this northern sub-species include the wall lizard, the green lizard, the slow worm, the black and Caspian whip snakes, the smooth snake and the Greek tortoise. In Croatia I was surprised to observe several, basking beside a hedgerow where the semi-aquatic dice snakes were also common. The locality was however rocky, and ideally situated between a barren scrubby area and a small river. In some parts of its range it co-habits with the adder. In Carinthia it sometimes shares its territory with the grass snake (Zapf, 1966).

Behaviour

The horned viper is fond of basking in the sun, and it likes to coil up on top of rocks, low stony walls or beside low bushes. Occasionally it climbs onto bushes or even the low branches of trees for this purpose. Sometimes it can be found in retreat under stones, or amid dry walling. Though much of its hunting is apparently done at night, it is often found during the day, and in cooler, mountainous regions it appears only when it is warm and sunny. At lower altitudes however it has been observed to crawl about by moonlight on suitably warm nights, sometimes in company with other specimens. In high summer it may become basically crepuscular or nocturnal, at least in some regions. It is known to enjoy the close warm atmosphere associated with thundery weather. Like the aspic viper its territory appears to be restricted to a comparatively small area. It is perhaps more socially inclined than many other snakes.

In its movements it is rather slow and clumsy, and consequently is usually quite easy to catch. It is none the less capable of striking very rapidly, though it is somewhat less inclined to bite than the adder or aspic viper.

Food

Its diet consists of small mammals, such as mice and moles; lizards and snakes, and occasionally small birds. Warm-blooded animals are usually killed by the effect of the venom. The snake strikes with unerring accuracy and allows the victim to scurry away until it is overcome by the venom. By using its forked tongue, the snake follows the scent to track down its quarry, which is soon able to offer little resistance. Cold-blooded prey is not infrequently swallowed alive, the fangs not having been used. This is sometimes the case as well with smaller warm-blooded prey. According to Staněk (1960) small birds are held in the jaws until they are completely paralysed.

One specimen was observed to regurgitate a semi-poisonous snake (*Malpolon monspessulanus*) which was much longer than itself. Bolkay (1922) has recorded an instance of cannibalism. Amphibians do not appear to form part of their diet. The young are said to eat lizards chiefly, but there is a record of a young specimen having eaten a large centipede. The horned viper drinks quite frequently.

A recent report gives an account of immature male specimens only 30 centimetres in length, which, on seeking the mice offered to them after a period of some 8 to 10 days without food, confronted each other in the manner associated with rival adult males in the breeding season. They raised the anterior part of their bodies and pushed against one another (Thomas, 1969b).

Enemies
Its enemies, apart from man, include predatory birds, polecats and wild boars. In many parts of its range extensive campaigns have been made with the objective of keeping its numbers down. In Bosnia and Hercegovina for example some 830,000 specimens were destroyed within six years. According to Boulenger (1913), over 7000 specimens were killed in a single district of southern Styria during the years 1892–3. Even today, however, it is still in some areas an abundant species.

Reproduction
The horned viper mates at the end of April or in May. Male rivalry, similar to that observed with adders (p. 202), occurs at this time. The young, numbering from 4 to 15 are born in August, September, or exceptionally October, and measure from 15 to 23 centimetres. Specimens measuring only 15 centimetres are however already dangerous to man.

Hybrids   A female specimen apparently obtained from Carinthia was released near Basle in Switzerland, and subsequently recaptured. It later produced a litter of four young whose characteristics in many ways resembled those of aspic vipers, thus strongly suggesting that the female had been fertilized by a male of the latter species while in the wild (Mertens, 1950). Specimens presumed to be hybrids have been found in areas where this species' range overlaps with that of the adder. The female is able to breed from its fifth year.

Hibernation
The hibernation period is variable, but normally lasts from October to March or early April. Though sensitive to the cold, the northern race may sometimes be seen about in mid-winter on sufficiently warm and sunny days.

General response
When approached it sometimes slithers silently off into the undergrowth, but quite often I have known it to remain stationary as though unaware of any intruder. One such individual lay motionless for a minute or so, even though I had gently prodded it several times with a stick. This species is able to hiss more loudly than the other vipers described, and more alert horned vipers

sometimes emit a prolonged hiss, which gets louder as one approaches. This is a rather fortunate habit from our point of view, as it gives advance warning of possible danger. On 22 April 1974 I found a male specimen partially concealed under loose vegetation, which held its ground for a while, hissing wildly, and striking several times in my direction.

If this species is to be picked up at all, it is advisable to wear thick gloves, or to use snake tongs. The newly-caught specimen will hiss and writhe somewhat, but soon calms down when placed inside a container.

Captivity   In captivity it does rather better than the other vipers, and if kept in a suitably warm and dry environment usually accepts food readily. However, great care must obviously be exercised with it, for abrupt movements can alarm it, and provoke it to strike. If offered dead food regularly, it may cease to use its poisonous fangs, and as the venom ducts become increasingly full, its bites are potentially more dangerous. Provided it is fed regularly with mammals, it normally lives well with other snakes. Being amenable to captive life it is frequently kept by medical institutes to assist in the production of anti-venomous serums.

The horned viper bite   This is not only the largest, but also probably the most dangerous viper living on the European mainland. In some localities it is at least potentially a serious hazard to man, and deaths due to its bite were formerly comparatively frequent in the Balkan region because of the peasants' habit of walking bare-footed. The fangs may sometimes reach a length of 10 millimetres, thus the venom can be deeply injected into the flesh of the victim. Anyone who is bitten should immediately seek medical attention.

I was fortunate in receiving fairly prompt hospital treatment following an accident in Yugoslavia in 1963. My right index finger had been penetrated by one fang only, and at first I observed merely a slight tingling sensation. Within a few minutes the finger had started to swell, though I still felt no pain. The accident occurred at 11.05 a.m. and by 11.20 I was already in hospital. At first I was given an antibiotic injection. About midday I got up out of bed and started to walk around, but suddenly became very giddy and collapsed onto the bed feeling very weak and ill. These effects wore off not long after I had settled down in bed again, and I was given anti-serum shortly before 1 p.m. By then the entire finger had become stiff and discoloured, and I felt a burning pain. The other fingers of that hand had also started to swell and this swelling continued throughout that day and the subsequent restless night. By the following morning the swelling had extended up the entire arm, and the glands in my armpit felt very hard. The whole hand had become very swollen, and all the fingers were stiff and discoloured. The pain was then at its worst—a burning ache—very unpleasant but never agonising. By the next day the swelling had started to recede, and the discomfort was no greater than that of the first day. By the fourth day the pain was much less. On the sixth day I was able to move all the digits somewhat, with the exception of the index finger which was completely numb. An operation was performed to remove a large, very hard, purple-black 'bubble' that had formed around the site where the fang had penetrated. By then I was experiencing no more pain and on the seventh day I left hospital. The index finger was completely numb for a few weeks and partially numb for several months. For several weeks the right hand always felt distinctly warmer than the left. Even 18 months after the accident, the finger felt slightly numb and tender. Never at any time did I experience the vomiting, diarrhoea and profuse cold sweating frequently associated with viper bites.

Mice, after having been bitten, may die at once, or exceptionally not for half an hour. I found that mice, having been bitten by a captive adult male, survived for a maximum of five and a half minutes. Small birds may not even survive ten seconds, while birds the size of a blackbird are said to die within four to nine minutes. Lizards normally die within half an hour. The venom is said to have less effect upon amphibians, which, according to Erber may even recover. The grass, dice, Aesculapian and smooth snakes are said to be immune to the venom of this species.

Distribution

Vipera ammodytes ammodytes is found in Austria where it occurs in Carinthia and Styria. In Carinthia it is fairly common, extending westwards to Arnoldstein and Gailitz, and as far north as Friesach. A little further north it occurs by Wildbach Einöd in south-western Styria. Elsewhere in Styria it has been mentioned from Leutschach near the Yugoslav border, though its presence there has not yet been verified. It is not known to occur anywhere within the present borders of Hungary, though a few isolated specimens have been reported from near Javorník in Moravia. Its existence there requires confirmation, according to Štěpánek (1949). It has apparently been found in Slovakia on several occasions (Ponec, 1965). In Romania it is confined to the south-western parts, where it inhabits the southern Banat and the Carpathian district, extending about as far north as Zlatna (near Deva), and eastwards to the regions of Olt and Argeş. It is absent from the Wallachian lowlands and most of Bulgaria, with the exception of the north-western part.

In Yugoslavia it is found in Slovenia, Croatia, where the river Sava forms the approximate northern border of its range, Bosnia, Hercegovina, and the islands of Pag, Šolta, Brač, Hvar, Vis, Korčula, Lastovo and Mljet. In western and southern Serbia, as well as the extreme north of Albania, its range overlaps with that of *Vipera ammodytes meridionalis*. In eastern Serbia and Macedonia the latter form predominates (Radovanović, 1964). Finally, it occurs in Italy, in the provinces of Trentino (Val di Cembra), and northern Venetia.

Other sub-species   Specimens from the southern Alto Adige district have recently been given sub-specific status, and are classified as *Vipera ammodytes ruffoi* **Bruno**. The other three known sub-species are *Vipera ammodytes meridionalis* **Boulenger** found, as already mentioned, in southern Yugoslavia, as well as in southern Bulgaria, Albania, the Grecian mainland and archipelago (including Euboea and the Cyclades), Turkey and Syria; *Vipera ammodytes montandoni* **Boulenger** found in European Turkey (Thrace), northern Bulgaria—especially in the Dobruja region, but extending westwards to the district of Pleven (Beškov and Beron, 1964), as well as the Romanian Dobruja; and *Vipera ammodytes transcaucasiana* **Boulenger** which inhabits north-east Anatolia and Transcaucasia.

Nomenclature *in northern and central Europe*
   English   Horned viper, Long-nosed viper, Nose-horned viper, Sand viper
   German   Sandotter, Hornotter
   French   Vipère ammodyte
   Italian   Vipera dal corno
   Czech   Zmije ružkatá, Zmije písečná
   Slovakian   Zmija rožkatá
   Romanian   Viperă cu corn
   Serbo-Croatian   Poskok
   Russian   Рогатая Гадюка

THE
TORTOISES

The Greek Tortoise
Testudo hermanni
(formerly *Testudo graeca*)

Sub-species found in eastern central Europe:
Testudo hermanni hermanni **Gmelin** 1789
Terra typica: Orşova in the Romanian Banat

Plate 43

This species is closely-related to the Mediterranean spur-thighed tortoise
(*Testudo graeca*), and these are the tortoises most commonly kept in captivity in
Europe. *Testudo hermanni* has a highly domed and very hard *carapace*. It
reaches a maximum total length of 28 to 30 centimetres, of which some 6
centimetres constitute the tail. It can reach a height of 25 centimetres, and the
maximum weight attained is 5 kilograms. In general females reach a greater
length than males, but have a slightly shorter tail. The short, thick tail is
proportionately the same in the adults and young; it is convex above, flat
below, and terminates with a horny, conical spur. Five (or sometimes four)
claws are present on each limb. The digits are not webbed.

Scales and plates
Carapace comprises 5 *vertebral* plates (the fifth of which is the largest) and 4
pairs of *costals*, and is bordered by 25 small *marginals*, including a narrow
nuchal and a divided *supracaudal*. (On rare occasions an irregular number of
plates may occur, *nuchal* may be absent or *supracaudal* may be undivided or
partially so.) *Plastron* rigidly joined to *carapace*, normally slightly concave in
males, flat or slightly convex in females; composed of 6 pairs of plates. Large
prefrontal; *frontal* considerably smaller; numerous other small plates on top of
head. Large *masseteric* and *tympanic* plates on side of head. Flattish scales on
limbs; tail also scaly.

This species is most readily distinguishable from *Testudo graeca* by its tail
spur, the divided (as opposed to single) supracaudal, and the absence of a
horny tubercle on the inside of the thigh.

Colouration
The basic colouration of the carapace is yellow, yellowish olive, greenish
yellow or light brown, and there are dark brown or black irregular patches

which often extend diagonally over, and cover more or less half the area of each of the plates. The plastron is duller in colour with two longitudinal series of dark, often black patches, which may sometimes connect. In older specimens however it becomes uniformly light. The head, throat and legs vary from a dirty yellow green to grey or brownish grey. The eyes are bluish black or brownish black.

In colour the young are similar to the adults.

(The south-western form *Testudo hermanni robertmertensi* is most readily distinguished from this race by the yellow fleck which occurs behind the eyes. In addition there is a greater contrast between the light and dark colouration, and the curvature of the carapace is more pronounced.)

Habitat
This species is an inhabitant of plains and low mountainous country, becoming scarce above 700 metres. However on very rare occasions in Bulgaria it ascends to 1300 metres (Beškov and Beron, 1964). It is found both in rocky and in sandy localities, in garrigues, in grassy, scrubby, thick bushy as well as forested regions. It is associated with warm and dry places, marshy and damp districts always being avoided. It is occasionally found in cemeteries.

Co-habiting species   In various parts of its range I have found this species sharing its habitat with the wall lizard, the meadow lizard, the green lizard, the three lined lizard (*Lacerta trilineata*), Erhard's wall lizard (*Podarcis erhardii*), the slow worm (eastern sub-species), the Caspian whip snake, Dahl's whip snake (*Coluber najadum dahlii*), and the horned viper. In some places its range overlaps with that of the Mediterranean spur-thighed tortoise (*Testudo graeca*), and the two species sometimes co-habit, which I have observed at a locality in Macedonia.

Behaviour
Diurnal in its habits, the Greek tortoise is a great sun-worshipper and can enjoy quite a hot sun. During the hottest hours of the day however it often stays in the shade, especially during the summer months. It is also very sensitive to the cold. It usually emerges comparatively late in the morning after the sun has fully established itself. Similarly it retires quite early in the late afternoon.

After hibernation much time is spent basking, with the head and limbs well stretched out. Usually it is found either basking, or slowly foraging about in search of food. Below a temperature of about 16°C. it becomes sluggish and its normal activities are curtailed. It can stay active up to a temperature of about 32°C. At the approach of rainy weather, it disappears into its retreat. Unlike the European pond tortoise this species is not a swimmer. It is very fond of digging, and frequently excavates a suitable hole into which it disappears during the hotter parts of the day and at night.

By nature it is quite a sociable species, and several can sometimes be found living in close proximity. More frequently however I have encountered single specimens. Like other land tortoises this species develops an attachment to a comparatively small area, particularly with increasing age. This can even be witnessed with captive specimens when offered the freedom of a garden, and they may regularly return to a favourite spot in order to sleep.

The principal periods of activity are in spring (mating) and in the autumn, when much time is spent searching for food in order to build up a sufficient reserve supply for the winter months.

Food
The Greek tortoise has a well-developed sense of smell. Although predominantly herbivorous, it is known to devour occasional earth-worms, slugs, snails, slow-moving insects and even carrion. In springtime young shoots are particularly favoured. It also eats roots and even decaying vegetation. There are frequent reports of its eating the excrement of other animals, and I once discovered a specimen in Romania eating human faeces. In captivity it will eat fruit, vegetables, especially lettuce leaves, and is known to be particularly fond of clover and dandelion leaves. Various other plants including grasses may also be taken. It will sometimes accept raw or even cooked meat. Schreiber's statement (1912) that it can be fed on kitchen refuse has to be modified in view of the high proportion of inedible packaging material also discarded nowadays!

It is said to drink very little when plenty of succulent food is available.

Enemies
Without doubt the worst enemy of this species is man. Every year many thousands of specimens together with those of *Testudo graeca* are imported into northern Europe. A high proportion of these are dead before they reach the pet-shops. As a result, many areas in the Mediterranean region have been depopulated. A recent report by Blatt and Müller (1974) concerning the exportation of tortoises from Yugoslavia makes sombre reading. During 1971 a total of 401,055 specimens were exported to nine European countries, of which 22,737 were sent to Britain and 124,236 to Germany. No fewer than 82.81 per cent of those monitored in the Saarland died during their first year. This mortality rate is probably quite typical. In previous centuries this tortoise was offered for sale as an item of food, as for example in the markets of Italy and Sicily.

The natural enemies of adult tortoises are relatively few, the hard bony shell offering a good protection. In the young however the shell is comparatively soft and can be eaten. The Egyptian vulture (*Neophron percnopterus*) apparently feeds largely on tortoises (Obst and Meusel, 1972).

Reproduction

Male rivalry　At the commencement of the mating season, usually in May, though sometimes earlier, there is much rivalry among the males. They struggle, biting one another's necks, and try to turn any rival over on to his back. Wounds may be inflicted during these fights.

Courtship　During courtship the male, continually in pursuit of an apparently disinterested female, knocks against her shell, bites her legs and tries to arouse her so that eventually she raises herself upwards on her hind legs ready for copulation. Courtship may last for several days. Their movements during this time are unexpectedly quick. Various observers have referred to frequent squeaking noises being emitted by the male during copulation.

Egg laying　Later, between May and July, the female lays from 2 to 12 hard-shelled, almost spherical, white eggs, which she carefully buries in a hole in the earth, excavated by herself. According to Kirsche (1967), the hole measures some 7 to 8 centimetres in depth. The eggs are laid at intervals of from one to two minutes. The female then fills up the hole and presses the earth down using her body weight. Some fifteen minutes are required to fill up the hole. The eggs are then abandoned. They measure about 3.5 centimetres in diameter, and weigh approximately 8 or 9 grams. Later in the year the female may produce a second clutch of eggs.

Hatching　The eggs normally hatch in September, the young making use of the well-developed egg caruncle. This process may require up to 18, or exceptionally up to 48 hours, according to Obst and Meusel (1972). They state that the body shell immediately stretches somewhat and measures some 2 to 4 millimetres longer than the egg. At this stage the shape of the shell is more or less deformed, though this adjusts itself within the first two years. Hatching is however unlikely to be successful when the shell is very deformed. Freshly hatched specimens weigh some 6 to 8 grams. Maturity is reached after from three to five years, depending on the general rate of growth. Well fed specimens develop very rapidly.

Hatching in captivity　Obst and Meusel (1972) refer to cases where the eggs of this sub-species were successfully incubated in captivity. A clutch kept at a temperature which fluctuated between 15 and 38°C. (averaging about 22°C.)

developed in 93 days. Those kept at a temperature varying from 30 to 33°C. required only 57 days. Some eggs kept by Kirsche (1967) in an incubator at a temperature of 28°C. hatched after from 58 to 73 days.

Abnormal behaviour Certain aspects of courtship behaviour have been observed among very young captive specimens, some of which were less than 8 weeks old, and they were seen to mount the carapace of other, similarly young, Greek tortoises. Some of the specimens involved were reared from the same batch of eggs. At this stage it was not possible however to identify their sexes. (Thomas, 1969a).

Hybrids In captivity hybrids have been produced as a result of the mating of this sub-species with the south-western form *Testudo hermanni robertmertensi* (Mertens, 1964), and also with the spur-thighed tortoise *Testudo graeca ibera* (Mertens, 1972b).

Hibernation

Hibernation usually begins in October or November. The winter months are spent in a hole in the ground, which the tortoise excavates for itself. This is dug with the fore-limbs and the earth is thrown away by the hind pair. Emergence takes place in March or April, sometimes as early as February in the south, while at higher altitudes its appearance may be delayed until May. In flat regions hibernation may last for only one or two months. Rarely is this species able to keep active throughout the winter months. In some areas it can sometimes be found about on mild sunny days during the winter. Shortly after hibernation it excretes the remainder of its intestinal contents, which according to Obst and Meusel (1972) includes a large number of parasites.

General response

Those that I have come across in the wild have shown little or no response on being found. Once while walking along a country path I encountered a specimen slowly ambling towards me. I stopped and waited as it approached. When about 1 metre in front of me it paused for a short while, then, making a slight detour around me, continued on its way along the path. Such a response may be regarded as typical. By nature it is very docile, and wild specimens can be picked up with the same ease as captive specimens.

It lives fairly well in captivity, even in climates not really suited to it, and has been known to reach ages of 33, 54 and even of about 100 years. One, it has been maintained, attained an age of 115 years (Grzimek, 1971). It is however more usual for it to survive up to 10 or 15 years. Its natural life span can be regarded as something in the region of 40 to 50 years (Obst and Meusel, 1972).

Captive specimens may show a fondness for bathing in suitably shallow water. It can be kept harmoniously with other species of reptile. Its diet should be varied as much as possible, for lack of vitamins and calcium deficiency can result in the softening of the shell, particularly in the young.

Distribution
Testudo hermanni appears to be confined to Europe. Two races are recognized.

Testudo hermanni hermanni   This form of tortoise mainly inhabits the Balkan region, but extends into south-western Romania—north of the river Danube, occurring in the southern Banat region and in the adjoining parts of Oltenia province. It is now protected in Romania. It is found in Yugoslavia (Macedonia, eastern and southern Serbia, Montenegro, Hercegovina, Dalmatia, Istria and the Adriatic islands of Hvar and Krk), extending into Italy near Trieste. Elsewhere it inhabits Albania, Bulgaria, where it is found throughout (Beškov and Beron, 1964), European Turkey and Greece, as far south as the Peloponnese. Its range includes Corfu, the Ionian, but probably not the Aegean islands. Efforts have been made to establish this species in Austria: near Vienna and also near Ferlach and Ponfeld, both near Klagenfurt in Carinthia (Eiselt, 1961).

Testudo hermanni robertmertensi   The remaining areas of the species' range are inhabited by *Testudo hermanni robertmertensi* **Wermuth**. This form is found in eastern Spain (the region of Valencia and the Balearic islands) and southern France, where it has now become very rare. It is further endangered by fires and collection. Its range comprises the *départements* of Bouches-du-Rhône, Var and Alpes-Maritimes, and possibly the province of Roussillon (Fretey, 1975). It is also found on the îles d'Hyères (Porquerolles and Port-Cros), where it was at one time common. It occurs in Italy, inhabiting the provinces of Liguria, Tuscany, Lazio, Campania, Calabria and Puglia, and the islands of Elba, Pianosa, Corsica and Sardinia, as well as the islands of Pantelleria and Lampedusa, south of Sicily (Lanza, 1968). Sicilian specimens probably also belong to this race. Finally, a thriving colony of Greek tortoises, presumably set free from captivity, has been discovered in the Normandy *département* of Calvados. According to Fretey this colony was imported before 1939.

Nomenclature *in northern and central Europe*
   English   Greek tortoise, Hermann's tortoise
   Dutch   Griekse landschildpad
   German   Griechische Landschildkröte
   French   Tortue grecque, Tortue d'Hermann

Italian   Testuggine comune, Testuggine di Hermann
Romanian   Broască țestoasă de uscat
Hungarian   Görög teknős
Czech   Želva řecká
Polish   Żółw grecki

The European Pond Tortoise
Emys orbicularis (**Linnaeus**) 1758
Terra typica: Southern Europe

Plate 44

The upper shell or *carapace* of this species is only moderately convex by comparison with that of the land tortoises. In the adult it is elliptical in shape, and is slightly broader at the rear than in the front. In the very young it is roundish, and a narrow, but very distinct longitudinal ridge runs along the vertebral region. Hints of this may still remain on some adults. This species is stated to reach a maximum total length of about 35 centimetres, though this length is not attained in the north of its range. The carapace in German specimens does not appear to exceed a length of 20 centimetres. One specimen found on the east coast of the Caspian Sea had a carapace length of 35 centimetres (Gläss and Meusel, 1969). The tail length was not given. In the young the tail is about the same length as the carapace. In the adult male it is about two thirds, while in the adult female it is only about half the length of the carapace (Hellmich, 1962). The limbs are well-developed, and the digits, unlike those of the land tortoises, are movable and webbed. They are provided with long claws—five on each fore-limb, and four on the hind-limbs. The maximum weight attained by this species is about 1 kilogram.

Scales and plates
Carapace comprises 5 broader than long *vertebral* plates and 4 pairs of *costals*, bordered by 25 *marginals*—including a narrow *nuchal* and 2 *supracaudals*. (Freak specimens recorded with 6–8 *vertebrals*, 5 or 6 pairs of *costals* or 26 or 27 *marginals*.) *Carapace* a little broader at rear than in front. *Plastron* comprising 6 pairs of plates (rarely irregularly divided), not rigidly joined to *carapace* but connected by cartilaginous ligament; usually concave in males, flat or slightly convex in females; fore-part hinged to rear-part behind third pair of plates;

both parts independently movable upwards, but not far enough to reach *carapace*. Triangular head covered with smooth skin; scales on neck and throat small, wart-like; large scales on limbs; tail also scaly.

Colouration

In colouration it is fairly variable. The carapace may be brown, dark reddish brown or black, and it is covered to a greater or lesser degree by yellow spots or streaks. The head is often pale brown in males and black in females. It is similarly spotted with yellow, as are the throat and neck. The plastron is yellowish and irregularly stained with brown or sometimes almost black. The dark staining may often predominate, especially in older specimens. The tail and limbs are mainly blackish and are spotted with yellow. In the young the carapace is dark brown or black, and there is a fairly large yellow spot on the outer edge of each of the shields of the predominantly black plastron. In general the yellow markings vary considerably from specimen to specimen. Not infrequently the markings fade with age on the carapace, which can become almost uniformly dark brown or black. On many specimens the surface of the carapace is uneven, and the pattern has eroded as a result of algae or other organisms. The pupil of the eye is round, and according to Fretey (1975) the iris is whitish or reddish in males and brown or yellow in females.

ALBINISM   Isolated cases of albinism are on record.

Habitat

This tortoise, or rather terrapin, is an inhabitant of bogs, marshy land, swamps, ditches, ponds, backwaters, streams, small slowly flowing rivers, and lakes. It is found mainly in muddy or even brackish water, which can be either stagnant or gently flowing, but not too deep. Clear water is frequently avoided, especially in rocky or stony districts, and it is accordingly not an inhabitant of mountain streams.

In general it does not occur near human habitation, but it can sometimes be found near farms, in watery ditches beside roads, and I have observed it in similar conditions beside railway embankments. In Hungary it can be met with in ricefields (Vásárhelyi, 1965). It prefers areas surrounded by thick vegetation, though it avoids ponds overgrown with reeds. Watery regions in woods are not avoided. It will soon leave areas which have become polluted.

Altitude   Though it is normally an inhabitant of relatively low altitudes, it has been found up to 1000 metres in Bulgaria (Beškov and Beron, 1964), and according to Pasteur and Bons (1960), in Morocco it ascends to 1700 metres.

Co-habiting species   This species is quite often found living in close proximity to the Spanish and Caspian terrapins (*Mauremys caspica*). I have observed it sharing streams and ponds with the grass and viperine snakes, and have also encountered it on nearby dry banks, where sand, green or wall lizards also occur.

Behaviour

Although largely aquatic in its habits, it spends much of its time sunning itself on tiny islands or on banks and suitable rocks at the edge of the water, into which it can quickly retreat when disturbed. It also enjoys sitting on a low branch of a tree which conveniently overhangs the water. Still, floating planks of wood make ideal basking spots for the pond tortoise. When relaxed it likes to stretch out all its limbs, exposing them to the sun, and will bask for hours in one place, and a favourite spot is often resorted to daily.

By nature it is both very shy and alert, and it is thus difficult to approach. It frequently basks with its eyes closed, yet the slightest disturbance will arouse it from an attitude of apparent repose, and it will quite suddenly plunge into the water, at the bottom of which it will hide among weeds, until all danger seems to have disappeared. Even a shadow may be sufficient to alarm it. On the other hand, one individual, basking on the surface of a small algae-covered river, neither noticed my presence, nor the hopping movements of frogs fleeing around it, while another remained basking, despite my having thrown twigs gently in its direction.

Its vision is keen both on land and in the water. It does not however respond to noises. Its specially adapted lungs enable it to remain submerged for long periods if necessary. When all seems safe it carefully rises towards the surface, allowing only its nostrils to protrude at first. Any sign of danger will send it down into the water again. If all is quiet however it will cautiously wait for a while near the surface, its nostrils still protruding. Then it will return to bask on dry land.

Frequently it may be found basking alone. Yet it is quite a sociable species, and it is not unusual to find up to six or more specimens basking together. I once counted nineteen basking together on a group of grassy tufts protruding from the water near the edge of a small, deserted lake. It is not unusual to see them basking on top of one another. If a specimen becomes alarmed, and flees into the water, it is immediately followed by the remainder. In cloudy weather it remains in retreat in the mud at the bottom of the water. During hot spells when the available water dries up, this species aestivates, digging its own burrow for this purpose. Compared with the land tortoises it is able to move quite quickly, even on land. It is a carnivorous species and has had to learn to fight for its food. Like all terrapins it swims by making kicking movements of the legs.

Food

The European pond tortoise is generally stated to reject all vegetable matter, even in captivity. Its diet, though mainly aquatic, is quite varied, and consists of small fish, frogs, newts and their larvae, as well as bivalves, snails, slugs, all kinds of worms, crustacea and various water insects in all stages of their development. It sometimes attempts to tackle prey larger than itself. Captive specimens will accept nestling mice and sparrows. Gläss and Meusel (1969) refer to one specimen which swallowed a dandelion leaf.

Food is recognized by sight, and seized by a sideways snap of the head. According to Gadow (1901), it prefers to smell its food before biting. Fish are stalked (Gadow), being approached along the bottom of the water, with a half swimming, half crawling motion, and are seized by the belly. Prey, having been bitten with the sharp horny beak, is soon rendered motionless. It is then torn up with the fore-limbs and beak and eaten piece by piece. Smaller prey may be swallowed whole. Eating takes place in the evening and at night, and always in the water. Even prey caught on land is taken to the water to be devoured.

Excretion, like feeding, takes place in the water.

Enemies

The adult has very few enemies. In times of danger it is quickly able to withdraw its head and limbs into its shell and can also conceal its tail under the edge of the back shields, thus leaving nothing except a hard and unappetising shell to be seized. Its only serious enemy appears to be man. The young however have far more enemies. These include predatory birds, crows, storks, herons, and such mammals as otters, foxes, polecats and rats, as well as cats and dogs. Even certain species of fish will devour them.

Reproduction

Mating Depending on latitude and weather, *Emys orbicularis* mates in March, or more usually in April and May, shortly after emergence from hibernation. It has also been observed to mate subsequently in late spring and during both summer and autumn. Rivalry has been reported among males at this time and fights between them have resulted in wounds being inflicted.

Courtship Copulation is preceded by a courtship display by the male, who continually swims around his seemingly disinterested mate. He tries to stimulate her by biting her head and limbs and by knocking his head upon hers. He also repeatedly tries to contact the female's cloaca with his nose. Such performances may continue for several hours or even days, until she is sufficiently aroused and he is then able to climb onto her back, though at first he is thrown off. He bites her firmly in the neck, which can cause wounding, and they swim, toad fashion, with outstretched legs. When he is on top of her back she swims around still with apparent disinterest, sometimes even eating. Eventually he bends his tail downwards in an effort to press his cloaca against hers, and copulation then takes place. This may require half an hour or more. The widespread belief that the male has a piping call during the mating period has now been discredited.

Egg laying   The whitish eggs, usually laid in June, number from 3 to 16—normally about 9. They are elliptical rather than circular in shape and measure approximately 30 to 39 millimetres by 18 to 22 millimetres. Their weight varies from 4 to 6 grams. The eggs when first laid are a transparent pale pink and have a soft but tough parchment-like shell, but they become harder on exposure to the air. They then become whitish and lose their transparency.

The eggs are buried in a hole specially prepared by the female who may return regularly each year to the same spot to lay her eggs. The site chosen is often a mound near the water's edge, which is devoid of vegetation, well drained and exposed to the sun. It can however be 100 metres or more from water (Gläss and Meusel, 1969). The female bores a hole, usually 8 centimetres deep, with the aid of her tail. After having positioned this vertically into the soil, she slowly and repeatedly revolves it, until eventually a funnel-shaped hole is formed. Her task is assisted by the fluid which she releases from her vent in order to make the soil moist. After having completed the initial hole, she then expands it to a width of about 12 centimetres by digging with the hind feet. In all the hole may take a day to prepare, and the eggs may be deposited on the following evening, though the whole operation can be completed in one night.

When the time has come to lay her eggs, she leans the rear part of her body over the edge of the hole and drops an egg onto a carefully positioned hind limb which then places it at the bottom of the hole. This performance is repeated until all the eggs have been similarly deposited. They are usually laid in rapid succession, at intervals of from one to three minutes. The female then fills up the hole with the excavated earth. Then, supporting herself with outstretched limbs, she lifts the rear of her body, and bounces it onto the earth until this is sufficiently firm and flat, the top layer being more firmly pressed than the lower layers.

Incubation   The incubation period is variable. According to Rollinat's (1934) observations in central France, in a hot and dry summer hatching will take place in about three months. If the summer has been cold or wet however, it may not take place at all. Hatching normally occurs in August, September or early October. Cooler weather may delay this until November and in the northern parts of its range the eggs may overwinter and hatch in the spring. Some eggs reared in the Zoological Gardens at Kiev required an incubation period of 11 months. Two clutches of eggs kept in captivity at a temperature of 30°C. required 55 to 57 and 59 to 60 days respectively.

Hatching   The hatching process can require two days or more and the young tortoise emerges from its egg by means of its well-developed egg-caruncle, and also with the aid of its head and forelimbs. The carapace and plastron are both fairly soft at this stage, the former measuring some 22 to 25 millimetres. They set off immediately in search of water, into which they swim and submerge straight away. The yolk sac shrinks soon after, and then is reabsorbed into the body.

Growth   Growth proceeds slowly, and after two years the carapace varies from 4 to 7 centimetres in length. The recorded weights of the young in successive years according to Rollinat (1934) are :

On hatching	4 to 6 grams
1 year	5 to 6 grams
2 years	13 to 20 grams
3 years	22 to 26 grams
4 years	30 to 33 grams
6 years	60 to 90 grams

A specimen kept by Gadow (1901) over a period of three years grew only from 11 to 13.2 centimetres in length, and from 8.3 to 10.6 centimetres in width. During this period no hibernation took place. According to Gläss and Meusel (1969) maturity is reached between the ages of about ten and twelve. Lanceau and Lanceau (1974) however state that the female rarely reproduces before the age of about twenty.

There have been several reports of very young specimens attempting to mate many years before maturity is reached. Mertens observed this habit with captive specimens which were hardly four weeks old.

Abnormal behaviour   Although the mating of this species with other European terrapins has been recorded in captivity, such behaviour does not normally occur in the wild, though Frommhold recently observed a male Caspian terrapin (*Mauremys caspica rivulata*) in a pond near Durrës in Albania, trying to copulate with a female *Emys orbicularis*. According to Gläss and Meusel (1969) rivalry has been reported between males of this species and males of *Mauremys caspica*, and in captivity such males have been known to attempt to pair with one another, though rivalry between them develops as soon as a female appears on the scene.

Hermaphroditism A case of hermaphroditism has been recorded from this species (Angel, 1946).

Longevity
The European pond tortoise is known to have a very long life span. An age of at least 70 years appears to have been confirmed (Grzimek, 1971), and one is reported to have survived for over 120 years in a botanical garden in the south of France.

Hibernation
This species hibernates in the mud at the bottom of the water, or in the banks of ponds and rivers, and it builds a special chamber for this purpose. Depending on the latitude and weather conditions, it usually disappears between the beginning of October and the beginning of November. As pointed out by Wermuth (1952), a low temperature can prove fatal, as water absorbed by the body may freeze and thus expand, killing the body cells. The critical temperature appears to be from minus 5 to minus 8°C. In southern Europe it may sometimes be met with on sufficiently mild days in the middle of winter, but it retreats well before there is any deterioration in the weather. In the north of its range the year's activities normally start at the beginning or middle of April. In a cold spring emergence may be delayed until May. Further south it may emerge as early as March. Some specimens kept by Rollinat in captivity hibernated amid heaps of manure. Weight loss estimated by him was only 10 to 15 grams. According to Mertens' observations (recorded in Grzimek, 1971), under a thick sheet of ice it appears to be able to obtain its small oxygen requirements from the water by breathing through its skin.

General response
If found some distance from the water's edge it presents little problem in catching. It often requries skill and patience however to seize one while it is basking right beside the water. When picked up, the newly-caught pond tortoise very rarely attempts to bite, but immediately withdraws its head, limbs and tail into the shell, and often releases a smelly mixture of excrement and water from the cloaca. Shortly afterwards however its head and legs tentatively emerge, and it becomes awkward to hold as it struggles to free itself using its sharp claws.

The pond tortoise usually does well in captivity, and tames easily. Occasionally old specimens may ignore all food however. Given a suitable

environment, it can survive captive life for many years. It will learn to accept
food from the hand, and even come up on to land in order to do so, though
according to Gläss and Meusel (1969) such behaviour ceases if it is
subsequently settled in a large open terrarium. In time it loses much of its
timidity. I once saw twelve specimens basking on a large floating board in a
pond at the Budapest Zoological Gardens, which displayed no reaction when a
large duck clambered up to share their basking site. It may learn to accept dead
food. European pond tortoises can be successfully kept in an outdoor pond,
and if the base is suitably muddy, they can even hibernate there. If the pond is
too shallow however, the water may freeze completely, and they are unlikely to
survive.

To ensure good health a wide variety of food should be offered, and
vertebrates should be provided to aid the development of the shell. Care should
be taken not to allow it to become over-exposed to the sun as it is easily stricken
by sun-stroke. Pneumonia can set in if the temperature of the surrounding air
is lower than that of the water. Gläss and Meusel (1969) state that it can be kept
with all of the European *Natrix* species. Gadow (1901) however refers to a
specimen of his which ate young grass snakes.

Distribution
The European pond tortoise has a very wide range, extending over much of
Europe and the adjacent parts of Africa and Asia. It is in fact the world's most
northerly distributed tortoise. Formerly it had an even greater range,
occurring in Britain, Holland, Denmark, southern Sweden, and also
extensively over the northern parts of the continent. More recently however it
has become increasingly rare in the north of its range, due to the intensive
development of its habitat by man, and also because of unfavourable climatic
changes.

Britain and Sweden   It has been extinct in Britain for thousands of years,
though it formerly occurred in Cambridgeshire and East Anglia (Smith, 1969).
Recent attempts have been made to re-establish this species in a locality in
Surrey, and on the Isle of Wight (Taylor, 1963).

In Sweden it appears to have been fairly common in Scania from the Stone to
the Bronze Ages, and it then extended northwards to Östergötland. Its
extinction there is estimated at about 500 B.C. (Gislén and Kauri, 1959). Its
present range on the continent is unfortunately still retreating, and there has
been a marked reduction in its numbers even within this century.

France   In France, according to Angel (1946), it is found mainly to the south
of a line extending from Angers to the *département* of Jura. It is however almost

entirely absent from the Massif central. The *départements* where it occurs include Vendée, Deux-Sèvres, Vienne, Indre, Gironde, Dordogne, Corrèze, Allier, Loire, Lot-et-Garonne, Landes and Gers. According to Lataste (1876), it is absent or very rare in the *département* of Charente-Maritime. Fretey (1975) however lists it from Royan and Marennes, and I myself have observed it near the village of St. Augustin. It also occurs in the Mediterranean *départements*. There have been isolated reports of it in northern France (Seine-et-Marne, Aisne and perhaps Bas-Rhin). According to Lanceau and Lanceau (1974) it is nowhere abundant in France. It has recently been introduced at Fontainebleau (Fretey, 1975).

Belgium, Holland and Germany   There are no recent records of its occurrence in Belgium and Holland, while in Germany it no longer survives as an indigenous species west of the Elbe, though a small colony (presumably introduced) exists near Frankfurt. In the Middle Ages it occurred throughout almost all Germany (Gläss and Meusel, 1969). Dürigen (1897) refers to numerous localities between the Elbe and Oder rivers. In the district of Oderbruch it could at one time be observed in abundance. Werner (1912–13) remarks that it was often reported in isolated numbers from the Havel and Spree districts. Nowadays it is found only on rare occasions in parts of Brandenburg, notably in the Märkische Schweiz district, as well as in the Mecklenburg lake region, though its chances of survival there do not seem good, despite the fact that it is protected by law.

Poland and Baltic States   Gadow (1901), remarking on its decline in Germany between the Elbe and Oder, states that it was at that time still common in Poland and East Prussia. This is alas no longer true, for though dispersed isolatedly all over Poland, with the exception of the mountainous regions of the south, it is now a rarity in that country (Berger, Jaskowska and Mlynarski, 1969). North-eastwards from Poland it extends sporadically through Lithuania to southern Latvia as far as the river Duna though it does not reach the Baltic Sea, nor Estonia.

Switzerland and Austria   Although occasional pond tortoises are found in Switzerland, presumably specimens which have escaped from captivity, this species is believed to have become extinct there in the nineteenth century (Stemmler, 1971). It no longer appears to be indigenous to Austria, though it has been reintroduced in certain areas in Lower Austria, Burgenland and Carinthia. Attempts have also been made to establish it near Innsbruck and near Linz (Eiselt, 1961).

Czechoslovakia and Hungary   According to Štěpánek (1949) it occurred in Bohemia only during interglacial periods. It has now become almost extinct in Moravia, although it still occurs in several places in Slovakia, but has now become rare there. It is found mainly in the eastern regions, notably near the rivers Latorica and Bodrog. Even here much of its habitat has been destroyed, because of agricultural development, and it is now rare even in places where it was formerly abundant (Ponec, 1965). In Hungary it is widespread, both in Transdanubia and on the Great Plain, and it can still be observed in undisturbed haunts beside the Danube and Tisza rivers. However, since the Second World War intensive land reclamation there has brought about a considerable reduction in the numbers of this species.

Romania and Soviet Union   It occurs sporadically throughout Romania. From Moldavia it expands eastwards across the Ukraine to the Caucasus and north-western Kazachstan, where it is known from as far east as the Aral Sea, and Kyzl-Orda on the river Syr Dar'ya. Its range in Turkmenistan extends to the rivers Uzboi, Atrek and Chandyr (Terent' ev and Cernov, 1949). Its northern limits in western Russia are Byelorussia, the Smolensk region, the upper course of the Don, and the middle Volga region.

Southern Europe   Elsewhere in Europe it lives throughout the Iberian, Apennine and Balkan peninsulas. In Spain it occurs almost throughout (Salvador, 1974b). Its range includes Majorca, Minorca, Corsica, Sardinia and Sicily, and the Yugoslav island of Mljet. According to Beškov and Beron (1964) it is found all over Bulgaria.

Outside Europe   It extends to north-west Africa north of the Sahara (northern Morocco, Algeria and Tunisia) and south-western Asia (Asia Minor, Kurdistan, the Caspian Sea region of Iran, and Kopet Dag).

Recent reports have noted a considerable reduction in the numbers of this species in Italy and Spain, even in those areas where it was formerly very abundant. This reduction is apparently only partly attributable to the fact that many thousands are exported annually to be sold in pet shops throughout northern Europe, since it has also declined in areas where there has been no collection. According to Lanworn (1972), half grown specimens and hatchlings of this species and of the Spanish terrapin (*Mauremys caspica leprosa*) are now arriving, a sign that the sources are being depleted.

Nearest relative
The nearest relative of this species is *Emydoidea blandingii* (**Holbrook**), a native of southern Canada and the northern and central parts of the United States.

Nomenclature *in northern and central Europe*

German   Europäische Sumpfschildkröte
Danish   Europaeisk Sumpskildpadde
Swedish   Europeiska Kärrsköldpadden
French   Tortue bourbeuse, Cistude d'Europe
Italian   Testuggine palustre
Romanian   Broască ţestoasă de apă
Hungarian   Mocsári teknős
Czech   Želva bahenní
Slovakian   Korytnačka bahenná
Polish   Żółw błotny
Russian   Болотная, Речная Черепаха

Appendix
The Reptiles of Southern Europe

This account gives an outline of the remaining species of reptiles occurring in Europe, including the southern part of European Russia. Reference is also made to the marine turtles, which are more usually encountered in the Mediterranean regions, but sometimes stray into north European waters.

Lizards
Lacertids

LACERTA AND PODARCIS The most conspicuous element in the reptilian fauna of southern Europe is the wide variety of lizards belonging to the family Lacertidae, especially those of the closely related genera *Lacerta* and *Podarcis*. Many of the latter genus are similar in appearance and habits to the wall lizard, and like this species are in suitable habitats, often found in abundance.

Several of these species are represented by a large number of insular races. *Podarcis hispanica* **Steindachner** and *Lacerta monticola* **Boulenger** are found on the Iberian peninsula, extending for a little way into southern France, while *P. lilfordi* (**Günther**) is indigenous to the Balearic islands. Majorca and the Pityusen islands are inhabited by *P. pityusensis* **Boscá**. Though a native of Madeira and the Canary islands, *L. dugesii* **Milne-Edwards** has been introduced to the Azores. Both *P. tiliguerta* **Gmelin** and *L. bedriagae* **Camerano** live on Corsica and Sardinia, while *P. wagleriana* (**Gistel**) is associated with Sicily, and *P. filfolensis* **Bedriaga** with Malta. *L. horvathi* **Méhely** is found in north-eastern Italy (Julian Alps), Slovenia, Istria and south-western Croatia. It does not penetrate into Austria. The Karst lizard *P. melisellensis* **Braun** extends from Gorizia, the Karst region and Istria along the Adriatic coast and islands to Dalmatia and Hercegovina.

Both *L. mosorensis* **Kolombatović** and *L. oxycephala* **Duméril & Bibron** occur in Dalmatia, Hercegovina and Montenegro, and the latter is also found on many of the Adriatic islands as well as in Istria. *P. erhardii* **Bedriaga** extends over Greece including many of the islands as far north as Albania, Kumanovo in southern Yugoslavia, and southern Bulgaria. The other species indigenous to Greece are *P. peloponnesiaca* **Bibron & Bory**, which resembles the ruin lizard, and *L. graeca* **Bedriaga**, a native of the Taygetos mountains in the Peloponnese. *P. milensis* **Bedriaga** is confined to Milos and the surrounding islands in the Cyclades. The Crimean peninsula and the western parts of the Caucasus are inhabited by *L. saxicola* **Eversmann**. Another Caucasian species is *L. derjugnini* **Nikol'skii**.

APPENDIX

In addition there are three species allied to the green lizard. These are Schreiber's lizard *L. schreiberi* **Bedriaga**, which occurs in the more humid western and southern parts of the Iberian peninsula; *L. trilineata* **Bedriaga**, a particularly large species which may attain 50 centimetres or more, and inhabits southern Romania (the Dobruja), the southern part of the Balkan peninsula including the Ionian islands, Crete and some of the Cyclades, as well as Asia Minor; and *L. strigata* **Eichwald** which is associated with the Caucasus and the Caspian Sea region. Finally one species from northern Africa, *L. perspicillata* **Duméril & Bibron** has successfully been introduced to Minorca.

SAND RACERS   Five other genera of this family are represented in Europe. These include two species of sand racers (*Psammodromus*). Such lizards have prominently keeled body scales. The Spanish sand racer *Psammodromus hispanicus* **Fitzinger** seldom exceeds a length of 12 centimetres, and is confined to Europe, occurring on the Iberian peninsula, and in certain Mediterranean regions of southern France. The Algerian sand racer *Psammodromus algirus* (**Linnaeus**) has a similar range, but also inhabits northern Africa. This species may reach a length of 25 centimetres or more.

FRINGE-FINGERED LIZARD   The fringe-fingered lizard *Acanthodactylus erythrurus* (**Schinz**) is distinguished by the fringes on its digits, which are composed of a row of little scales. It inhabits the Iberian peninsula as well as north-western Africa. Reports of its occurrence in southern France appear to be based upon faulty identification.

ALGYROIDES   Members of the genus *Algyroides* possess very prominently keeled, overlapping scales on top of the back. Four species are European. *A. marchi* **Valverde** is indigenous to south-eastern Spain, *A. fitzingeri* (**Wiegmann**) to Corsica and Sardinia, while *A. nigropunctatus* (**Duméril & Bibron**) is found by Gorizia and Trieste, and in Carniola, Istria, western and southern Yugoslavia, Albania, the Ionian islands and Epirus in northern Greece. The fourth species is *A. moreoticus* **Bibron & Bory**, an inhabitant of the Ionian islands, and the Peloponnese.

SNAKE-EYED LIZARD   The snake-eyed lizard *Ophisops elegans* **Ménétriés** is associated with south-eastern Bulgaria, north-eastern Greece and the Sporades as well as south-western Asia. Its eyes are protected by a transparent layer of skin as in snakes, the eyelids being absent. It reaches a maximum length of about 16 centimetres.

DESERT RACERS   Finally there are two species of desert racers. *Eremias arguta deserti* (**Gmelin**) extends from south-eastern Romania (southern Moldavia and the Dobruja) eastwards across southern Russia to the Ural mountains and into the northern Caucasus. In the region of Saratov it extends to about as far north as 52°. It grows to some 15 centimetres. *Eremias velox* (**Pallas**) is a larger, more slender species occurring in the region of Volgograd, and on the northern and eastern shores of the Caspian Sea.

Skinks   Four further species of skink are present in the southern parts of Europe, three of them being members of the genus *Chalcides*. The round-bodied skink *Chalcides bedriagai* (**Boscá**) grows to about 12 centimetres and has five digits on each of the limbs. It lives on the Iberian peninsula. The ocellated skink *Chalcides ocellatus* (**Forskål**) reaches a maximum length of 20 centimetres, and inhabits Sardinia, Sicily, Malta, Pantelleria, Greece, Crete, Cyprus, south-western Asia and northern Africa. Like the previous species it possesses five digits on each limb. *Chalcides moseri* **Ahl** is restricted to the island of Santorin. It does not appear to have been observed there since it was found in 1937. The remaining skink *Ophiomorus punctatissimus* (**Bibron & Bory**) is found in Greece and Asia Minor. It is devoid of limbs, and resembles a slow worm; it reaches a maximum length of about 18 centimetres.

Glass snake   Apart from the slow worm, the remaining European member of the family Anguidae is the glass snake, *Ophisaurus apodus* (**Pallas**), a species which normally attains a maximum length of 1.25 metres. Apart from its length it is most easily distinguished from the former species by its rudimentary hind legs, by a longitudinal furrow on either side of the flanks, and by the comparative roughness of its scales. It is on record from Trieste and Istria, but otherwise is known from western and southern Yugoslavia, Albania, Greece, the Black Sea region of Bulgaria, the Crimean peninsula, Transcaucasia, central and south-western Asia.

Three other families of lizards are represented in Europe. These are the agamas (Agamidae), chameleons (Chamaeleontidae) and geckos (Gekkonidae).

Agamas   Six species of agamas are indigenous to the south-eastern parts of Europe. The most well known is the sling-tailed agama *Agama stellio* (**Linnaeus**), an inhabitant of Corfu, Salonica, the Cyclades, Sporades and south-western Asia. The remaining five species are *Agama caucasia* (**Eichwald**) from Daghestan and Transcaucasia, *Agama sanguinolenta* (**Pallas**) from the Caspian Sea region, *Phrynocephalus mystaceus* (**Pallas**) from southern Russia, where it extends as far west as the lower Don and Volga regions, *Phrynocephalus helioscopus* (**Pallas**) from the eastern Caucasus and the lower Volga region, ranging as far north as Volgograd and Chklalov, and *Phrynocephalus guttatus* (**Gmelin**) which occurs to the north and north-west of the Caspian Sea.

Chameleon   The chameleons are well known for their ability to change colour. One species *Chamaeleo chamaeleon* (**Linnaeus**) is found in Europe, inhabiting southern Spain, a few Greek islands, as well as south-western Asia and northern Africa.

Geckos   Geckos are small lizards with a very thin though scaly skin. The transparent lower eyelid is usually fused to the upper one, and there is a finely slit vertical pupil. In most species adhesive pads are present on the digits, and they are therefore able to scale walls and ceilings without difficulty. When seized they protest by squeaking.

The Moorish gecko *Tarentola mauritanica* (**Linnaeus**) is found in northern Africa, and in the Mediterranean regions of Spain, France, Italy and along the Adriatic coast from Yugoslavia to Greece. Its range includes the Ionian islands and Crete. This species is relatively large, growing up to 18 centimetres.

The Turkish gecko *Hemidactylus turcicus* (**Linnaeus**) reaches a maximum length of 10 centimetres. It is widely distributed in the Mediterranean coastal regions of Europe, south-western Asia and northern Africa.

Corsica and Sardinia are the home of the leaf-fingered gecko *Phyllodactylus europaeus* **Gené,** a species which also occurs on a few islands off the south coast of France and on Monte Argentario on the western coast of Italy. It does not appear to exceed 7 centimetres in length.

The naked-fingered gecko *Cyrtodactylus kotschyi* **Steindachner** lives in the southern Balkan region, extending as far north as central Macedonia and central Bulgaria. Its range includes the Cyclades and Sporades as well as southern Italy and the south of the Crimean peninsula.

Two further species of gecko occur in European Russia. These are *Gymnodactylus russowii* **Strauch** known from the eastern Caucasus region and *Alsophylax pipiens* (**Pallas**), a mainly central Asian species which is also present in Transcaspia.

Amphisbaenid

Blanus cinereus (**Vandelli**) is the sole European representative of the order **Amphisbaenia.** Its long, limbless body may reach a length of 30 centimetres. In its habits it is fossorial. Its range is limited to northern Africa and the southern parts of the Iberian peninsula.

Snakes

In addition to those species of snakes already dealt with, a further 23 inhabit Europe, of which 15 are colubrids, 12 belonging to the sub-family Colubrinae, 3 to the sub-family Boiginae. The latter are back fanged (*opisthoglyphous*) species, whose venom is relatively mild and without serious consequences for man.

Harmless colubrids The first group includes a further six species of the genus *Elaphe*. The ladder snake *Elaphe scalaris* (**Schinz**) is confined to Europe, being represented in the Iberian peninsula, Minorca and the Mediterranean coastal region of France. The ladder-like pattern on top of the back, very prominent in young specimens, fades considerably with increasing age.

The four-lined snake *Elaphe quatuorlineata* (**Lacépède**) is found in Italy, mainly in the central and southern parts and Sicily, although it is also known from the provinces of Trentino and Venezia Giulia in northern Italy. It occurs on the Balkan peninsula, southern Romania (Galaţi and in the Dobruja), south-western Russia, the Caucasus, Asia Minor and Iran. It has been known to attain a length of 2 metres.

Perhaps the most beautiful of all European snakes is the leopard snake *Elaphe situla* (**Linnaeus**), characterized by a long row of reddish or brownish blotches on top of the back. It is an inhabitant of southern Italy, Sicily, the south of the Balkan peninsula, Asia Minor, the Crimean peninsula and parts of the Caucasus. The island of Amorgos in the Cyclades has its own endemic species, *Elaphe rechingeri* **Werner**. The remaining species of this genus in Europe are *Elaphe dione* (**Pallas**) from the steppelands of the eastern Ukraine, European and Asiatic Russia, and *Elaphe hohenackeri* (**Strauch**) known from Daghestan, the Caucasus, Asia Minor and north-western Iran.

Three additional species of whip snake are found on the mainland of southern Europe. These are the horseshoe whip snake *Coluber hippocrepis* (**Linnaeus**) from Spain, Portugal, Sardinia, Pantelleria and north-western Africa, a handsome species which can attain a length of 1.75 metres; Dahl's whip snake *Coluber najadum* (**Eichwald**), a long, very slender snake known from Istria, the Adriatic Balkan coast, and other parts of that peninsula as far north as Hercegovina, Macedonia and southern Bulgaria, as well as Cyprus, western Turkey and the Caucasus; and *Coluber gemonensis* (**Laurenti**), a close relative of *Coluber viridiflavus*, which is found mainly in Greece and Crete, but also occurs in the coastal regions of Yugoslavia and in Albania. In addition to those found on the mainland, one north African species *Coluber florulentus algirus* (**Jan**) appears to have established itself on Malta (Lanza, 1968).

Two species of dwarf snakes inhabit south-western Asia mainly, though their ranges slightly overlap into European territory. These are *Eirenis modestus* (**Martin**) which extends into Daghestan and a few Greek islands, and *Eirenis collaris* (**Ménétriés**), which is likewise known from Daghestan. These species rarely exceed 40 centimetres in length.

Semi-poisonous Colubrids The largest of the back fanged snakes is the Montpellier snake *Malpolon monspessulanus* (**Hermann**) which has been known to exceed 2 metres in length. It inhabits the Iberian peninsula, the

Mediterranean region of France, Liguria, Piedmont, the southern part of the province of Alto Adige, Istria and the Adriatic coastal district, and the southern part of the Balkan peninsula as far north as Macedonia and southern Bulgaria. According to Cantuel (1949) it is found in the southern part of the Massif central (Lot and Lozère). Its occurrence in the *département* of Haute-Vienne is open to doubt. Outside Europe it occurs in south-western Asia, and in Africa north of the Sahara.

The hooded or false smooth snake *Macroprotodon cucullatus* (**Geoffroy**) is very similar in appearance to the southern smooth snake. It is most readily distinguished by the dark blotch on the back of the head. It is found in the central and southern parts of the Iberian peninsula, on the Balearic islands, Lampedusa and in northern Africa.

The European cat snake *Telescopus fallax* (**Fleischmann**) is indigenous to Malta, Greece, Albania, Macedonia, Hercegovina and the Adriatic coastal region of Yugoslavia. Outside Europe it inhabits south-western Asia. It grows to about 80 centimetres.

Vipers   Four additional species of vipers and one pit viper are European. The snub-nosed viper *Vipera latasti* **Boscá** has a scaly horn protuding from the snout, though this is less developed than in *Vipera ammodytes*. Its range covers most of the Iberian peninsula as well as north-western Africa. Its venom is relatively mild in effect.

The largest of the European vipers is *Vipera lebetina* (**Linnaeus**) which can reach a length of 1.5 metres. It is found mainly in south-western Asia and in northern Africa, with the exception of Egypt. It is also known from the Caucasus and from some of the Cyclades. Its venom is very potent.

The remaining species are *Vipera xanthina* (**Gray**) from European Turkey and some of the southern Sporades, and *Vipera kaznakovi* **Nikol'skii** whose range is restricted to the western parts of the Caucasus.

Pit viper   The one European representative of the pit vipers (*Crotalidae*) is *Agkistrodon halys caraganus* (**Eichwald**) which is found in the Volga delta region in Russia, and extends eastwards to the Pacific coast. It is an inhabitant of steppeland and semi-desert regions.

Sand boas   Two species of sand boa may be found in parts of south-eastern Europe. These are relatively short in length, normally less than 1 metre, and are largely fossorial in their habits. *Eryx jaculus* (**Linnaeus**) the javelin sand boa occurs in southern Romania (the Dobruja region), Bulgaria, southern Yugoslavia, Albania, Greece including the islands, the Caucasus district, south-western Asia and northern Africa. *Eryx miliaris* (**Pallas**) is mainly a central Asian species, but extends westwards into Europe, occurring to the north of the Caspian Sea.

European blind snake   The European blind snake *Typhlops vermicularis* **Merrem**, which normally grows to only 25 centimetres, is a primitive burrowing species with vestigial eyes. Though the snakes of this family possess a relatively long forked tongue, they are regarded by some authorities as being lizards. The European range of this species includes Albania, southern Yugoslavia, southern Bulgaria and Greece. Elsewhere it inhabits Egypt and south-western Asia.

Tortoises
Land tortoises   Three additional species of land tortoise are European. The Mediterranean spur-thighed tortoise *Testudo graeca* **Linnaeus** inhabits southern Spain, the Pityusen islands, southern Romania (the Dobruja), the southern parts of the Balkan peninsula, south-western Asia and northern Africa. It is similar in appearance to *Testudo hermanni*. (The points which differentiate the two species are given on p. 225.)

The marginated tortoise *Testudo marginata* **Schoepff** is similar to both of these species, and is most readily distinguished from them by its marginal plates, which turn outwards in the rear part of the carapace. There are no horny tubercles on the thighs as there are in *T. graeca*. Its home is in Sardinia and southern Greece.

The third species is Horsefield's tortoise *Agrionemys horsfieldii* **Gray**, which is mainly a central Asian species, but has been found isolatedly in European Russia (Samara province).

Terrapins   Another species of pond tortoise *Mauremys caspica* is indigenous to Europe, being represented by two forms: the Spanish terrapin, found on the Iberian peninsula, in the French Camargue region (according to Weber and Hoffmann, 1970), in north-western Africa, extending as far south as Gambia (13°N.); and the Caspian terrapin found in the south of the Balkan peninsula and its islands, as well as south-western Asia.

Marine turtles   Marine turtles spend almost their entire lives in the sea, and are mostly inhabitants of tropical and sub-tropical seas. The females always come ashore to lay their eggs, however. The fore-limbs are adapted to serve as flippers. Five species appear in European waters, and occasional individuals find themselves stranded on the coasts of northern Europe. Four of these species belong to the family Cheloniidae.

Kemp's Ridley *Lepidochelys olivacea kempii* (**Garman**) has a strikingly broad carapace which reaches a maximum length of 75 centimetres. It has been recorded off the coasts of Britain, Ireland, Jersey and Holland. Only rarely has it been observed in the Mediterranean.

The common loggerhead *Caretta caretta caretta* (**Linnaeus**) has a long oval-shaped carapace which grows to about 1 metre. This species inhabits the Mediterranean, Black Sea and Atlantic waters, but has occasionally been observed by the coasts of France, Belgium, Holland and the British Isles.

Much rarer now is the green turtle *Chelonia mydas mydas* (**Linnaeus**), a species which has been much in demand for its fat, which is used in the production of turtle soup. Like the previous species it has a long oval-shaped carapace, and attains a maximum length of 1.4 metres. Its range includes the Atlantic and Mediterranean regions and it has occasionally been sighted off the coasts of Belgium and Holland.

The hawksbill turtle *Eretmochelys imbricata imbricata* (**Linnaeus**) is distinguished by its long, narrow and pointed head, and its strongly hooked beak. The carapace grows to a length of about 90 centimetres. Like the previous species it occurs in the Atlantic and Mediterranean regions, and at least one specimen has been recovered from the English Channel.

The remaining species (family Dermochelydidae) is the leathery turtle or luth, *Dermochelys coriacea coriacea* (**Linnaeus**), whose carapace may reach a length of 2 metres. This species is the largest of all the turtles. The strongly tapering carapace is covered by leathery skin. Occasional individuals have been found in the Mediterranean and even off the coasts of western Europe, including the British Isles and Norway.

Bibliography

Andrén, C. and Nilson, G. (1976), *Hasselsnoken* (Coronella austriaca) *en utrotningshotad ormart!* Fauna och Flora 71 No. 2 pp. 61–76, Stockholm

Angel, F. (1946), *Faune de France* 45: *Reptiles et Amphibiens.* Paul Lechevalier, Paris

Appleby, L. G. (1971), *British Snakes.* John Baker, London

Arnold, E. N. (1973), *Relationships of the Palaeartic lizards assigned to the genera* Lacerta, Algyroides *and* Psammodromus. Bull. Brit. Mus. Nat. Hist. 25(8) pp. 291–366, London

Arnold, E. N., and Burton, J. A. (1978), *A field guide to the Reptiles and Amphibians of Britain and Europe.* Collins, London

Arnold, H. (1973), *Provisional Atlas of the Amphibians and Reptiles of the British Isles.* Biological Records Centre, Monks Wood, Abbots Ripton, Huntingdon

Avery, R. A. (1962), *Notes on the ecology of* Lacerta vivipara. Brit. J. Herpet. Vol. 3 pp. 36–38

Avery, R. A. and McArdle, B. H. (1973), *The morning emergence of the common lizard* Lacerta vivipara. Brit. J. Herpet. Vol. 5 pp. 363–368

Bechtle, W. (1970), *Wie steht es mit der Aeskulapnatter?* Kosmos 9. 9. 1970, Stuttgart

Bellairs, A. d'A. and Attridge, J. (1975), *Reptiles.* Hutchinson University Library, London

Bellairs, A. d'A. and Carrington, R. (1966), *The World of Reptiles.* Chatto & Windus, London

Berger, L., Jaskowska, J. and Młynarski, M. (1969) *Katalog Fauny Polski* Vol. 39. *Płazy i Gady.* Państwowe Wydawnictwo Naukowe, Warsaw

Beškov, V. (1961), *Beitrag zur zoogeographischen Untersuchung der Herpetofauna in Bulgarien.* Bull. Inst. Zool. 10 pp. 373–380, Sofia

Beškov, V. and Beron, P. (1964), *Catalogue et Bibliographie des Amphibiens et des Reptiles en Bulgarie.* Ed. Acad. Bulg. Sci. pp. 1–39, Sofia

Bieling, R. (1936), *Die europäischen und mediterranen Ottern und ihre Gifte.* Behringwerk Mitt. Fasc. 7. Marburg/Lahn

Blatt, G. and Müller, P. (1974), *Die Mortalitätsrate importierter Schildkröten im Saarland.* Salamandra 15.12.1974, Frankfurt am Main

Bodenheimer, F. (1944), *Introduction into the knowledge of the Amphibia and Reptiles of Turkey.* Rev. Fac. Sci. Univ., Istanbul

Bolkay, S. J. (1922), *On a case of cannibalism among* Vipera ammodytes *L.* Glasnik. Hrv. Prirod. Društ XXXIV, Zagreb

Bolkay, S. J. (1924), *A list of the Amphibians and Reptiles preserved in the Bosnian Hercegovinian Land-Museum, with morphological, biological and zoogeographical notes.* Mem. Serb. Ac. V. 61 pp. 1–37, Belgrade

Bolkay, S. J. (1929), *Die Amphibien und Reptilien von Sarajevo und Umgebung.* Glasnik. Zem. Mus. Bos. Her. V. 41 pp. 57–77, Sarajevo

Boulenger, G. A. (1913), *The snakes of Europe.* Methuen, London

Boulenger, G. A. (1920), *Monograph of the Lacertidae* (Vol I). Brit. Mus. Nat. Hist., London

Brongersma, L. D. (1967), *British Turtles.* Brit Mus. Nat. Hist., London

Bruno, S. (1966), *Sulle specie del genere* Coronella **Laurenti** *viventi in Italia.* (Terzo contributo alla conoscenza degli Ofidi Italiana) Atti Acc. Gioenia de Scienze Naturalia (6) 18. pp. 99–117, Catania

Bruno, S. (1970), *Anfibi e rettili di Sicilia.* Atti della Accademia Gioenia di Scienze Naturalia, Catania

Bund, C. F. van de (1964), *De Verspreiding van de reptielen en amphibieen in Nederland.* Lacerta 22 No. 4/5 Vierde Herpetografisch Verslag, Lekkerkerke

Buresch, I. and Zonkov, J. *Untersuchungen über die Verbreitung der Reptilien und Amphibien in Bulgarien und auf der Balkanhalbinsel:* (1933) I Schildkröten (*Testudinata*) und Eidechsen (*Sauria*) (1934) II Schlangen (*Serpentes*). Mitt. kgl. Naturw. Inst., Sofia

Cantuel, P. (1949), *Faune des Vertébrés du Massif Central de la France.* Encycl. bio. Paul Lechevalier, Paris

Capocaccia, L. (1966), *Osservazioni su* Chalcides chalcides striatus (Cuv) *in Liguria.* Doriana 4 (172), pp. 1–6, Genoa

Capocaccia, L. (1968), *Anfibi e Rettili.* A Mondadori, Milan

Cloudsley-Thompson, J. L. (1971), *The temperature and water relations of reptiles.* Merrow, Watford

Colbert, E. H. (1965), *The Age of Reptiles.* Weidenfeld and Nicolson, London

Cyrén, O. (1933), *Lacertiden der Südöstlichen Balkanhalbinsel.* Mitt. kgl. Naturw. Inst., Sofia

Dalton, R. F. (1950), *A preliminary resurvey of the distribution of the Dorset Amphibia and Reptilia.* Proc. Dorset. Nat. Hist. Archaeol. Soc. 72, pp. 135–143

Davies, M. (1967), *A case of* Anguis fragilis *devouring newly-born young.* Brit. J. Herpet., Vol. 4, p. 20

Davies, M. (1974), *A double-headed grass snake* Natrix natrix helveticus, *found at Ladock, Truro, Cornwall.* Brit. J. Herpet., Vol. 5, pp. 452–453

Dely, O. G. (1965), Notes herpétologiques I. *Quatre lieux de récolte récemment découverts du lézard taurique* (Lacerta taurica **Pall.**) *en Hongrie.* Vertebr. Hung., pp. 9–11, Budapest

Dely, O. G. (1972), *Beiträge zur Verbreitung und Systematik der Blindschleiche* (Anguis fragilis **Linnaeus**) *im Karpatenbecken.* Vertebr. Hung., pp. 60–67, Budapest

Dely, O. G. and Marián, M. (1960), *Contributions à l'étude de la répartition de la Vipère commune* (Vipera berus **Linné**) *en Hongrie.* Vertebr. Hung., pp. 175–188, Budapest

De Witte, G-F. (1948), *Faune de Belgique: Amphibiens et Reptiles.* Patrimoine du Musée royal d'Histoire naturelle de Belgique, Brussels

Ditmars, R. (1931), *Snakes of the World.* Macmillan, New York

Dottrens, E. (1963), *Batraciens et Reptiles d'Europe.* Delachaux et Niestlé, Paris and Neuchâtel

Dreux, P. and Saint Girons, H. (1951), *Ecologie des Vipères* II: Vipera ursinii. Bon. Bull. Soc. Zool., France 76 pp. 47–54

Dürigen, B. (1897), *Deutschlands Amphibien und Reptilien.* Creutz'sche Verlagsbuchhandlung, Magdeburg

Edlin, H. L. (1960), *Wild life of wood and forest.* Hutchinson, London

Eiselt, J. (1961), Catalogus Faunae Austriae XXI ab: *Amphibia, Reptilia.* Springer-Verlag, Vienna

Eiselt, J. (1970), *Ergebnisse Zoologischer Sammelreisen in der Türkei*: Bemerkenswerte Funde von Reptilien I. Ann. Naturhist. Mus. 74, pp. 343–355, Vienna

Fejérváry, G. J. de (1923), *On the occurrence of* Vipera berus **L.** *in the county of Zala, S. Hungary.* Ann. Mus. Nat. Hung. XX, pp. 135–140

Fejérváry-Lángh, A. M. (1943), *Beiträge und Berichtigungen zum Reptilien-Teil des ungarischen Faunenkataloges.* Fragm. Fauna Hungar., V. 6, pp. 81–98

Ferrant, V. (1922), *Faune du Grand-Duché de Luxembourg* (2e partie) Amphibies et Reptiles. P. Worré-Mertens, Luxembourg

Franz, W. R. (1973), *Beobachtungen über die Verbreitung einiger Reptilienarten in Kärnten.* Carinthia II V. 83, pp. 609–615, Mitt. Naturw. Ver. Kärnten, Klagenfurt

Frazer, J. F. D. (1949), *The Reptiles and Amphibia of the Channel Isles and their distribution.* Brit. J. Herpet. Vol. I, pp. 51–53

Frazer, J. F. D. (1964), *Introduced species of Amphibians and Reptiles in mainland Britain.* Brit. J. Herpet., Vol. 3, pp. 145–150

Fretey, J. (1975), *Guide des Reptiles et Batraciens de France*. Hatier, Paris

Fritzsche, J. and Obst, F. J. (1966) Vipera berus bosniensis **Boettger** *auch in Ungarn*. Zool. Abh. Mus. Tierk. Vol. 28, pp. 281–283, Dresden

Frommhold, E. (1959), *Wir bestimmen Lurche und Kriechtiere Mitteleuropas*. Neumann Verlag, Radebeul

Frommhold, E. (1965), *Heimische Lurche und Kriechtiere*. 3rd ed. Neue Brehm-Bücherei 49, A. Ziemsen Verlag, Wittenberg Lutherstadt

Frommhold, E. (1969), *Die Kreuzotter*. 2nd ed. Neue Brehm-Bücherei 332, A Ziemsen Verlag, Wittenberg Lutherstadt

Fuhn, I. E. (1961), *Die systematische Stellung der rumänischen Blindschleiche* (Anguis fragilis **L**.). Zool. Beitr. (N.F.) 6, 3, pp. 377–378

Fuhn, I. E. (1969), *Broaște, șerpi, șopîrle*. Natura și Omul Editura știjnțifică, Bucharest

Fuhn, I. E. (1970), *Über die Unterarten von* Ablepharus kitaibelii (**Bibron & Bory de St. Vincent**, 1833). Vĕst. Česko. Spol. Zool. Acta Soc. Zool. Boh. XXXIV. I, pp. 9–17

Fuhn, I. E. and Vancea, S. (1961), *Fauna Republicci Populare Romîne (Reptilia)*. Eitura Academiei Republicci Populare, Romîne, Bucharest

Gadow, H. (1901), *Amphibia and Reptiles*. Cambridge Natural History, Vol. 8, Macmillan, London

Gans, C. ed. (1969–77), *Biology of the Reptilia*. 6 vols. Academic Press, London and New York

Gislén, T. and Kauri, H. (1959), *Zoogeography of the Swedish Amphibians and Reptiles*. Acta Vertebr. pp. 197–397, Almqvist & Wiksell, Stockholm

Gläss, H. and Meusel, W. (1969), *Die Süsswasserschildkröten Europas*. Neue Brehm-Bücherei 418, A. Ziemsen Verlag, Wittenberg Lutherstadt

Grzimek, B. (1971), *Grzimeks Tierleben*. Enzyklopädie des Tierreiches, Bd. 6. Kindler Verlag, Zurich

Guglia, O. and Festetics, A. (1969), *Pflanzen und Tiere des Burgenlandes*. Österreichischer Bundesverlag, Vienna

Halfpenny, G. and Bellairs, A. d'A. (1976), *A black grass snake*. Brit. J. Herpet., Vol. 5, pp. 541–542

Hecht, G. (1928), *Zur Kenntnis der Nordgrenzen der mitteleuropäischen Reptilien*. Zoolog. Mus. Berlin 14, pp. 503–595

Hediger, H. (1937), *Die Schlangen Mitteleuropas*. Benno Schwabe & Co., Basel

Hellmich, W. (1962), *Reptiles and Amphibians of Europe*. Eng. translation by A. Leutscher. Blandford Press, London

Herter, K. (1960), *Das Tierreich*. VII/4 Kriechtiere Sammlung Göschen. Walter de Gruyter & Co., Berlin

Holder, L. A. and Bellairs, A. d'A. (1963), *Litter records for common lizard and slow worm*. Brit. J. Herpet., Vol. 3, p. 133

Hopkins, P. W. (1957), *Additions to the Literature on Devonshire Amphibians and Reptiles*. Brit. J. Herpet., Vol. 2, pp. 90–92

Hvass, H. (1972), *Reptiles and Amphibians in Colour*. Blandford Press, London

Jaeschke, J. (1971), *Zur Einbürgerung der Äskulapnatter in Oberhessen*. Salamandra 15.9.1971, Frankfurt am Main

Janisch, M. (1973), *Occurrence of the ringed snake of peculiar shape and designs along the Upper Tisza*. Tiscia, Vol. 8, p. 95, Szeged

Kabisch, K. (1966), *Zur Lebensweise der Würfelnatter* Natrix tessellata (**Laurenti**) *in Bulgarien*. Bd. 28, No. 16, Zoo. Abh. St. Mus. Trk., Dresden

Kabisch, K. (1967), *Massen-Eiablageplätze der Ringelnatter* Natrix natrix (L.) *in Mecklenburg*. Salamandra, 1.8.1967, Frankfurt am Main

Kabisch, K. and Engelmann, W-E. (1970), *Zur Ernährung von* Lacerta taurica *in Ostbulgarien*. Salamandra, 30.12.1970, Frankfurt am Main

Karaman, S. (1921), *Beitrag zur Herpetologie von Jugoslawien*. Glasnik. Hrv. Prirod Društ. XXXII, Zagreb

Karaman, S. (1939), *Über die Verbreitung der Reptilien in Jugoslawien*. Edidit Museum Serbiae Meridionalis, Skopje

Kauri, H. (1946), *Die Verbreitung der Amphibien und Reptilien in Estland*. Kungl Fys. Sällsk. Förh. 16, No. 18, pp. 1–20

Kirsche, W. (1967), *Zur Haltung, Zucht und Ethologie der Griechischen Landschildkröte* (Testudo hermanni hermanni). Salamandra, 1.8.1967, Frankfurt am Main

Klemmer, K. (1964), *Die westlichen Randformen der Mauereidechse*. Senckenbergiana, 1.12.1964, Frankfurt am Main

Knight, M. (1965), *Reptiles in Britain*. Brockhampton Press, Leicester

Knoeppfler, L-P. (1961), *Contribution a l'étude des Amphibiens et des Reptiles de Provence*. Vie et Milieu XII Fasc. I

Koenig, O. (1961), *Das Buch vom Neusiedlersee*. Wollzeilen Verlag, Vienna

Kopstein, F. & Wettstein, O. (1920), *Reptilien und Amphibien aus Albanien*. Verh. Zool.-bot. Ges. 70 H. 9–10, pp. 387–457

Kramer, E. (1961), *Variation, Sexualdimorphismus, Wachstum und Taxionomie von* Vipera ursinii (**Bonaparte** 1835) *und* Vipera kaznakovi **Nikolskij** 1909. Rev. Suisse. Zool. 68. 41. pp. 627–725, Geneva

Kramer, E. (1970), *Revalidierte und neue Rassen der europäischen Schlangenfauna*. Lavori Soc. ital. Biogeogr. n.s. I, pp. 667–676

Kramer, G. and Mertens, R. (1938), *Zur Verbreitung und Systematik der Festländischen Mauer-Eidechsen Istriens*. Senckenbergiana, 21.3.1938, Frankfurt am Main

Lanceau, M-T. and Lanceau Y. (1974), *Á la découverte des reptiles*. Fleurus, Paris

Lanworn, R. A. (1972), *The book of reptiles*. Hamlyn, London

Lanza, B. see: Tortonese, and Lanza, B.

Lataste, F. (1876), *Essai d'une Faune herpétologique de la Gironde*. V Cadoret, Bordeaux

Leighton, G. (1901), *The life history of British serpents and their local distribution in the British Isles*. Blackwell & Son, London

Leighton, G. (1903), *The life history of British lizards and their local distribution in the British Isles*. G. A. Morton, Edinburgh

Lockley, R. M. (1970), *The naturalist in Wales*. David & Charles, Newton Abbot

Lombardi, G. and Bianco, F.(1974), *La Vipera*. Nardini Editore, Florence

Lopes Vieira, A. X. (1897), *Catalogo dos Reptis e Amphibios do Continente de Portugal*. Imprensa da Universidade, Coimbra

Lydekker, R. (ed.) (1896), *The Royal Natural History*. Vol. 5, Warne, London & New York

Marián, M. (1956), *Adatok a keresztes vipera* (Vipera b. berus **L.**) *somogyi elterjedési viszonyaihoz*. Ann. hist. nat. Mus. Nat. Hung., Budapest

Marián, M. (1963), *Néhány adat a keresztes vipera* (Vipera b. berus **L.**) *szaporodás biológiájához*. Vertebr. Hung. p. 55, Budapest

Méhely, L. von (1911), *Systematisch-Phylogenetische Studien an Viperiden*. Ann. Hist.-Nat. Mus. Hungar. 9, pp. 186–243 Budapest

Mertens, R. (1925), *Amphibien und Reptilien aus dem nördlichen und östlichen Spanien*. Abh. Senckenb. Naturf. Ges., 39 Frankfurt am Main

Mertens, R. (1947a), *Die Lurche und Kriechtiere des Rhein-Main Gebietes*. Verlag Dr. Waldemar Kramer, Frankfurt am Main

Mertens, R. (1947b), *Studien zur Eidonomie und Taxonomie der Ringelnatter* (Natrix natrix). Abh. Senckenb. Naturf. Ges. 476, pp. 1–38, Frankfurt am Main

Mertens, R. (1950), *Über Reptilienbastarde*. Senckenbergiana 31.10.1950, Frankfurt am Main

Mertens, R. (1952), *Amphibien und Reptilien aus der Türkei*. Revue de la Faculté des Sciences de L'Université d'Istanbul, Serie B Vol. XVII. Fasc. I

Mertens, R. (1956), *Über Reptilienbastarde II* Senckenbergiana 19.5.1956, Frankfurt am Main

Mertens, R. (1964), *Über Reptilienbastarde III* Senckenbergiana 13.3.1964, Frankfurt am Main

Mertens, R. (1964), *Welches Tier ist das? Kriechtiere und Lurche*. 3rd ed. Kosmos. Franckh'sche Verlagshandlung, Stuttgart

Mertens, R. (1972a), *Nachträge zum 'Kosmos-Naturführer' Kriechtiere und Lurche*. Salamandra 15.9.1972, Frankfurt am Main

Mertens, R. (1972b), *Über Reptilienbastarde V* Senckenbergiana 14.4.1972, Frankfurt am Main

Mertens, R. and Wermuth, H. (1960), *Die Amphibien und Reptilien Europas*. Verlag Waldemar Kramer, Frankfurt am Main

Młynarski, M. (1966), *Płazy i Gady Polski. Atlas*. Państwowe Zakłady Wydawnictw Szkolnych, Warsaw

Młynarski, M. (1971), *Nasze Gady*. Pánstwowe Zakłady Wydawnictw Szkolnych, Warsaw

Müller, P. (1969), *Einige Bemerkungen zur Verbreitung von* Vipera aspis (Serpentes, Viperidae) *in Spanien*. Salamandra 30.6.1969, Frankfurt am Main

Müller, P. (1973), *Monomorphismus und Polymorphismus italienischer* Chalcides chalcides—*Populationen* (Sauria, Scincidae). Salamandra 15.6.1974, Frankfurt am Main

Müller, P. (1974), *Bemerkungen zur Verbreitung von Amphibien und Reptilien im Abruzzen-Nationalpark (Italien)*. Salamandra 15.9.1974, Frankfurt am Main

Nettmann, H-K. and Rykene, S. (1974), *Eine gelungene Kreuzung von* Lacerta trilineata trilineata *mit* Lacerta viridis viridis. Salamandra 15.6.1974, Frankfurt am Main

Nikol'skii, A. M. (1915), *Reptiles* vol. I *Chelonia & Sauria*. Eng. translation from Russian (Israel Program for scientific translations, 1963), Jerusalem

Nikol'skii, A. M. (1916), *Reptiles* vol. II *Ophidia*. (Israel Program for scientific translations, 1964), Jerusalem

Obst, F. J. and Meusel, W. (1972), *Die Landschildkröten Europas*. 4th ed. Neue Brehm-Bücherei 319. A. Ziemsen Verlag, Wittenberg Lutherstadt

Pasteur, G. and Bons, J. (1960), *Catalogue des Reptiles Actuels du Maroc*. Travaux de l'Institut Scientifique Chérifien, Rabat

Pénzes, B. (1972), *Terrárium*. Natura, Budapest

Peters, G. (1959), *Zur Taxionomie und Oekologie der Zauneidechsen zwischen Peipus- und Onega-See*. Zool. Beitr. (N.F.) Bd. 4 (H.2) pp. 205–232

Peters, G. (1962a), *Ein Beitrag zur Ökologie der Perleidechse* (Lacerta l. lepida **Daudin**) Mitt. Zool. Mus. Ber. Bd. 38 (H.2) pp. 401–413, Berlin

Peters, G. (1962b), *Studien zur Taxionomie, Verbreitung und Oekologie der Smaragdeidechsen* I Lacerta trilineata, viridis *und* strigata *als selbständige Arten*. Mitt. Zool. Mus. Ber. Bd. 38 (H.1) pp. 127–152, Berlin

Peters, G. (1970), *Studien zur Taxionomie, Verbreitung und Oekologie der Smaragdeidechsen. IV Zur Oekologie und Geschichte der Populationen von* Lacerta v. viridis (**Laurenti**) *im mitteleuropäischen Flachland.* Bezirksheimatmuseum, Potsdam

Petzold, H-G. (1971), *Blindschleiche und Scheltopusik.* Neue Brehm-Bücherei 448. A Ziemsen Verlag, Wittenberg Lutherstadt

Petzold, H-G. (1972), *Eine total-melanotische Zauneidechse* (Lacerta agilis) *aus dem Raum Berlin.* Salamandra 15.12.1972, Frankfurt am Main

Pfaff, J. R. (1950), *List of Danish Vertebrates* Dansk Videnskabs Forlag, Copenhagen

Phisalix, M. (1922), *Animaux venimeux et venins.* Vol. 2, Masson, Paris

Pitman, R. (1940), *The smooth snake* (Coronella levis) *in Wiltshire.* Wiltsh. Archael. Nat. Hist. Mag. 49 pp. 238–9

Ponec, J. (1965), V Ríši Plazov. Obzor, Bratislava

Pope, C. H. (1956), *The Reptile World.* Routledge & Kegan Paul, London

Pozzi, A. (1966), *Geonemia e catalogo ragionato degli Anfibi e Rettili della Jugoslavia.* Natura, 51(i) pp. 1–55, Milan

Prestt, I. (1971) *An ecological study of the viper* Vipera berus berus *in southern England.* J. Zool. 164. pp. 373–418, London

Race, D. (1971), *Green lizards* (Lacerta viridis). Newsletter No. 3 Brit. Herp. Soc., London

Radovanović, M. (1941), *Zur Kenntnis der Herpetofauna des Balkans.* Zool. Anz. 1.12.1941. Bd. 136 H. 7/8 Akad. Ver. Becker & Erler Kom-Ges., Leipzig

Radovanović, M. (1951), *Vodozemci i Gmizavci naše Zemlje.* Izdavačko Preduzeče Narodne Republike Srbije, pp. 1–249, Belgrade

Radovanović, M. (1964), *Die Verbreitung der Amphibien und Reptilien in Jugoslawien.* Senckenbergiana 1.12.1964, Frankfurt am Main

Raehmel, C-A. (1977), *Zum Vorkommen von* Natrix tessellata *an der Ahr (Rheinland-Pfalz).* Salamandra, 15.3.1977, Frankfurt am Main

Reichenbach-Klinke, H-H. (1963), *Krankheiten der Reptilien* Gustav Fischer Verlag, Stuttgart

Reuss, T. (1930), *Ueber die neurotoxische Otterngruppe Europas* Mesocoronis *1927.* Glasnik Zem. Mus. Bosn. 42, pp. 57–114

Rollinat, R. (1934), *La vie des Reptiles de la France centrale* Librarie Delagrave, Paris

Rühmekorf, E. (1970), *Die Verbreitung der Amphibien und Reptilien in Niedersachsen.* Natur, Kultur und Jagd. Beit. Naturkunde Niedersachsen 22 pp. 67–131

Saint-Girons, H. (1956), *Les Serpents du Maroc.* Var. Scient. Soc. Nat. Phys. Maroc 8.

Salvador, A. (1974a), *Die Äskulapnatter* (Elaphe longissima) *in Spanien.* Salamandra 15.3.1974, Frankfurt am Main

Salvador, A. (1974b), *Guia de los anfibios y reptiles Españoles.* Instituto Nacional para la Conservacion de la Naturaleza, Madrid

Schmidt, K. and Inger, R. F. (1957), *Living Reptiles of the World* Hamish Hamilton, London

Schreiber, E. (1912), *Herpetologia europaea.* 2nd ed. Verlag Gustav Fischer, Jena

Schwarz, E. (1936), *Untersuchungen über Systematik und Verbreitung der europäischen und mediterranen Ottern.* Behringwerk-Mitt. Fasc 7 pp. 159-362, Marburg/Lahn

Schweizer, H. (1962), *Beitrag zur Kenntnis der schwarzen Würfelnatter am Luganer See.* Die Aquarium und Terrarien Zeitschrift. Feb. 1962. Alfred Kernen Verlag, Stuttgart

Shcherbak, N. N. (1966), *Amphibians and Reptiles of the Crimea.* (In Russian) Naukova Dumka, Kiev

Sievers, K. (1969), *Doppelte Eiablage einer Vipernatter* (Natrix maura) Salamandra 30.12.1969, Frankfurt am Main

Simms, C. (1971), *Lives of British Lizards.* Goose, Norwich

Smith, M. (1949), *British Reptiles and Amphibia.* King Penguin Books, Harmondsworth

Smith, M. (1969), *The British Amphibians and Reptiles.* 4th ed. The New Naturalist. Collins, London

Sochurek, E. (1953), *Irrtümer um* Vipera berus bosniensis. Carinthia II V. 63, pp. 103-104. Mit. naturw. Ver. Kärnten, Klagenfurt

Sochurek, E. (1957), *Liste der Lurche und Kriechtiere* Kärntens, Carinthia II V. 67, pp. 150-152. Mit. naturw. Ver. Kärnten, Klagenfurt

Staněk, V. J. (1960), *Introducing poisonous snakes.* Spring Books (Artia), London

Staněk, V. J. (1962), *Introducing non-poisonous snakes.* Golden Pleasure Books (Artia), London

Stemmler, O. (1971), *Die Reptilien der Schweiz mit besonderer Berücksichtigung der Basler Region.* 2nd. ed. Veröff. Naturh Mus. Basel. No. 5

Štěpánek, O. (1949), *Obojživelníci a plazi zemí českých.* Archiv pro Přírodovědecký Výz., Prague

Sternfeld, R. and Steiner, G. (1952), *Die Reptilien und Amphibien Mitteleuropas.* Quelle & Meyer, Heidelberg

Steward, J. W. (1958), *The Dice Snake* (Natrix tessellata) *in captivity.* Brit. J. Herpet. Vol. 2 pp. 122-125

Steward, J. W. (1971), *The Snakes of Europe*. David & Charles, Newton Abbot

Stonehouse, B. (1973), *Young Animals*. Peter Lowe, London

Street, D. J. (1967), *The smooth snake* (Animal of the month). Animals Vol. 9 pp. 660–661.

Street, D. J. (1973), *Notes on the reproduction of the southern smooth snake* (Coronella girondica). Brit. J. Herpet. Vol. 4 pp. 335–337

Street, D. J. (1976), *Brief report on some reptiles found in the Sava valley (Jugoslavia)*. Brit. J. Herpet. Vol. 5 pp. 558–559

Street, D. J. (1976), *Hungary's pacifist viper*. Country Life. Vol. 160 p. 1304. London

Street, D. J. (1976), *Reptiles in Hungary*. Wildlife Vol. 18 pp. 512–516. London

Street, D. J. (1977), *Britain's extinct terrapin. The European pond tortoise*. Country Life Vol. 162 pp. 1768–1771. London

Street, D. J. (In press), *New locality records for reptiles in France*. Brit. J. Herpet.

Stugren, B. (1961), *Systematik der Wieseneidechse* Lacerta praticola **Eversmann**. Zool. Beitr. (N.F.) 6, 3, pp. 379–390

Stugren, B. Fuhn, I. E. and Popovici, N. (1962), *Untersuchungen über die Systematik der Blindschleichen* (Anguis fragilis Linn) in *Rumänien*. Zool. Anz. 169 11/12 pp. 460–466

Taylor, R. H. R. (1948), *The distribution of Reptiles and Amphibia in the British Isles, with notes on species recently introduced*. Brit. J. Herpet. Vol. 1 pp. 1–38

Taylor, R. H. R. (1963), *The distribution of Amphibians and Reptiles in England and Wales, Scotland and Ireland and the Channel islands: a revised survey*. Brit. J. Herpet. Vol. 3. pp. 95–115

Terent'ev, P. V. and Cernov, S. A. (1949), *Key to the reptiles and amphibia of the USSR*. 3rd ed. (Israel Program for scientific translations, 1965) Jerusalem

Thomas, E. (1969a), *Fortpflanzungsverhalten bei jungen griechischen Landschildkröten* (Testudo hermanni hermanni). Salamandra 30.12.1969, Frankfurt am Main

Thomas, E. (1969b), *Jungtierkämpfe bei* Vipera ammodytes ammodytes (Serpentes, Viperidae). Salamandra 30.12.1969, Frankfurt am Main

Tortonese, E. & Lanza, B. (1968), *Pesci, Anfibi e Rettili* (Piccola Fauna Italiana). Aldo Martello Editore, Milan

Trutnau, L. (1975), *Europäische Amphibien und Reptilien*. Belser Verlag, Stuttgart

Vainio, I. (1932), *Zur Verbreitung und Biologie der Kreuzotter in Finnland*. Ann. Soc. Zool.-bot. Fenn 12 pp. 1–19

Vásárhelyi, I. (1965), *A kétéltűek és hüllők hasznáról, káráról.* Mezőgazdasági Kiadó, Budapest

Viitanen, P. (1967), *Hibernation and seasonal movements of the viper* Vipera berus berus *in southern Finland.* Ann. Zoo. Fennici 4, p. 472–546

Vogel, Z. (1954), *Aus dem Leben der Reptilien.* Artia, Prague

Vogel, Z. (1964), *Reptiles and Amphibians. Their care and behaviour.* Eng. translation by G. Vevers Studio Vista, London

Voipio, P. (1956), *On the blue-spotted morph of the Slow-worm* (Anguis fragilis) *in Finland* Arch. Soc. zool-bot. Fenn. 11, pp. 5–11

Voipio, P. (1962), *Multiple Phaneromorphism in the European Slow-worm* (Anguis fragilis). Ann. zool. Soc. Vanamo 23, pp 1–20

Weber, K. and Hoffmann, L. (1970), *Camargue.* Eng. translation by E. Osers. Harrap, London

Wermuth, H. (1952), *Die Europäische Sumpfschildkröte.* Die Neue Brehm-Bücherei 81. Geest & Portig, Leipzig

Werner, F. (1897), *Die Reptilien und Amphibien Österreich-Ungarns und der Occupationsländer.* A. Pichlers Witwe & Sohn, Vienna

Werner, F. (1912–13), *Brehms Tierleben,* Vol. 4 & 5 *Die Lurche und Kriechtiere.* Bibliographisches Institut, Leipzig

Wettstein, O. (1953), *Herpetologia aegaea.* Sitzber. Akad. Wiss. 162, Abt. 1, pp. 651–833

Zapf, J. (1966), *Unsere beiden Giftschlangen, ein Vergleich.* Carinthia II. V. 76 pp. 87–90. Mitt. naturw. Ver. Kärnten, Klagenfurt

Zapf, J. (1969), *Unsere Nattern.* Carinthia II V 79 pp. 173–176 Mitt. naturw Ver. Kärnten, Klagenfurt

Index